IMAGES
of America

AROUND REMSEN AND STEUBEN

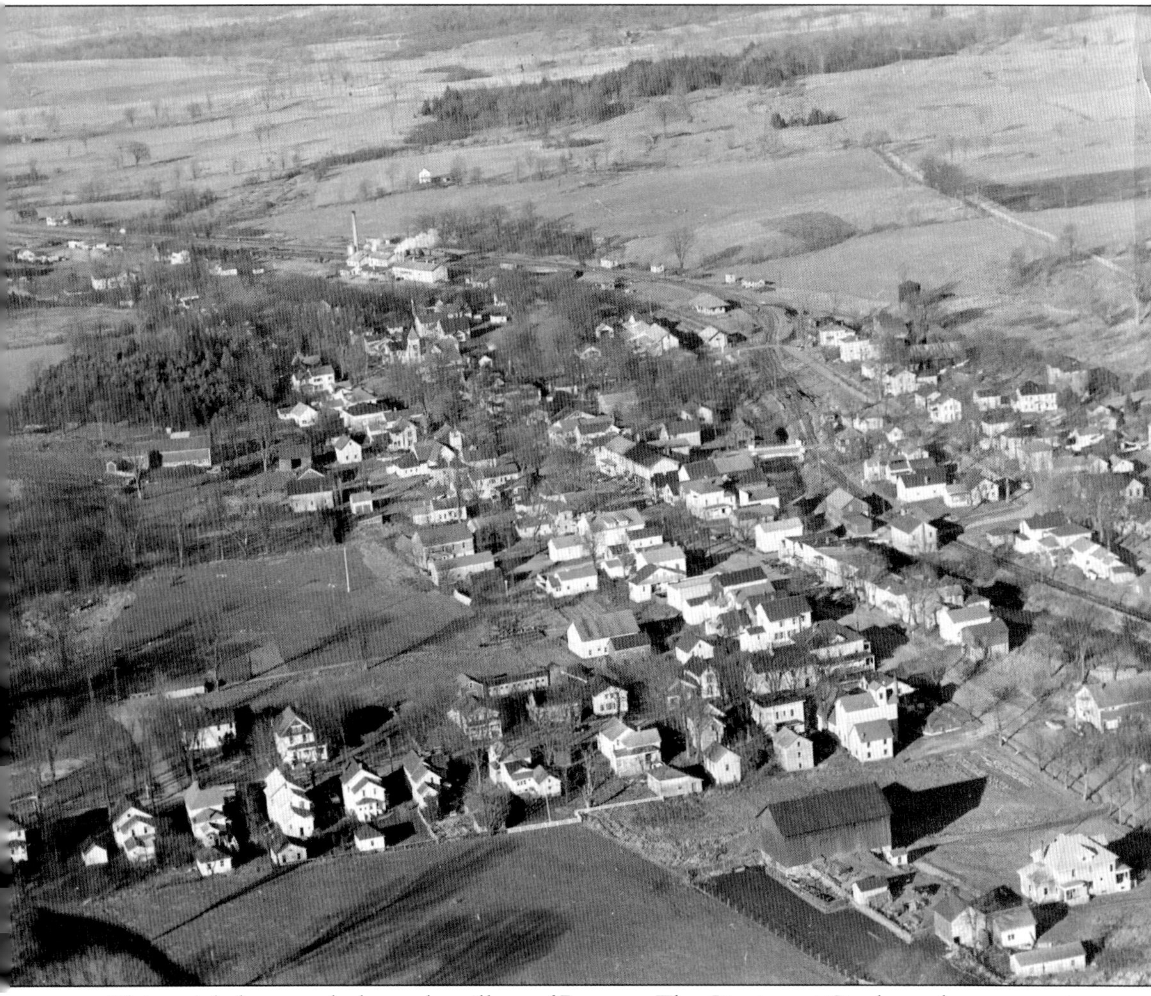

This aerial photograph shows the village of Remsen. The Cincinnati Creek can be seen cutting through the town park on the right side of the photograph. Notice the railroad tracks running parallel to the creek. The town park is pictured on the left side of the photograph. (Photograph by Henry DeWolf, courtesy of Jeanette Walter.)

On the Cover: The Bristol House, otherwise known as Bill's Gainsway House, was built by Dr. Earl Bill in 1814. The proprietor in the 1840s was Jacob Lewis, who was affectionately known by locals as "Uncle Jake." Frank Gainsway owned and operated it from 1906 until 1947. The photograph shows the Gainsway family on the porch and, in front, from left to right, Ernest Worden, Ingraham Griffith, and Fred Worden. (Courtesy of Jeanette Walter.)

IMAGES
of America

AROUND REMSEN AND STEUBEN

Megan Plete Postol

ARCADIA PUBLISHING

ISBN 978-1-4671-1714-2

Published by Arcadia Publishing
Charleston, South Carolina

Printed in the United States of America

Library of Congress Control Number: 2016932901

For all general information, please contact Arcadia Publishing:
Telephone 843-853-2070
Fax 843-853-0044
E-mail sales@arcadiapublishing.com
For customer service and orders:
Toll-Free 1-888-313-2665

Visit us on the Internet at www.arcadiapublishing.com

To Gummie, whose never-ending love and support has carried me through the crafting of this book, and life

Contents

Acknowledgments		6
Introduction		7
1.	Remsen City: The Village	9
2.	No Law East of Ninety Five Hill: The Rambling Countryside and Surrounding Communities	51
3.	Old Gang Mills: The Hinckley Area	87
Bibliography		127

Acknowledgments

I am deeply grateful to the many people who had a role in this book coming to fruition. Jeanette Walter generously granted permission for many of the images within these pages and offered a wealth of knowledge. Without her, this book would not be possible. Linda Bailey generously provided her own research on the Hinckley area. The staff at the Didymus Thomas Library was consistently gracious and helpful. Art Johnson provided insight and more help than he realized. A thank-you goes to Pat Hill, who edited my work for historical accuracy. Travis Leigh continues to lend me his books, even after the unfortunate coffee-spilling incident. My father, Ron Plete, encouraged my interest in history, both local and national, which ultimately led to this book. My brother, Bill Plete, could always be counted on to deliver harsh encouragement guaranteed to pull me out of procrastination. And my husband, Dale, keeps me laughing through the chaos and continues to surprise me.

Introduction

As the dust settled in the years after the American Revolution, the areas that are now Remsen and Steuben were first settled by the hearty few that were brave enough to delve into the uncultivated wilds north of Utica, which was then known as Fort Schuyler.

The first settlers of this rugged wilderness that became the towns of Remsen and Steuben were hearty pioneers, Welsh immigrants, and a famous Revolutionary War hero. The untamed forest of Oneida County proved challenging but not insurmountable.

The Revolutionary War hero Baron von Steuben, whose full name was Friedrich Wilhelm August Heinrich Ferdinand Steuben, came to the area in approximately 1790. He had earlier gained fame as the "Drillmaster of the American Revolution" and was awarded approximately 16,000 acres of upstate wilderness for his service. Steuben had the land surveyed by James Cockburn and divided up into 160 lots of about 100 acres each. At this time, one of the baron's closest friends, Benjamin Walker, was working at the Port Authority in New York City. He helped his friend get tenants to live on his property by directing the influx of Welsh immigrants to the hills of Steuben. These families arrived to an untamed forest to clear land with crude implements and build shelters with scarce comforts.

Baron von Steuben built a humble two-room log cabin on the site, where he summered with trusted aides until his death in 1794. In his will, Steuben requested an unmarked grave, but his remains were later transferred to what is now known as the Sacred Grove. A monument marks his final resting place. Steuben left his property to his former aides, William North and Benjamin Walker. It is now owned by the National Park Service.

From the day in 1792 when pioneer Barnabas Mitchell trudged from Meriden, Connecticut, to the rugged wilderness of Upstate New York, Remsen was a place of unforgiving elements and indomitable spirits. Mitchell and his family were joined by a party of five Welsh families in 1795. In that same year, settler James Smith constructed the first business, a public house for travelers. In the early years of the 19th century, Welsh immigrants arrived in the Remsen and Steuben areas by the score. It was said that the area was as well-known in Wales as in Central New York and perhaps even more so.

The first child to be born in Remsen was Polly, the daughter of Barnabas Mitchell and his wife, Mary. Of the eight children in the Mitchell family, Clarissa, Olive, and Tyler were born before the family came to Remsen, and Polly, Milo, Melissa, Charlotte, and Amanda were born in Remsen. Barnabas died in 1813 and was buried in Fairchild Cemetery. His daughter Polly married a Mr. VanSlyke. His son Milo became one of the most successful farmers in Oneida County and was known as a man of enterprise, perseverance, and industry. Milo established the first cheese factory in the township. It was the second in the entire United States; the first was in Rome, New York, and was established by Jesse Williams. Milo first married Catherine Hinckley. After her death, he married Anna Humphreys, widow of John Humphreys.

The first settler in what came to be the village was Peter Becker. He first built a log cabin and then established the Peter Becker Inn, which burned to the ground in 1796.

The first store was opened in 1803 by Broughton White, a surveyor who had worked for Baron von Steuben. His business partner was Lemuel Hough. They established an ashery and grocery store on the north side of the corner of Steuben and Main Streets. Jacob Betticher succeeded them in operating the business. The spot was known as "Jack," as the Welsh pronounced it with the hard "a" sound.

The area flourished into a place of farming, manufacturing, business, and religion. Churches were built to be within walking distance of outlying clusters of homes. The settlers were deeply religious and fiercely loyal to their specific denominations. There were so many churches that the lands of Steuben became known as "the singing hills," as the melodic sounds of the old hymns could be heard for miles.

It has been said that the courage of a Welshman rises in proportion to the obstacles thrown in his path. The same could be said for those who braved an unknown wilderness to build a life in this rugged place. Remsen and Steuben were built by sturdy hands, both Welsh and not.

Remsen was incorporated by an act of legislature in 1798 that established Oneida County. This was unusual because it came to pass without petitioning from the people who inhabited the settlement.

Business flourished in Remsen for a time. Residents could acquire any necessary goods at any of the numerous general stores, hardware stores, groceries, or specialty stores. By 1851, the Remsen village boasted five general stores, one hotel, one grocery, one hardware store, two tailor shops, one harness shop, two blacksmiths, two wagon and carriage shops, a butter tub factory, two shoe repair shops, two shoe stores, two gristmills, one cooper, three doctors, one paint shop, one foundry and machine shop, one small tannery, one marble shop, four churches, and a two-story school.

By 1855, the Black River & Utica Railroad was complete, with tracks extending from Utica to Boonville, New York. Following a foreclosure sale in 1858, it was reorganized as the Utica & Black River Railroad (U&BR) and extended to Carthage, with connections to Lake Ontario and the St. Lawrence River. The railroad was leased to the Rome, Watertown & Ogdensburg Railroad (RW&O) in 1886. The Mohawk & Malone Railroad (M&M), built by Dr. William Seward Webb, was completed in 1892. These tracks had a junction at Remsen. Webb's railroad made the interior of the Adirondacks accessible to the public. When Webb leased the M&M to the New York Central Railroad (NYC) two years later, Remsen became a very busy rail hub. It was the only station between Utica and Watertown where all three NYC divisions converged and a turntable was operated. Many notable passengers passed through Remsen, including the Webbs, Rockefellers, Whitneys, Roosevelts, and Vanderbilts, en route to their lavish Adirondack camps. The railroads prospered until the invention of the automobile. By 1926, passenger train traffic had dwindled to about 10 per day, and it decreased steadily until it ceased in the 1930s.

The spirit of Remsen and Steuben's residents remains one of independence, ingenuity, and grit. These people who inhabit the Adirondack Foothills work hard, stand up for what they believe in, and have a sense of community. The area exemplifies the pioneering and persevering spirit that our country was built on and continues to operate with today.

One

Remsen City

The Village

After Baron von Steuben died, many of the settlers of his patent removed to the village, according to *A Narrative History of Remsen, New York*, by Millard Roberts. He states that "in every instance, these were intelligent, capable men."

Between the mid-1800s and mid-1900s, Remsen had become a bustling and self-sustaining center of business. A rugged sense of independence fueled the village forward. Many entrepreneurs established businesses that led to successful careers. Many products were crafted within the village or surrounding town. There was pride in hard work. There was little need to travel away from the Remsen and Steuben community and into the cities for goods. Timber and dairy were thriving industries that employed many local people. This was a time when lives were based on home, church, and community. Neighbors knew neighbors.

The people who inhabited this place were hearty. They met the challenges of winter elements with determined resolve. They also knew how to enjoy life. There were community picnics and church revivals in the summertime. It was the rising use of automobiles and mechanized industry that led to businesses moving to the cities. Remsen then lost most of the daily commerce that used to make the village buzz with activity.

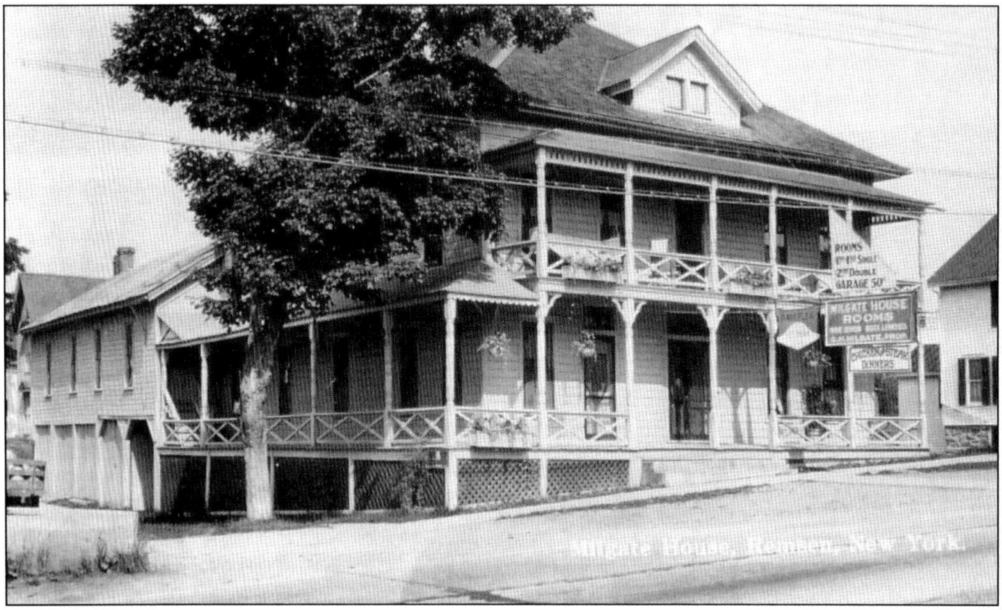

This 1906 photograph shows the Pierce House on the corner of Steuben Street and Main Street. The large structure with a wraparound porch had many rooms that were rented out. The proprietors also operated a kitchen. The building still stands, but the porch has been removed. (Courtesy of Jeanette Walter.)

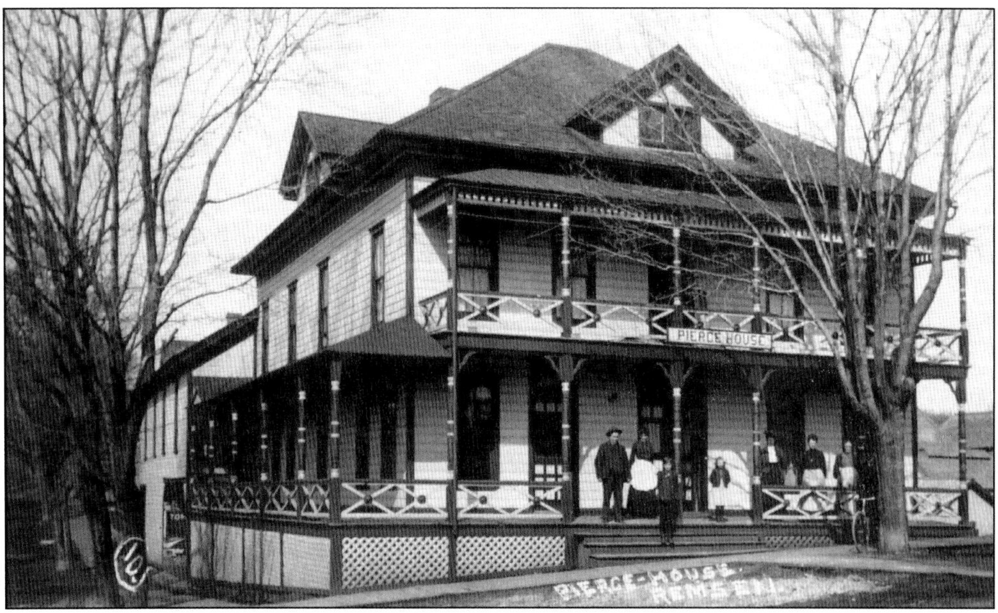

Originally built as the Dynes Hotel for Pierce Dynes, the Pierce House changed hands many times and was later known as the Hotel Edward and then Milgate House. Presently, the structure houses rental apartments. A watering trough stood in the street in front of the building. It was on this site that Jacob "Jake" Betticher operated an ashery and grocery. (Courtesy of Jeanette Walter.)

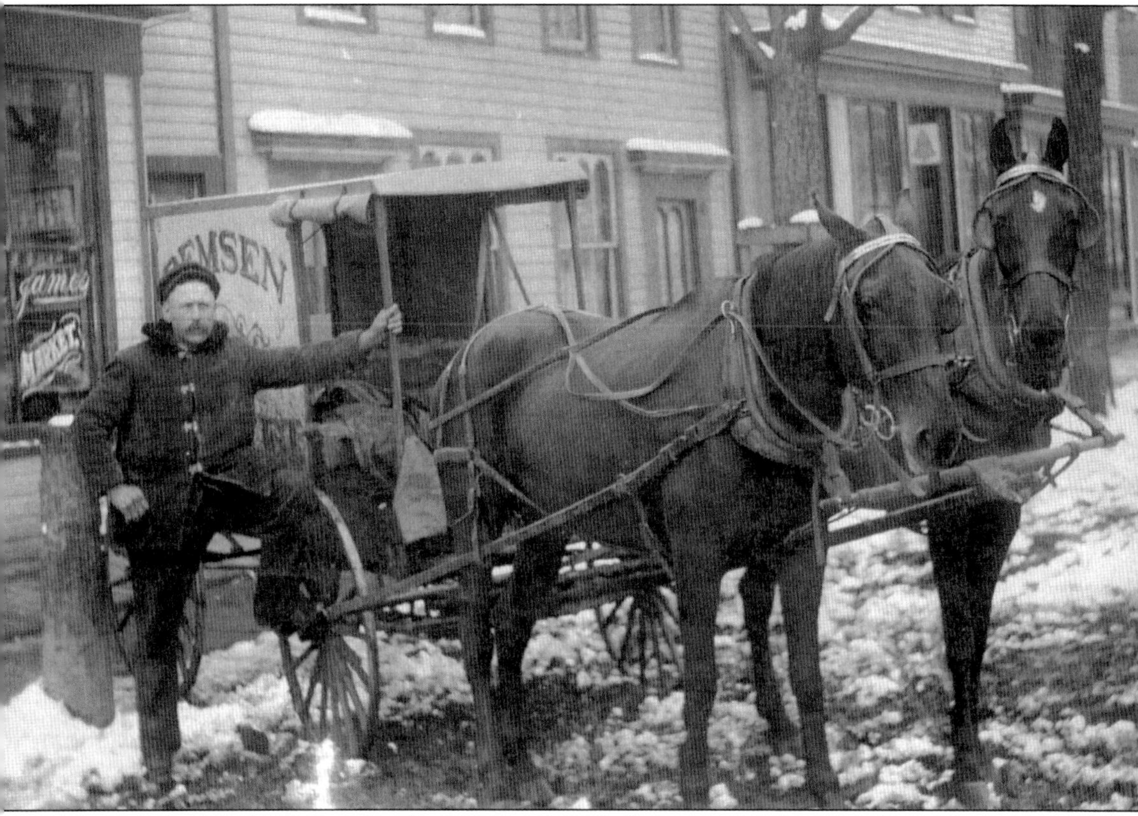

This photograph shows driver Willard James of the Robert L. James Meat Market and Country Delivery supplying goods with his team of workhorses around the end of the 19th century. Demand for goods was high in Remsen, and not everyone had the means to travel to the store. Before automobiles, people relied on their horses for transportation, business, and work. (Courtesy of Jeanette Walter.)

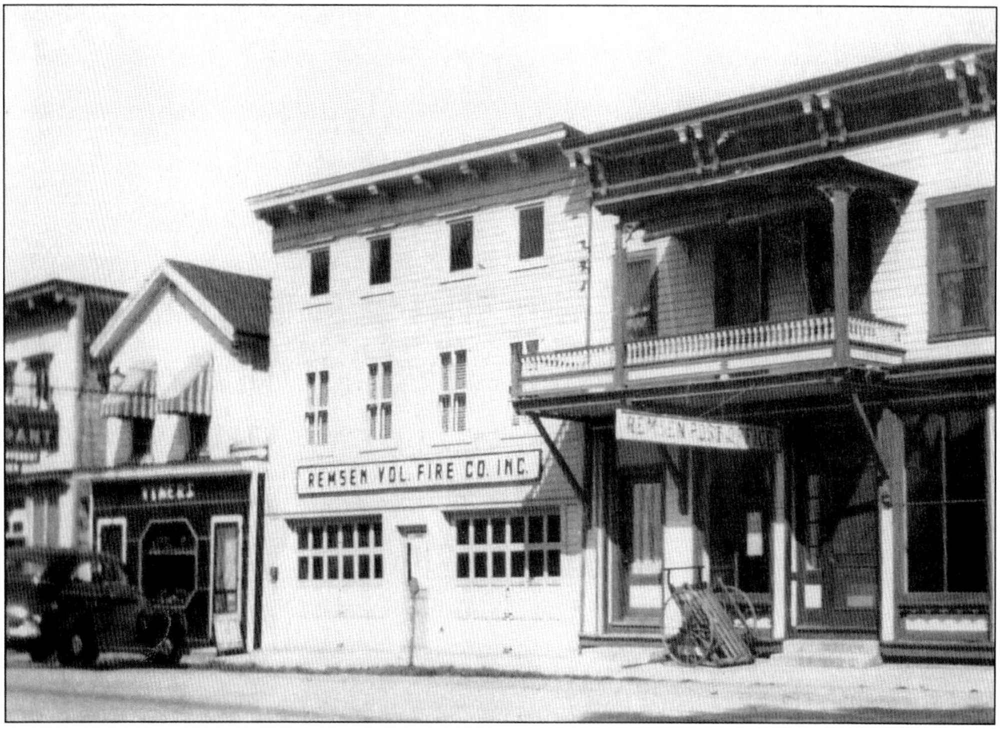

The Remsen Volunteer Fire Company was organized in 1923 with 20 original members. They purchased their first fire truck the following year. By 1942, the fire company had grown, and it had two fire trucks, Engine No. 1 and Engine No. 2. The chief at the time was Hap Howard. Deputy chiefs included Edwin Milgate and Vaughn Roberts. Captains included Frank Davis, Lyle Walter, and George Thomas. Drivers included Stanley Shufelt, William Rowlands, Trevor Williams, and Edward Clemens. Firemen included Harold Horn, Henry Stone Jr., Albert Harriman, William Schrader, Thomas Allen Jr., R.C. Jones, Roy Brant, C.N. Brown, Carl Kelly, Ira Barnard, Lloyd Mortice, Francis Putney, Harold Seaman, Clark Phelps, Geo Francis, Charles Delong, Ken Beagle, John Griswold, Malcolm Walter, Joe Cardessi, Charles Horton, Henry Stone, W.J. Watson, Arch Williams, Clarence Ingersoll, and others. (Both, courtesy of Jeanette Walter.)

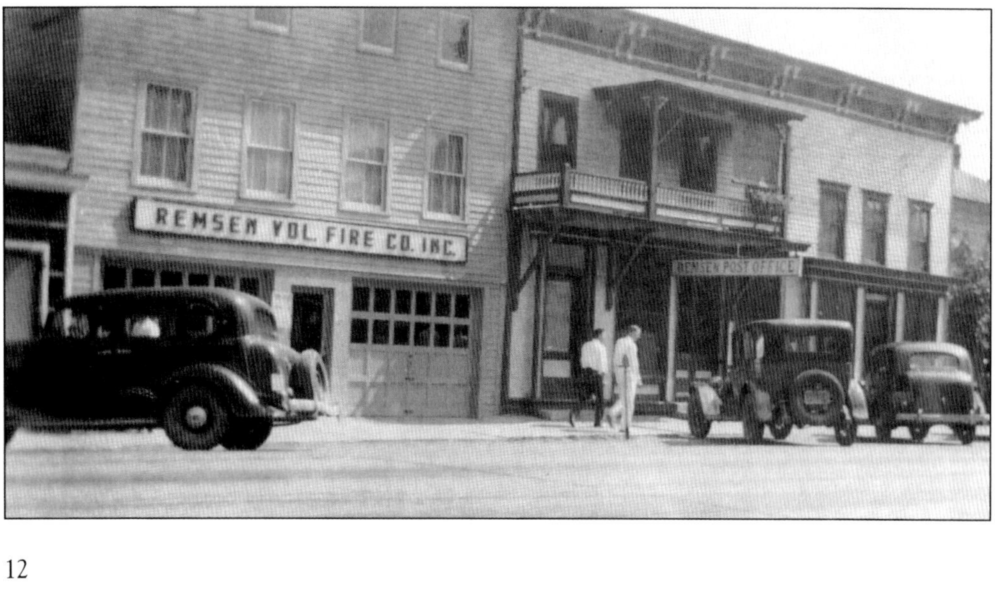

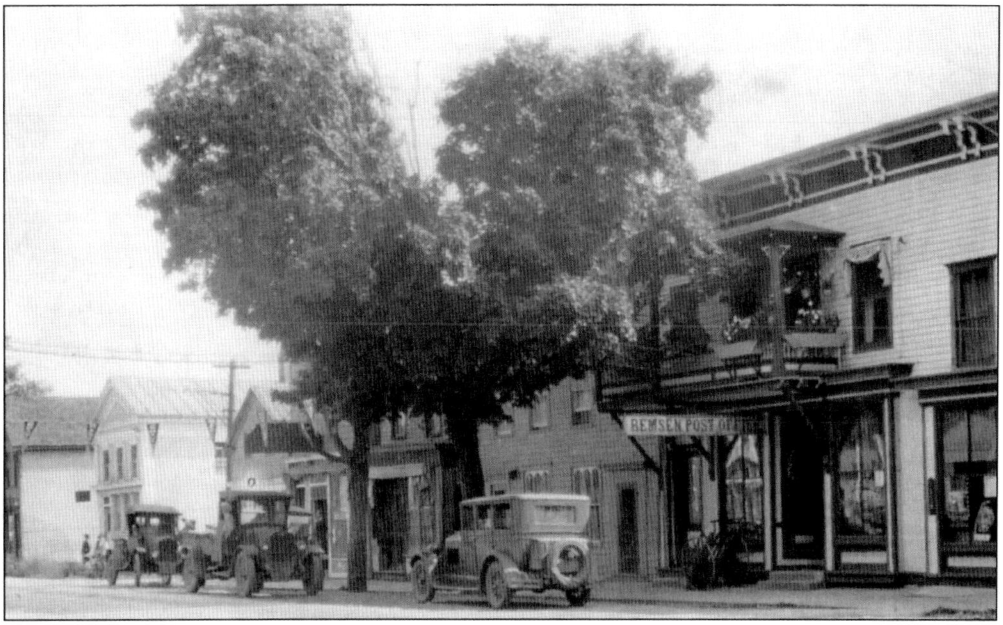

The post office was located in the business district on lower Main Street in Remsen. It was near the fire department and businesses including Vyner's Restaurant. Postmasters between 1853 and 1921 include Obadiah J. Owen, Nathan C. Phelps, Morgan Owen, Owen S. Evans, John B. Jones, Albert S. Jones, R.R. Jones, Edward Pirnie, John Pritchard, and Walter Brown. (Courtesy of Jeanette Walter.)

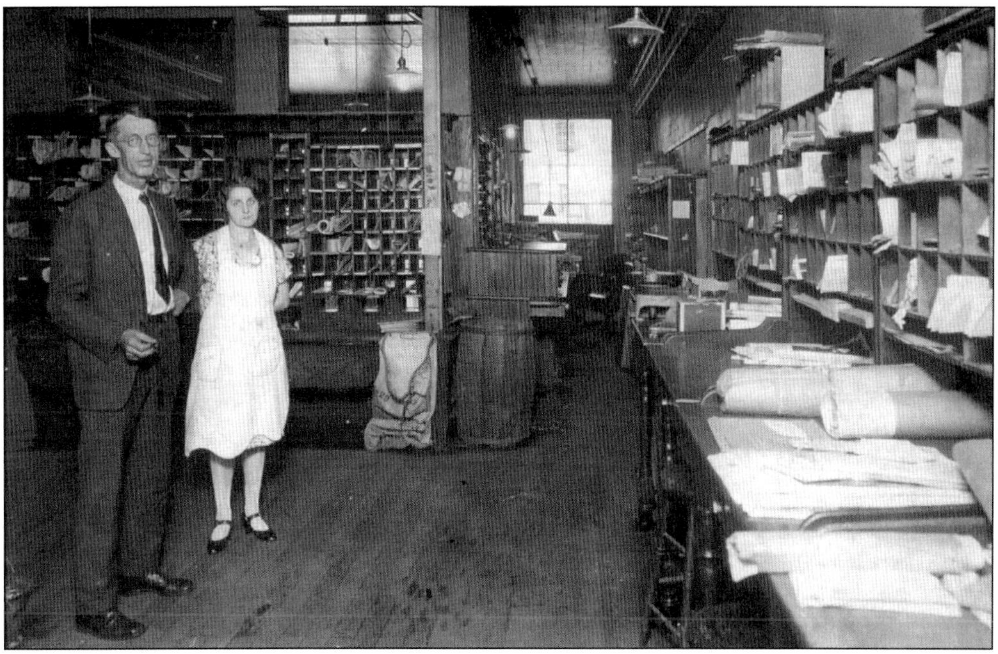

This photograph shows the interior of the post office. Workers pictured are postmaster O.J. Griffith and Helen Rowlands. Griffith was postmaster between 1921 and 1934. The post office was a very busy place during Remsen's peak years. A new post office was built on Steuben Street around 1960. (Courtesy of Jeanette Walter.)

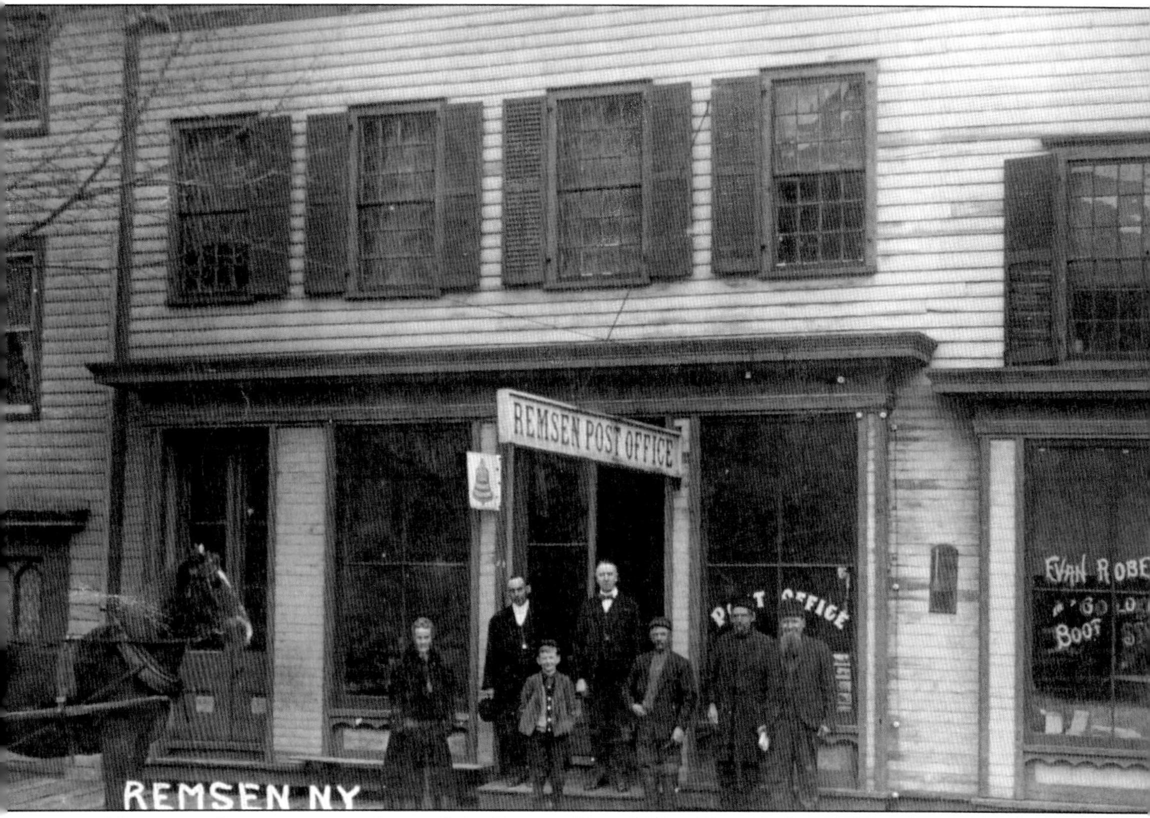

These people are posing in front of the Remsen Post Office. Evan Roberts's boot shop is to the right. Many notable names in Remsen held the position of town of Remsen supervisor. These include, in order of procession from 1798 until 1917, Ephraim Hollister, Gershom Hinckley, Broughton White, James Sheldon, Zalmon White, Luther Conkling, Lemuel Hough, Henry R. Sheldon, Mathew Beecher, Evan Owens, Thomas White, Obadiah J. Owens, Griffith O. Griffith, Andrew Billings, William H. Thomas, Evan Owens, Joseph Montague, Didymus Thomas, Samuel Lamb, John J. Vaughn, William Owen, James Mitchell, William Owen, Silas Morse, William A. Thomas, James Mitchell, Evan G. Williams, Richard R. Jones, Hohn R. Thomas, Evan G. Williams, William G. Griffith, John S. Kent, William A. Thomas, William J. Jones, David Jones, Griffith Morris, B.H. Kent, Clinton R. Thomas, D.H. Reed, Owen Thomas, John Pritchard, Chauncy Williams, Charles M. Williams, and Arthur Jones. (Courtesy of Jeanette Walter.)

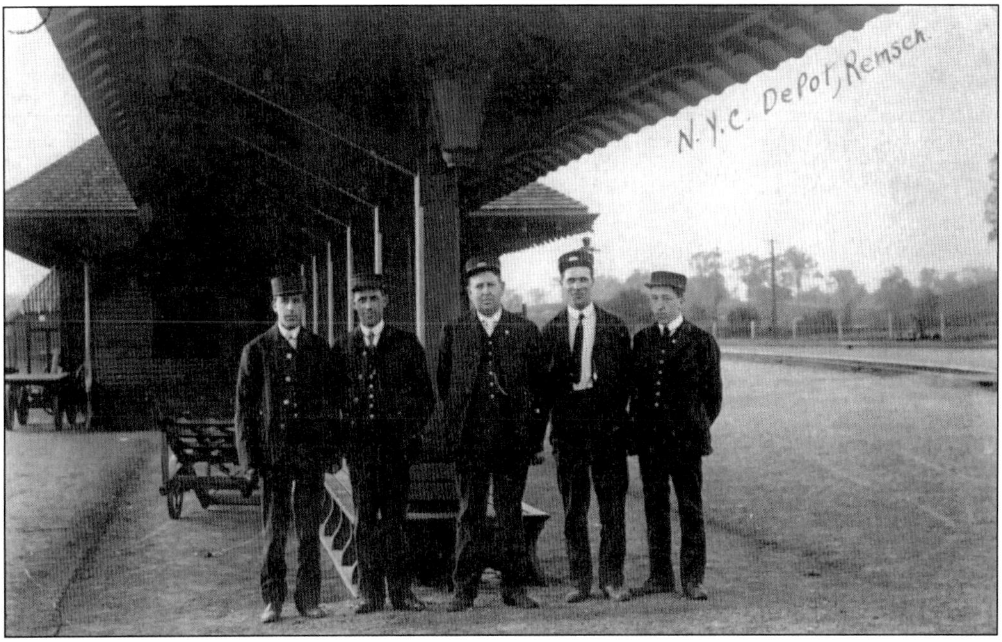

The railroad brought additional commerce to Remsen. The Black River & Utica Railroad opened its tracks from Utica to Boonville, New York, in December 1855. It operated under this name until 1858. Then it was reorganized as the Utica & Black River Railroad (U&BR) following a foreclosure. The railroad line was then extended to Carthage, with connections to Lake Ontario and the St. Lawrence River. The rail line was leased in perpetuity to the Rome, Watertown & Ogdensburg Railroad (RW&O) in 1886. This lease was transferred to the New York Central Railroad in 1891. (Both, courtesy of Jeanette Walter.)

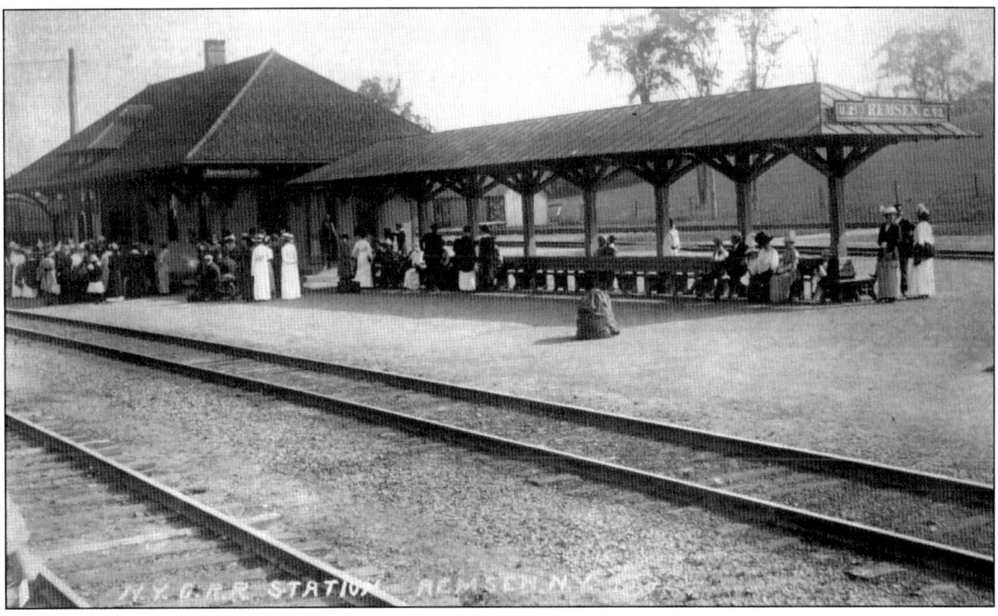

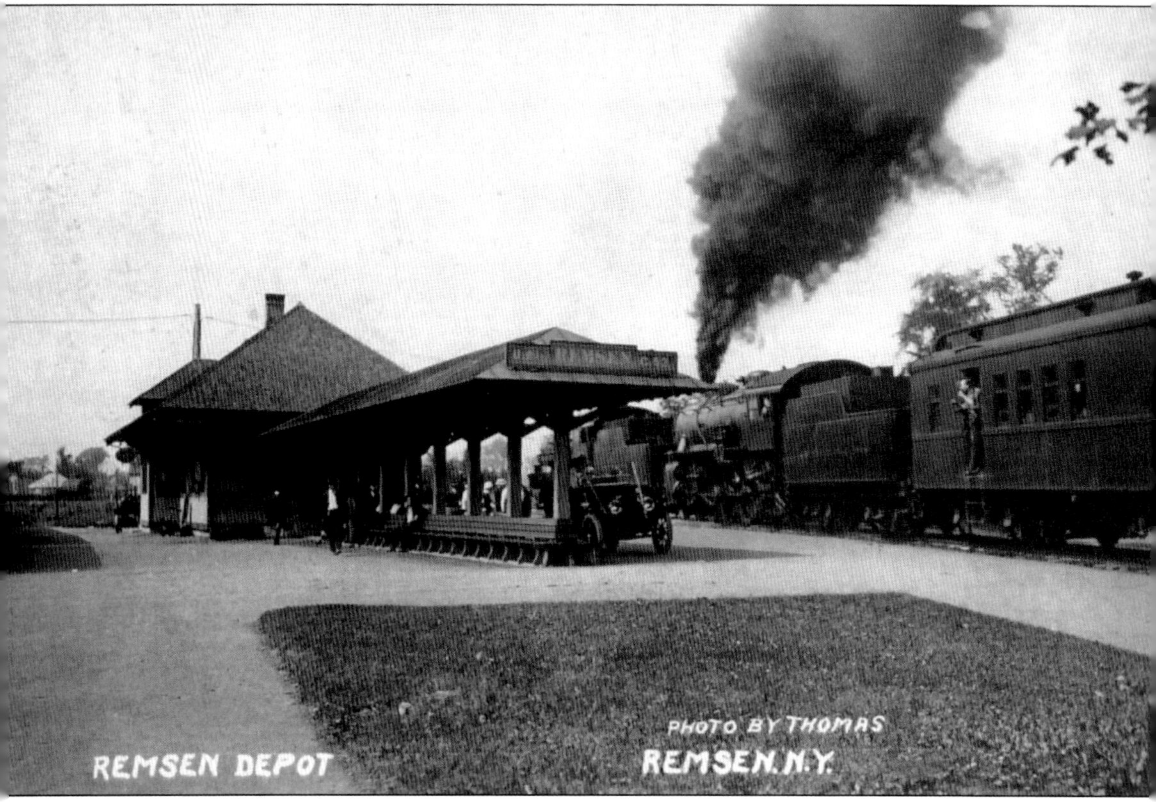

Remsen became a very busy rail hub in the 1890s and into the early 1900s. It happened to be the only station between Utica and Watertown where all three New York Central railroad divisions converged and a turntable was operated. The original Remsen train station was destroyed by fire in the late 1890s. Its replacement served as many as 40 passenger trains per day. Notable passengers, many with private cars, included the Vanderbilts, Webbs, Rockefellers, Whitneys, and Roosevelts. These wealthy families were traveling to their lavish Adirondack lodges. Many other tourists came to Remsen to board trains, sustaining the flourishing local hotel and restaurant operations. The Remsen rail yard at one time contained nine tracks. At least 17 turnouts were used by many local businesses and industries associated with the railroad, including a stockyard, coal yard, milk plant, feed mill, lumberyard, and cold storage plant. (Photograph by LeRoy Thomas, courtesy of Jeanette Walter.)

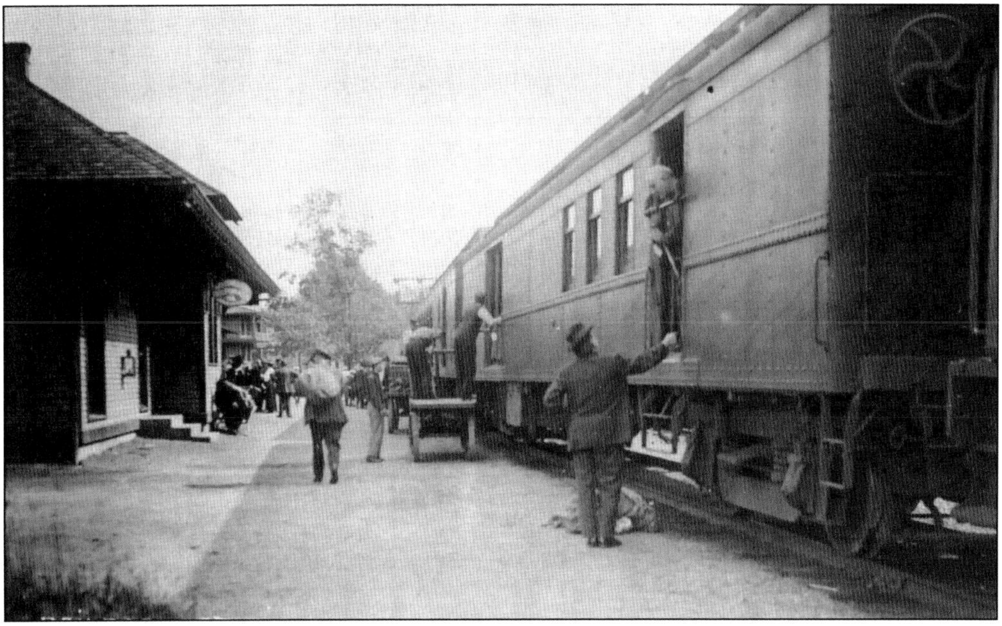

The train station was a regular meeting place. The addition of Webb's Mohawk & Malone rail line made the inner Adirondacks accessible to those who wished to travel there. This line passed through Remsen and brought many tourists with it. The Mohawk & Malone was opposed by conservationists of the time, who claimed it would ruin the hunting and fishing in the Adirondacks. (Courtesy of Jeanette Walter.)

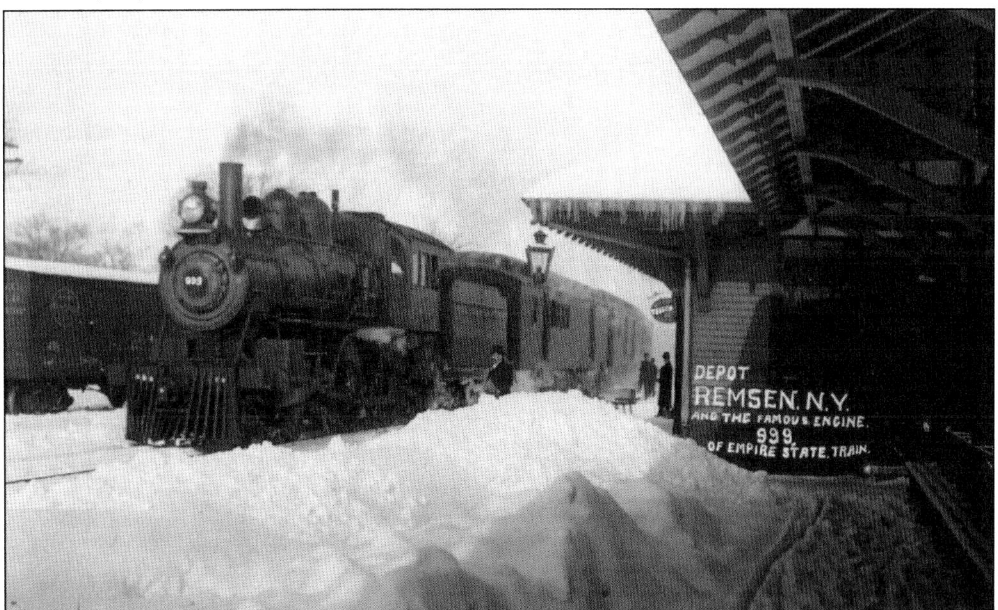

This wintertime image of the Remsen depot shows the "Famous Engine 999 of Empire State Train." Using a Herkimer–Remsen line, the Mohawk & Malone Railroad offered service from New York City to Montreal via Albany, Utica, Remsen, Saranac Lake, and Malone. Later, the Herkimer line was replaced by a Utica–Remsen route using RW&O track. This railroad opened the interior of the Adirondacks to the public. (Photograph by LeRoy Thomas, courtesy of Jeanette Walter.)

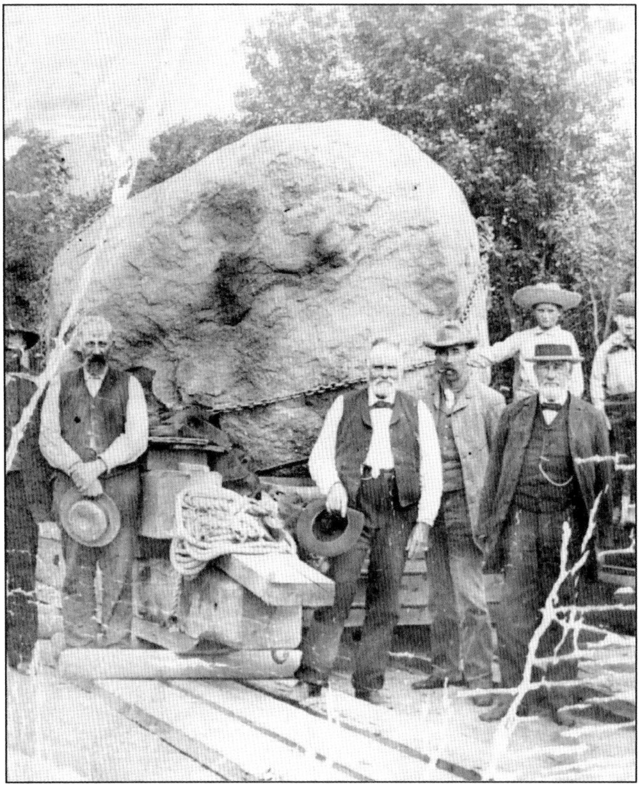

The boulder that served as the base for the Gen. Nicholas Herkimer monument in the Herkimer village park was harvested from the Pirnie farm, south of the Remsen village. It was transported by rail to Herkimer in the summer of 1907. There was much excitement in Remsen, and many people came out to view the boulder's transport. (Courtesy of Jeanette Walter.)

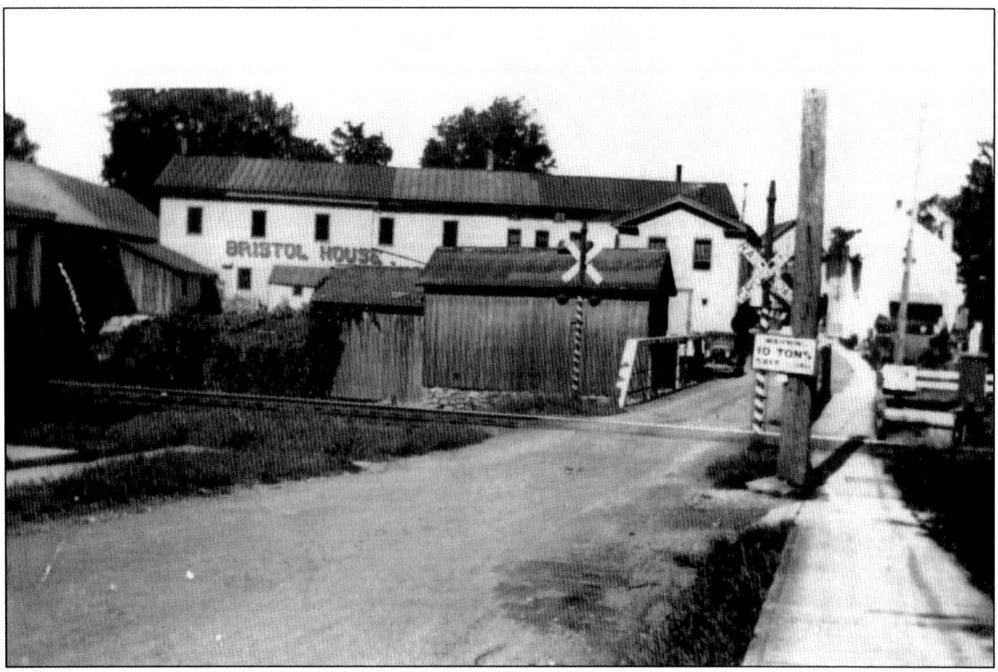

This image shows Prospect Street at the bridge crossing the Cincinnati Creek. The railroad also crosses the street here and can be seen directly in front of the bridge. The rear of the Bristol House is in the background. (Courtesy of Jeanette Walter.)

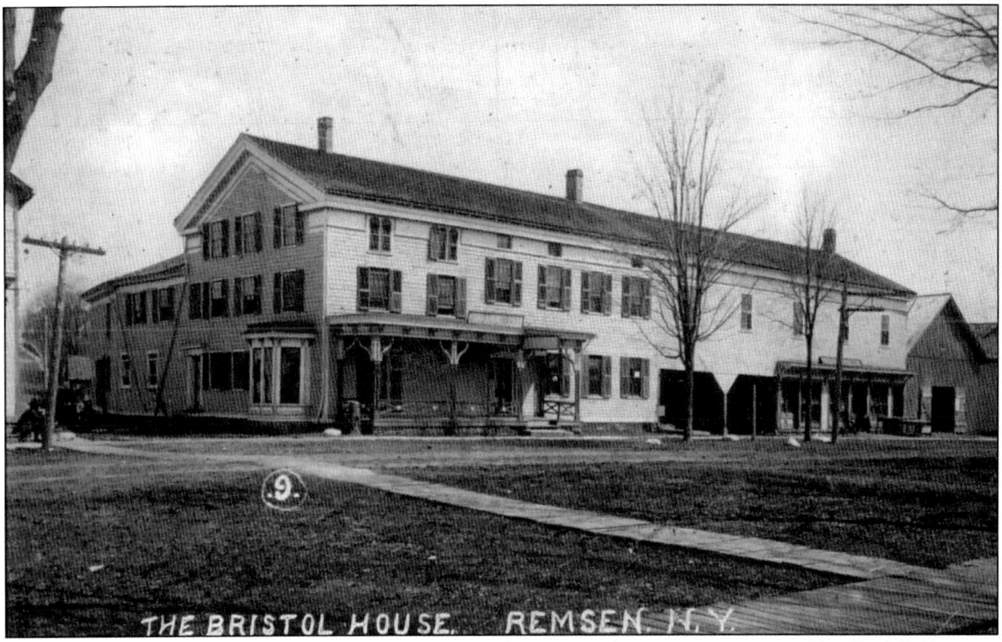

The Bristol House was located on the corner of Main and Prospect Streets. Dr. Earl Bill came to Remsen from the Steuben countryside in 1814. He operated it as an inn. Bill was succeeded by Jacob "Uncle Jake" Lewis, known as a fun-loving storyteller who made up outlandish tales to entertain his companions. Lewis was succeeded in business by George Dawson and then Friend Bristol, who later sold the property to John Brant and Frank Gainsway. In October 1905, the Third District Republican Convention was held there. The ballroom was often used as a theater and voting hall. Church suppers were also held there. Gainsway sold the Bristol House to Orville Davis in 1947. It became the Remsen Hotel and burned down on January 28, 1977. It housed the Harold Evans barbershop, the Gainsway Electrical Shop, the Victory Store, a Laundromat, a beauty shop, and upstairs apartments. (Both, courtesy of Jeanette Walter.)

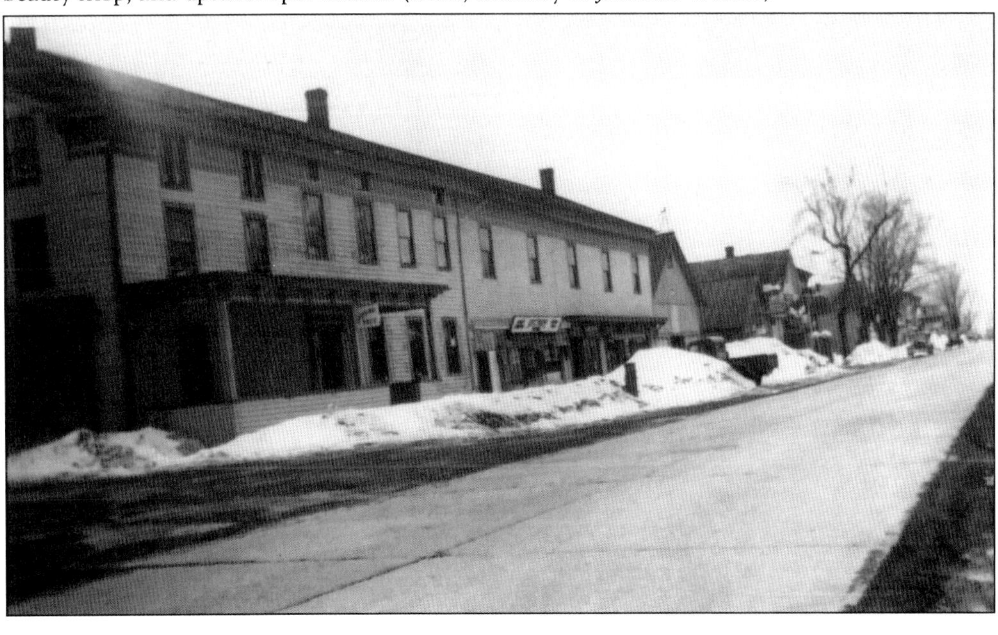

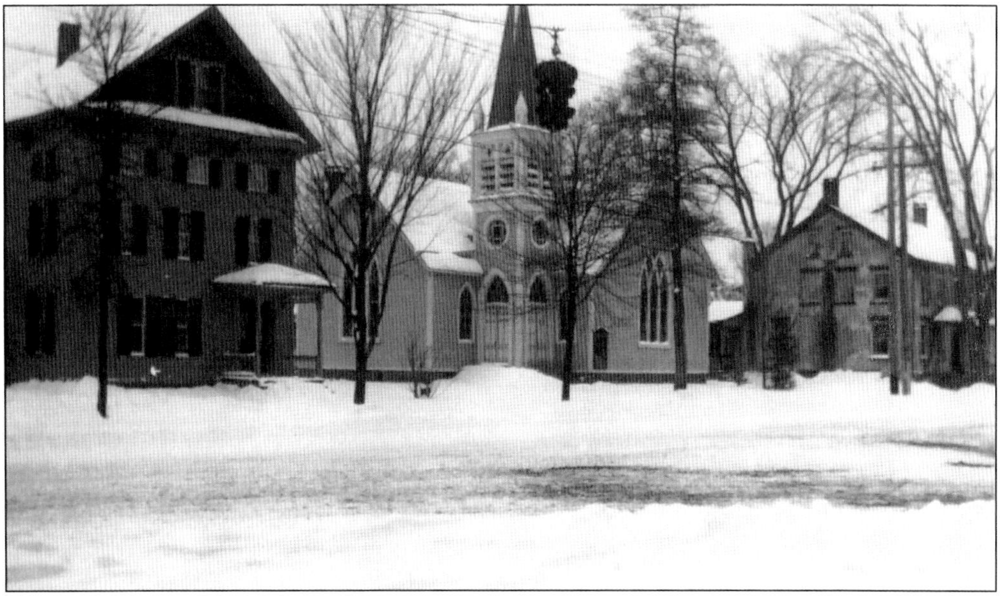

The Baptist church on Main Street was built in 1893. The Remsen Volunteer Fire Department built a firehouse next door to the church in 1965. Notice the traffic light, which no longer exists in the intersection. It was one of two in the village. The church building is currently the Remsen Performing and Visual Arts Center. (Courtesy of Jeanette Walter.)

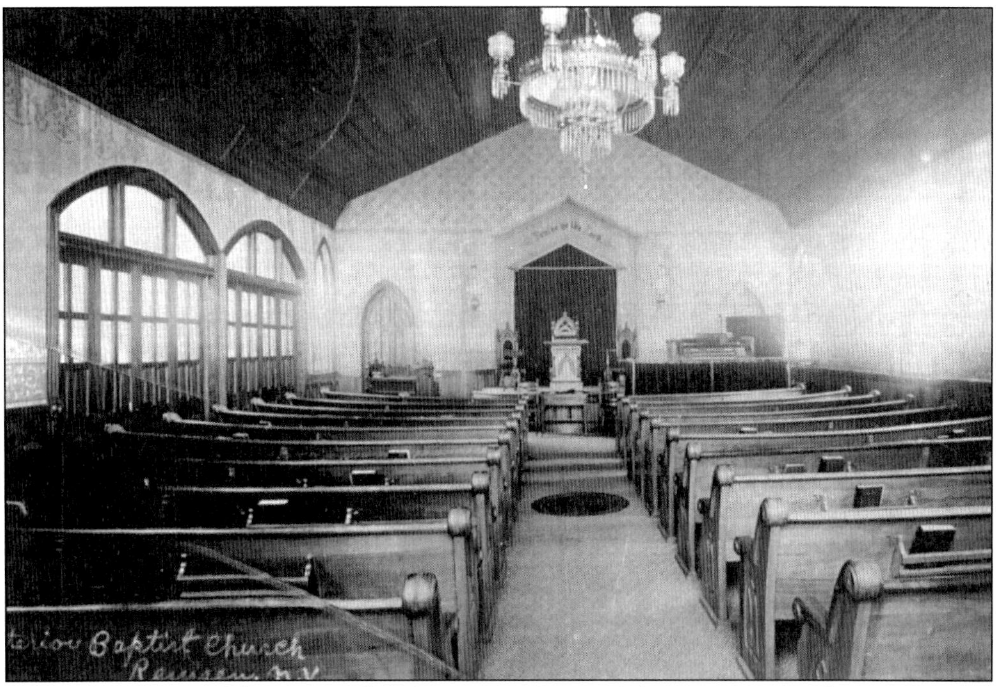

This is the interior of the Baptist church on Main Street while it was in use. The congregation became too small to sustain, so the church was closed. The building remained empty for a number of years until its 2011 revitalization as the arts center. (Courtesy of Jeanette Walter.)

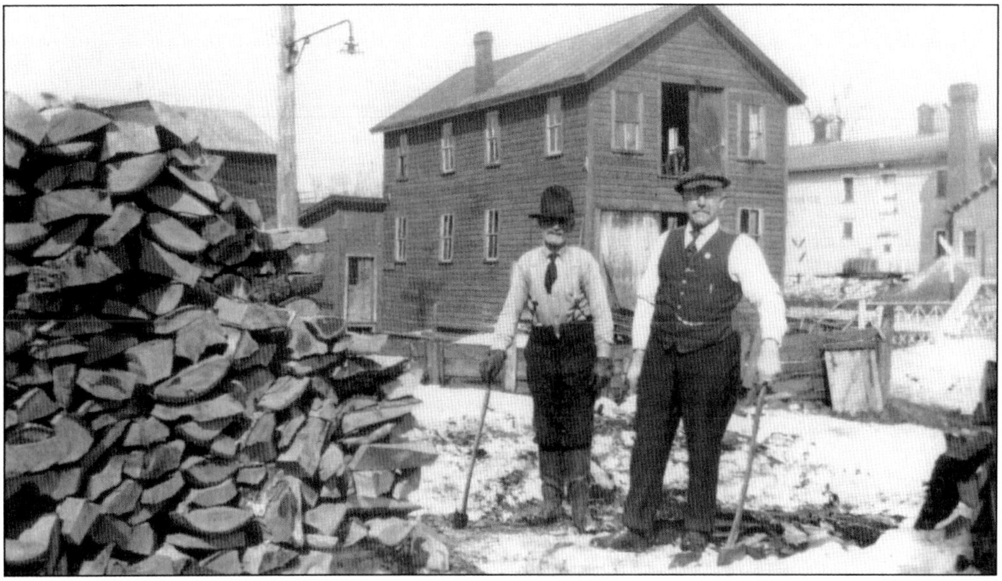

In the early part of the 20th century, cutting firewood in the warmer months was crucial to winter comfort and survival. Remsen's winters typically had many days and nights when the temperature never got above minus 30 degrees. Jim Reed (left) and an unidentified man are pictured in front of Reed's woodworking shop, where they have piled firewood higher than they stand. This building was later Doug Hughes's Service Shop. (Courtesy of Jeanette Walter.)

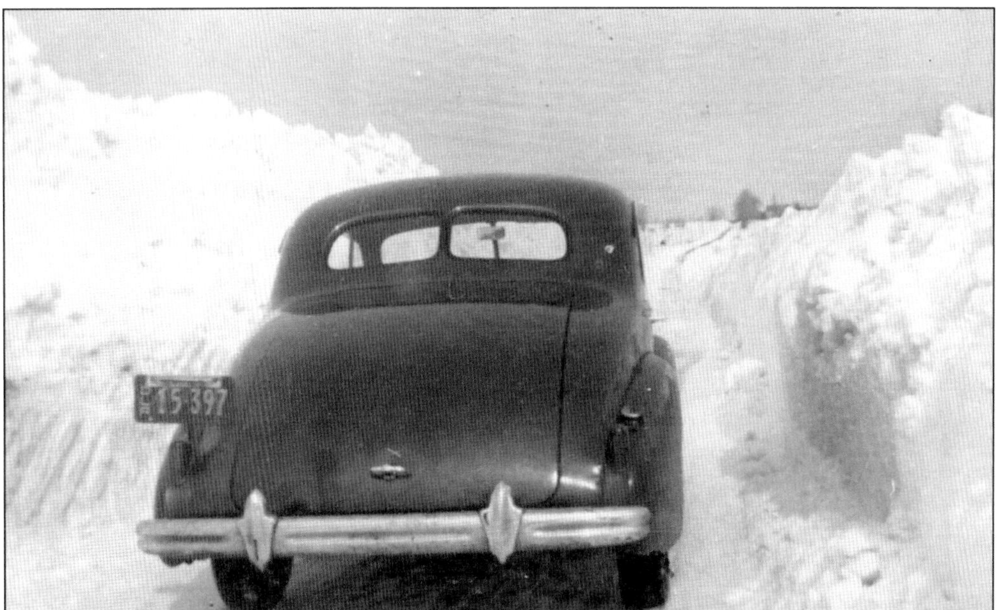

One thing that has remained constant is the heavy Upstate New York winters. The snowbanks here are piled much higher than the rooftop of the automobile. (Author's collection.)

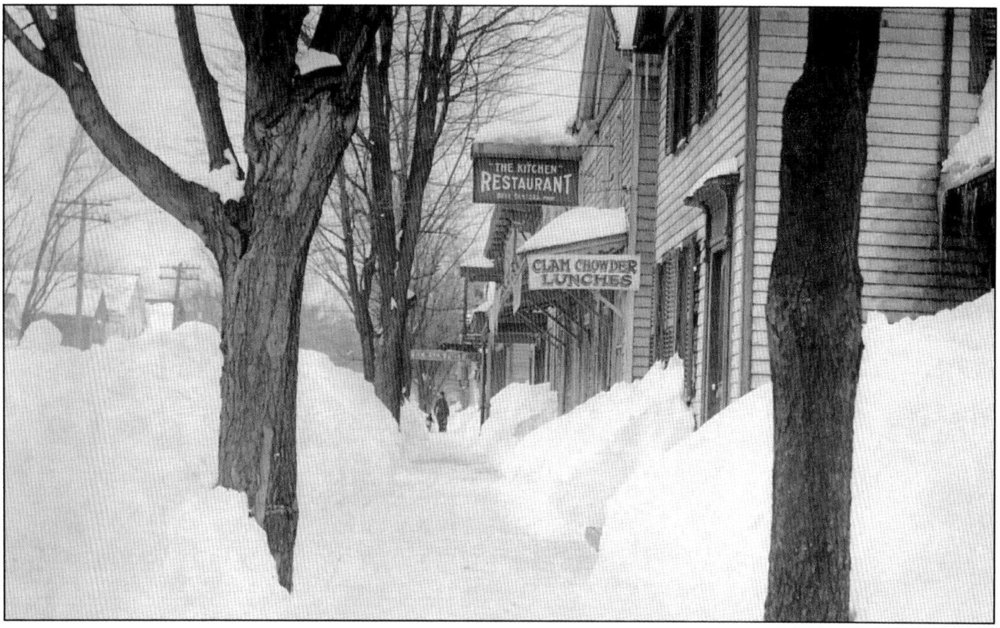

In the early 1900s, a typical restaurant menu would feature meat, potatoes, vegetables, and dessert. At this time, many American diets were based on meat and potatoes. An example of a common meal would be ham, mashed potatoes, wax beans, applesauce, and a roll with butter. Pie was a common dessert. By the 1920s, a lunch would cost between 35¢ and 50¢, a moderate price in the post–World War I economy. Around this time, processed foods were becoming more popular. The Baby Ruth candy bar and Wonder Bread both debuted. Yoo-hoo chocolate drink and Reese's Peanut Butter Cups came to the market. Velveeta Cheese was introduced. This same decade, ice cream rose rapidly in popularity. Vyner's Restaurant and the Kitchen Restaurant were both located downtown in the village of Remsen. (Both, courtesy of Jeanette Walter.)

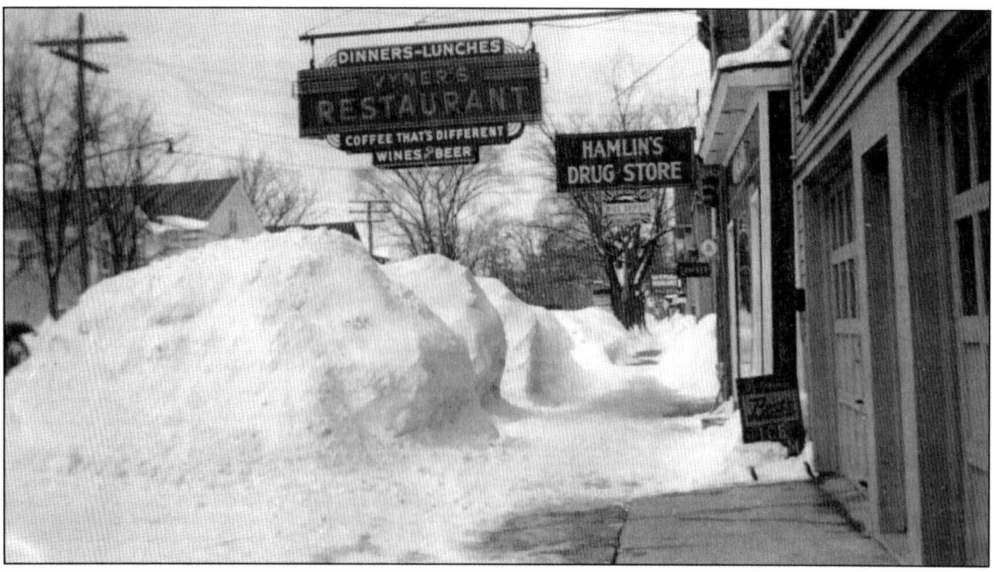

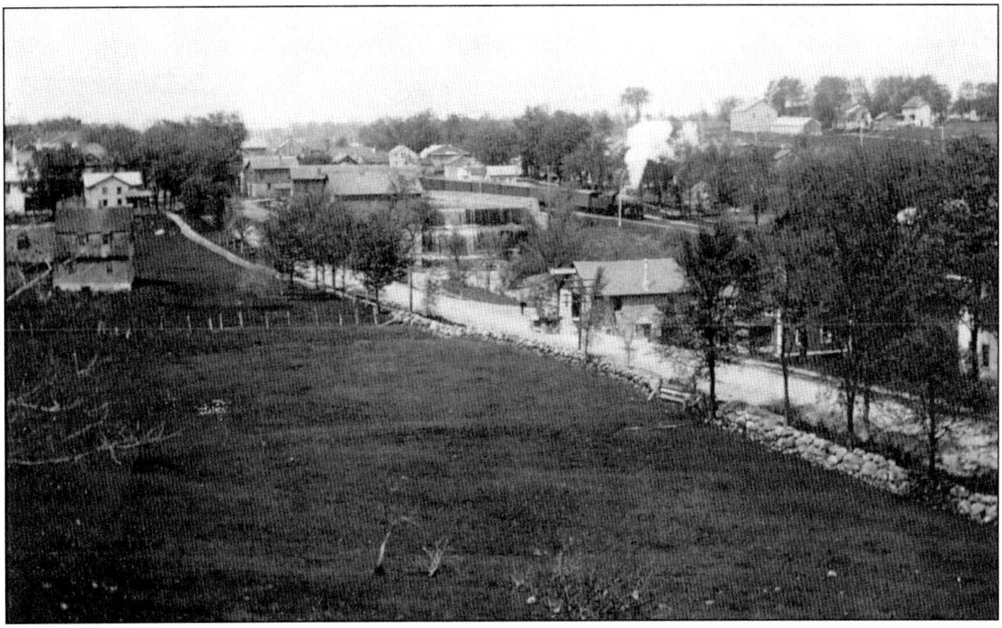

This 1920 photograph shows the edge of Remsen in a view looking down from a hilltop at the southern end of the village. The landscape has changed somewhat, but many of the structures remain. Notice the train passing near the falls. (Photograph by LeRoy Thomas, courtesy of Jeanette Walter.)

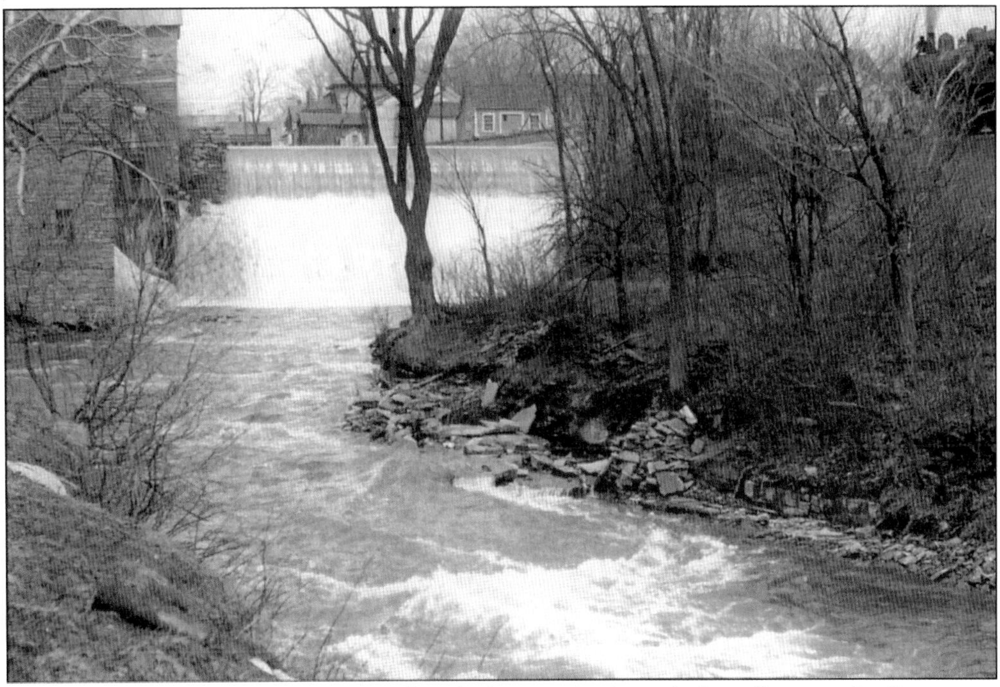

Mills were built around the Remsen Falls, which cut right through the village via the Cincinnati Creek. One of these was a gristmill built by Cornelius Jones in the 1850s. It featured a horizontal waterwheel located in the cellar instead of the typical vertical wheel usually found outside of the building. Another was a sawmill built shortly after. (Courtesy of Jeanette Walter.)

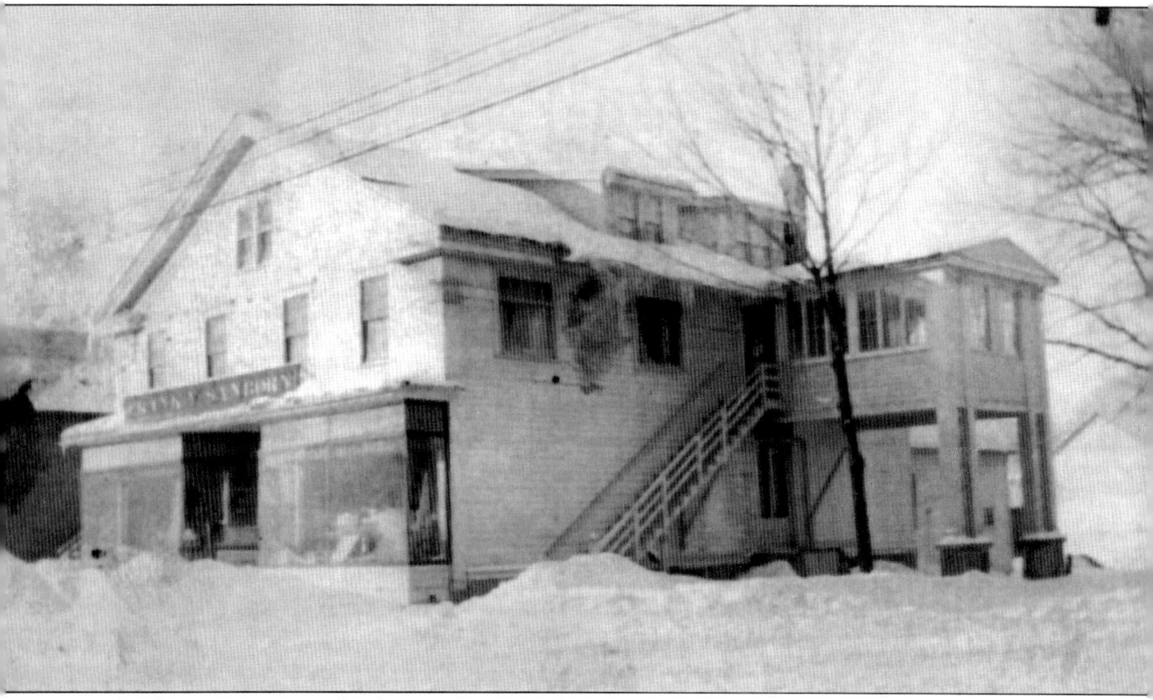

The first proprietor at this location was Jonah Howe. Before operating here, Howe was a partner in a store called Howe & Billings, located on the north corner of Main and Prospect Streets, approximately where the Remsen Country Bakery stands today. Howe was followed in this location by James P. Owen. William H. Griffith and Robert G. Griffith bought the business in 1863 and operated it for five years. In 1868, "R.G." Griffith became sole proprietor, and he continued for 47 years. His retirement was announced in a local newspaper: "R.G. Griffith, one of the stalwart citizens of the village and town, it is here printed to signalize his retirement from business after 50 years of close attention to the work and duties of mercantile establishment, the reputation of which was second to none in that section." It is believed that Frank and Ida Sanborn were the next in line to conduct business in the present Ackley-Mills Funeral Home. They were the proprietors when this photograph was taken on February 22, 1927. (Courtesy of Jeanette Walter.)

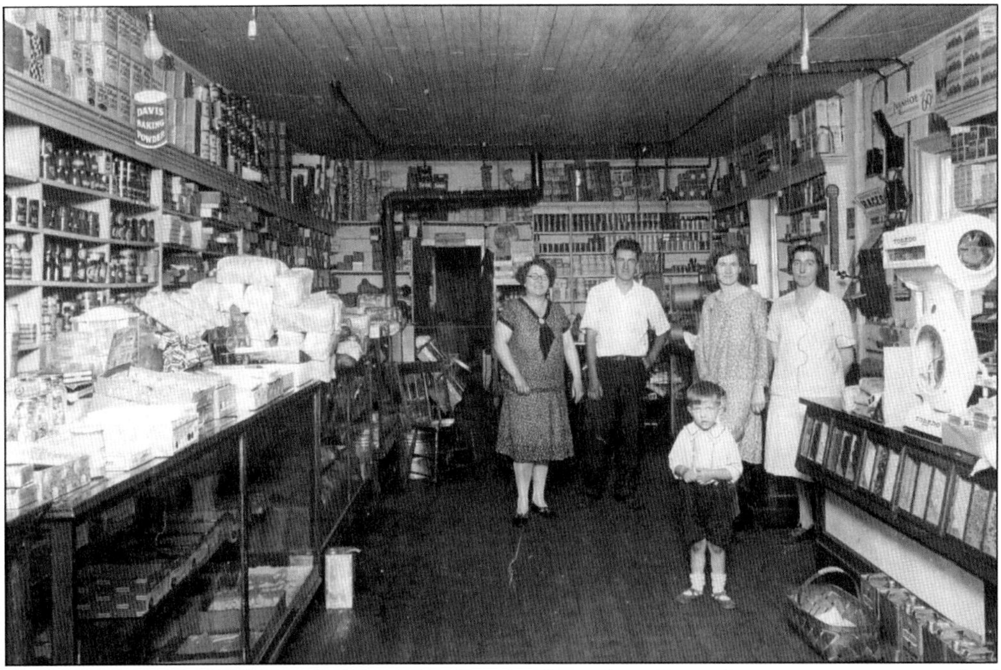

This country store is fully stocked from the floor to the ceiling. Even the countertops are stacked high with goods. From left to right are Abby Jones Evans, Lawrence Beagle, a Mrs. Lane, Charlie "Boy" Lane, who later drowned in B.K. Brown Pond, and an unidentified woman. (Courtesy of Jeanette Walter.)

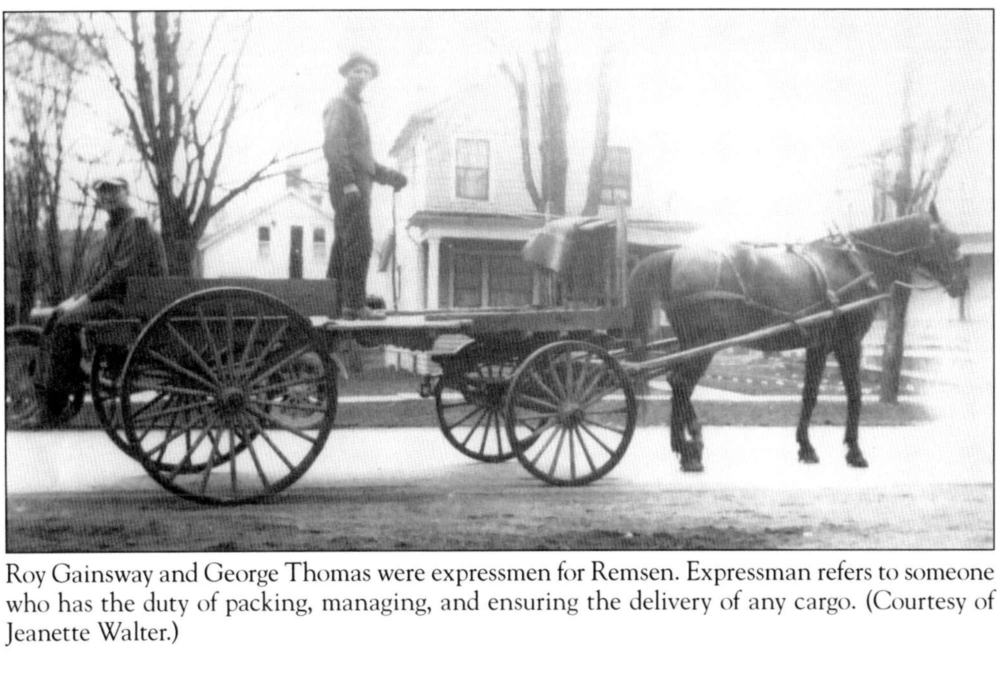

Roy Gainsway and George Thomas were expressmen for Remsen. Expressman refers to someone who has the duty of packing, managing, and ensuring the delivery of any cargo. (Courtesy of Jeanette Walter.)

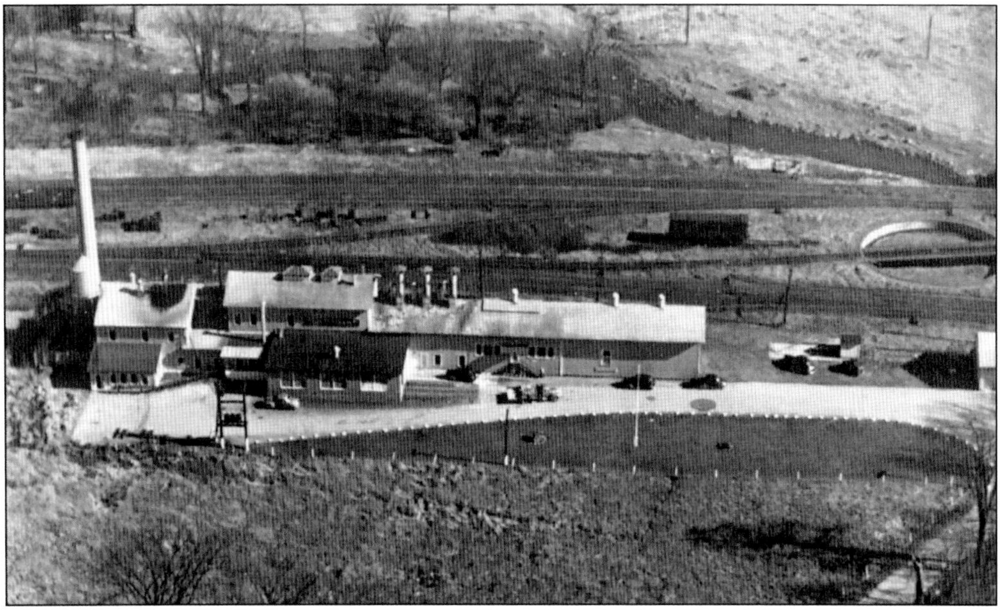

The Dairymen's League in Remsen was built in the 1920s. It was a part of the larger Dairymen's League Co-op, which was formed in response to New York State dairy farmers' dissatisfaction with outlets for marketing their milk. Remsen dairy farmers wanted to take their milk to a station close to their farms. Notice the old railroad turntable in the upper right corner. (Courtesy of Jeanette Walter.)

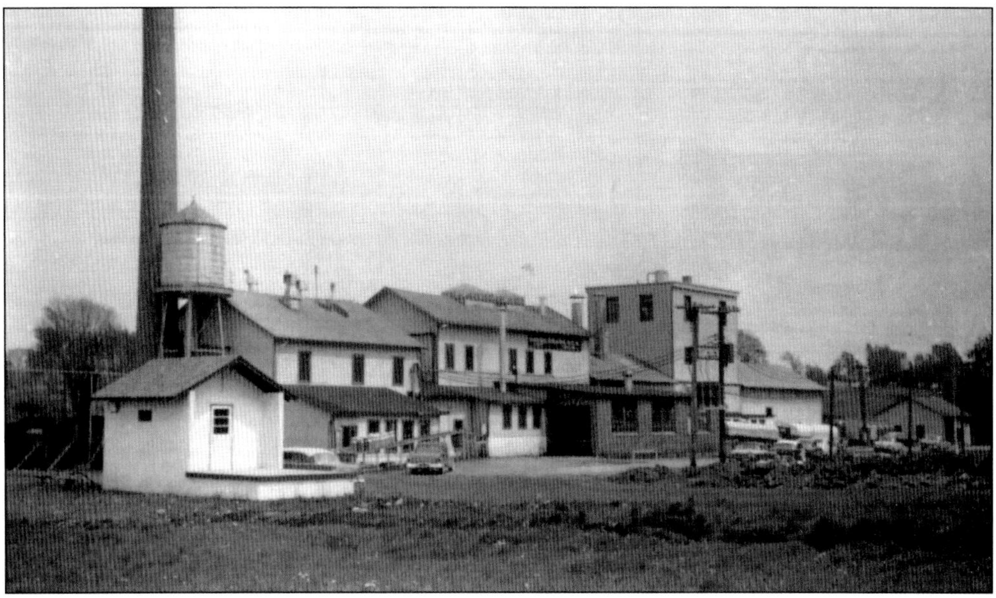

The Dairymen's League operated a plant on the north end of the Remsen village from the 1920s until the 1960s. The daily capacity of the plant was about 225,000 pounds of milk. It was one of the largest employers in the village, and its closure devastated many. The building is currently a multiple-unit rental property. (Courtesy of Jeanette Walter.)

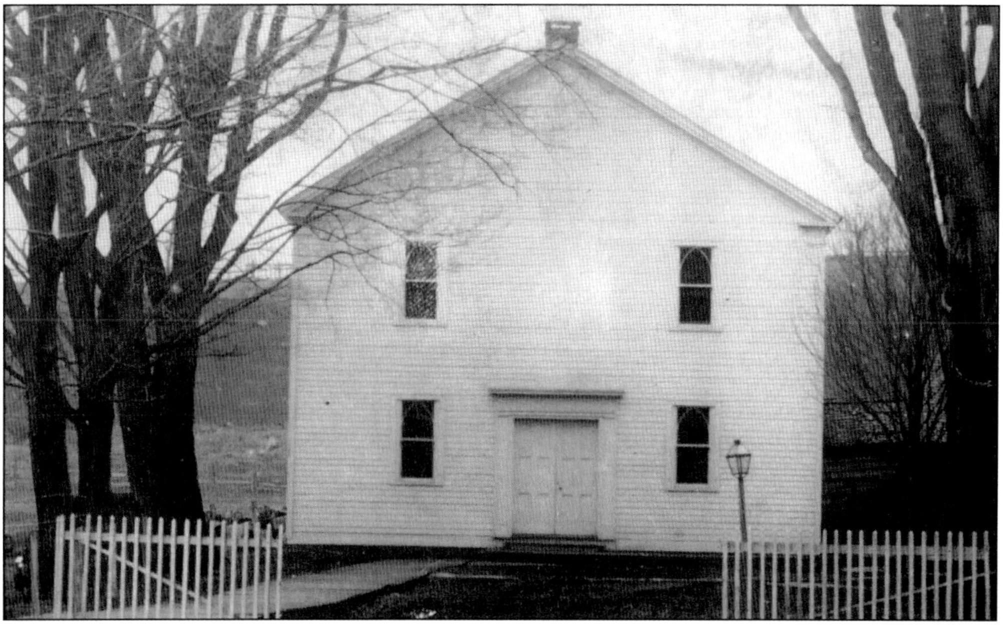

The building behind the present Ackley-Mills Funeral Home was the former Peniel Church. It was built in 1839 under the leadership of Rev. Morris Roberts, who preached at Bethel Church in Steuben for more than 30 years. "Old Morris" was something of a legend in the Remsen-Steuben area. He was highly respected and was known for his powerful personality and community service. (Courtesy of Jeanette Walter.)

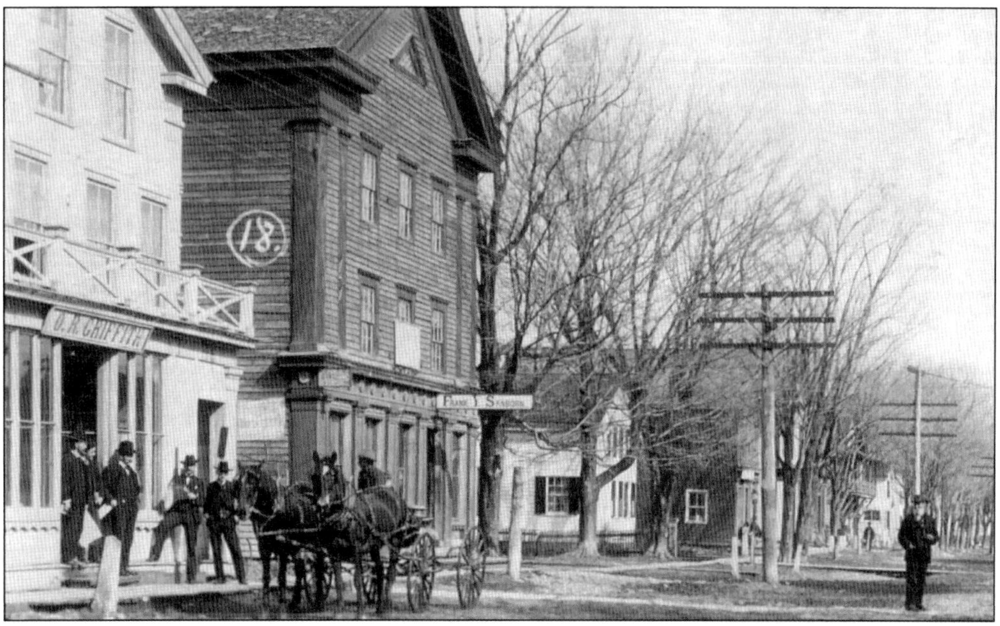

This photograph depicts the downtown business district in Remsen in the early 1900s. In the photograph are the Griffith and Sanborn businesses. The Griffith store was built by merchant Griffith W. Roberts and, at the time of this photograph, was operated by O.R. Griffith. The photographer would have been standing on Main Street. Notice the gentleman standing in the street. (Photograph by LeRoy Thomas, courtesy of Jeanette Walter.)

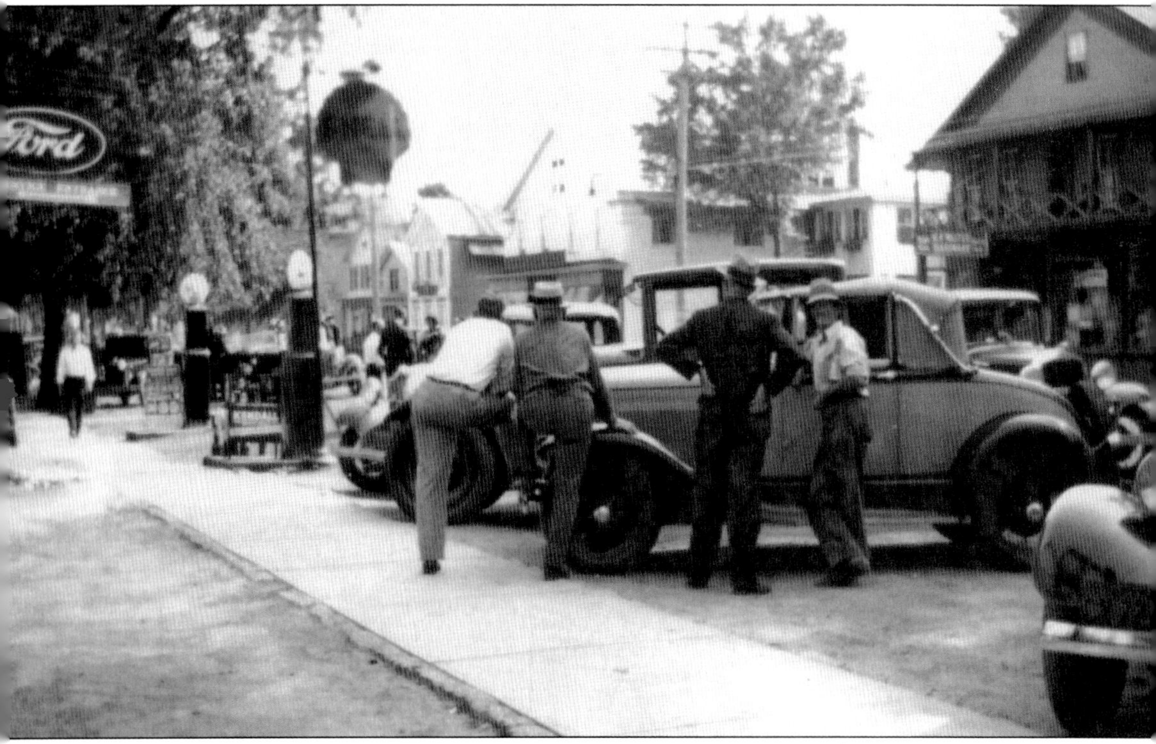

This photograph of Dairyman's League employees gathering during the milk strike was taken from the east side of Main Street, in front of the Williams Ford garage and next to the current location of Stinger's bar. The Stinger's bar building was a grocery and confectionery store run by John J. Owens at one point, and after that was a Grand Union grocery store operated by George W. Jones and O.B. Ferguson. The funeral parlor and Walter's Hardware can be seen in the background. (Courtesy of Jeanette Walter.)

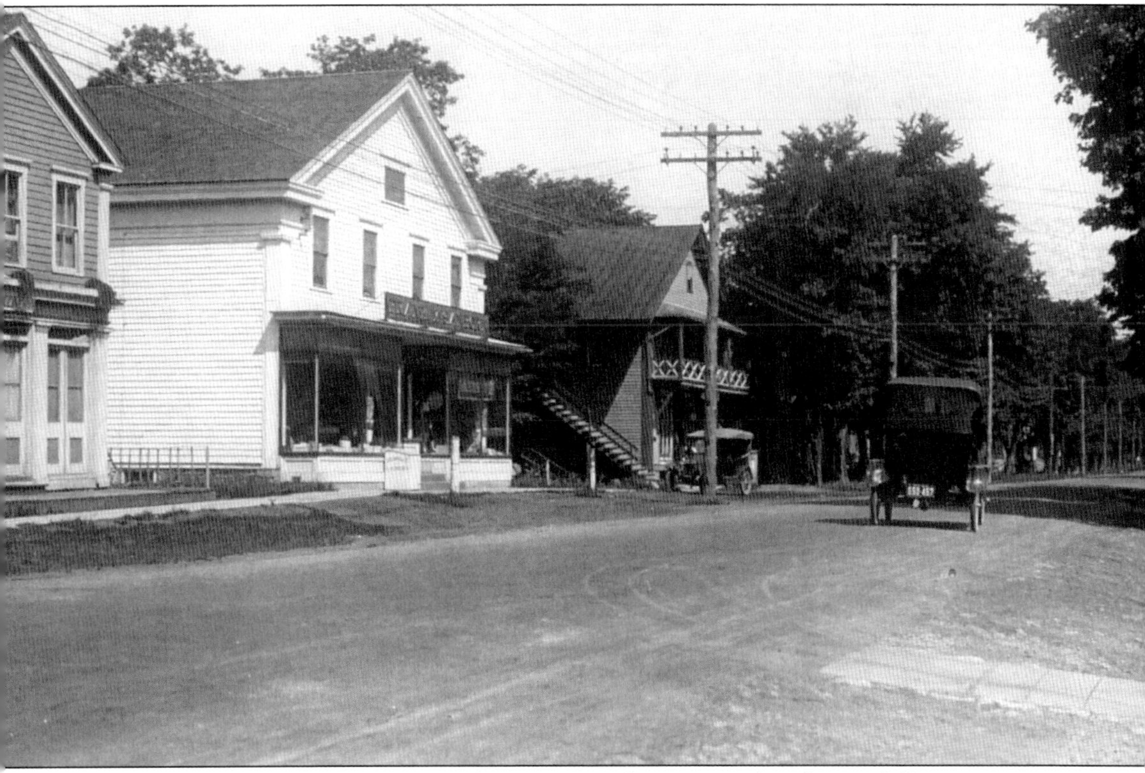

This photograph shows the same area of Main Street, but it was taken from a different vantage point—southeasterly, looking north. The building on the left is the millinery store of Katherine E. Jones. It was later used by the American Legion and referred to as "the Legion rooms." For a short time, it was used as school classrooms. (Courtesy of Jeanette Walter.)

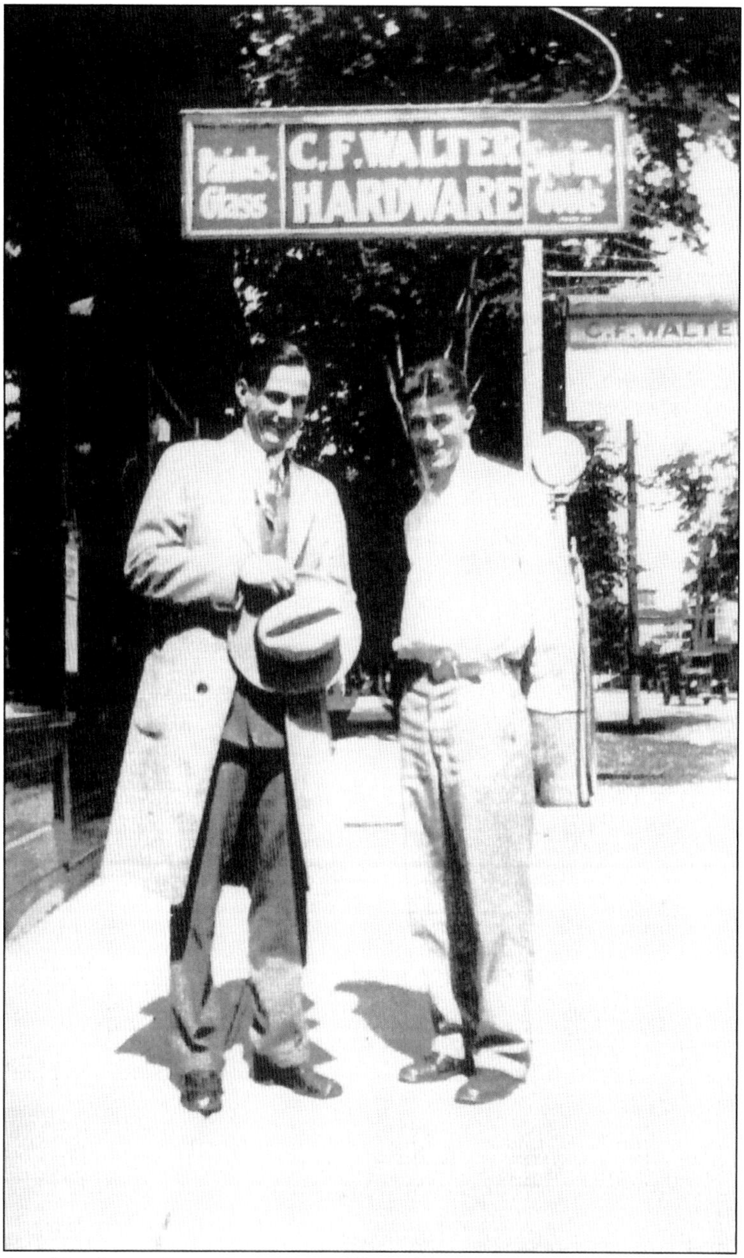

The C.F. Walter Hardware Store was operated by Clifton F. Walter (left), one of Remsen's most esteemed citizens. He was deeply involved in community affairs, held the office of town clerk for about 10 years, and was a director of the First National Bank of Remsen. Walter, originally from Clifton Springs, married Mary LaMunion in 1906. He then came to Remsen to purchase his father-in-law's hardware store, which he operated successfully until his death. His untimely passing in 1933 shocked and bereaved the village. The *Boonville Herald* reported: "A deep, heartfelt sorrow is felt. Generous, kindly to the needy, obliging in all his business relations, he will be greatly missed here." Pall bearers at his funeral included many of Remsen's notable citizens: Frank Davis, Allan Brown, Milton Cole, Edwin Milgate, Reginald Park, and Hubert Arthur. Walter was buried in Prospect Cemetery. (Courtesy of Jeanette Walter.)

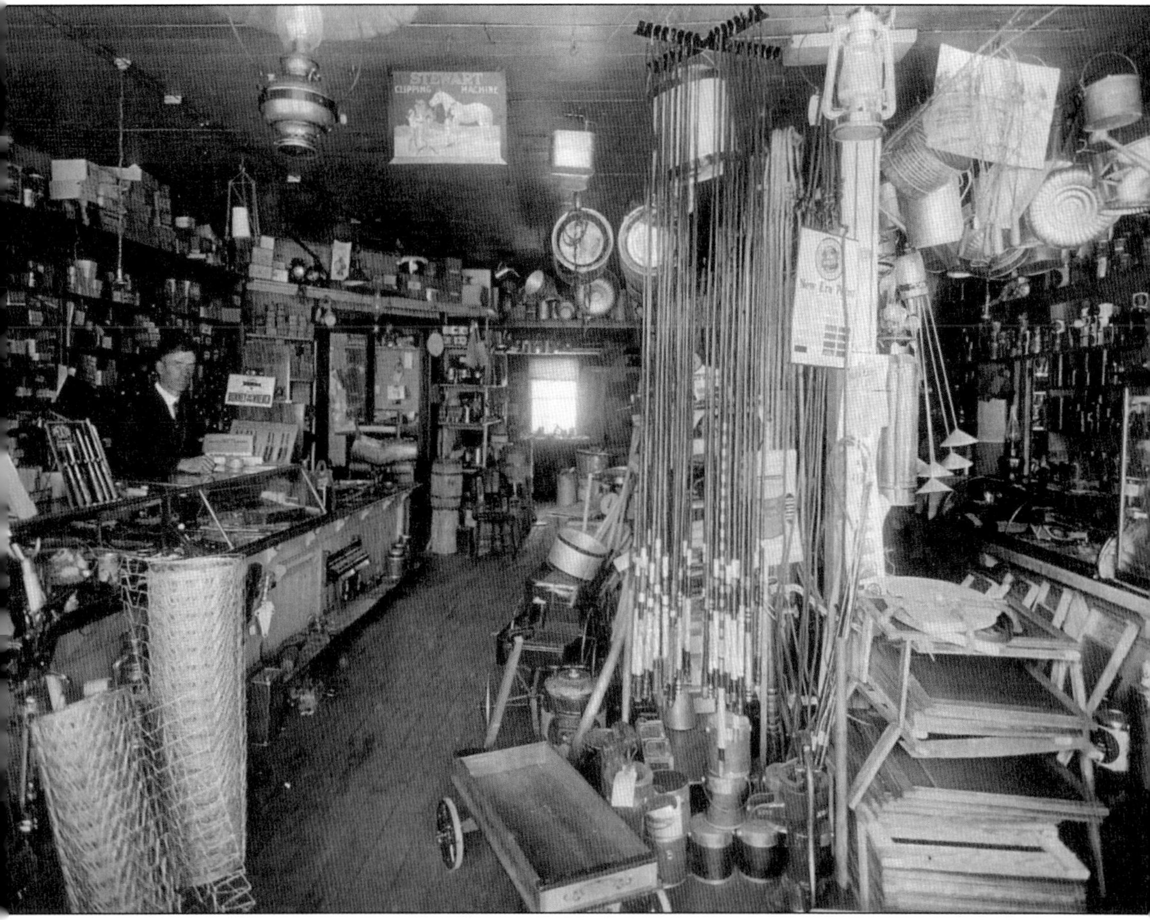

The general stores in Remsen, much like those in other small towns, were historically a one-stop destination for village and rural residents' shopping for the farm, home, and business. The clerks often came to know all of the customers and forge congenial relationships. It was common practice to spend hours at the general store talking to neighbors or catching up on village gossip. General stores stocked everything from buttons and pins to tires and wheels. Many stores gave away paper fans or yardsticks with the business name printed on them. Around the late 19th century, advertising became important to manufacturers and they began to brand their products. At that time, country stores began to display all types of signs, calendars, lights, fixtures, and even murals on the sides of their buildings advertising soft drinks, tobacco, farm implements, and more. (Courtesy of Jeanette Walter.)

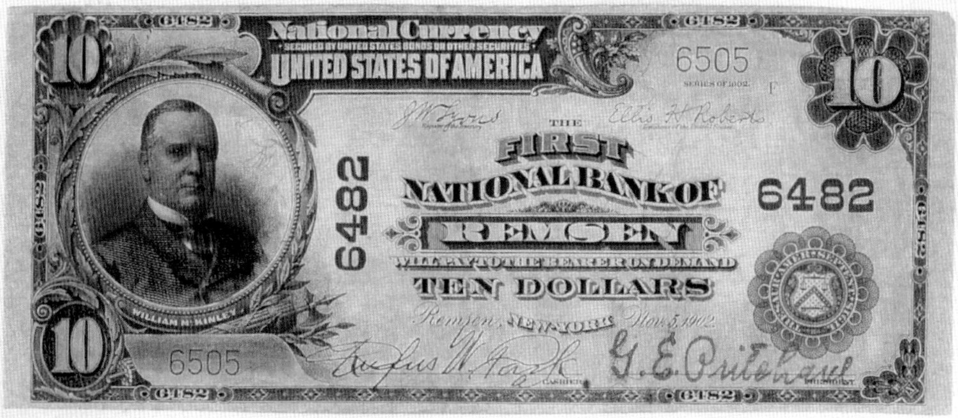

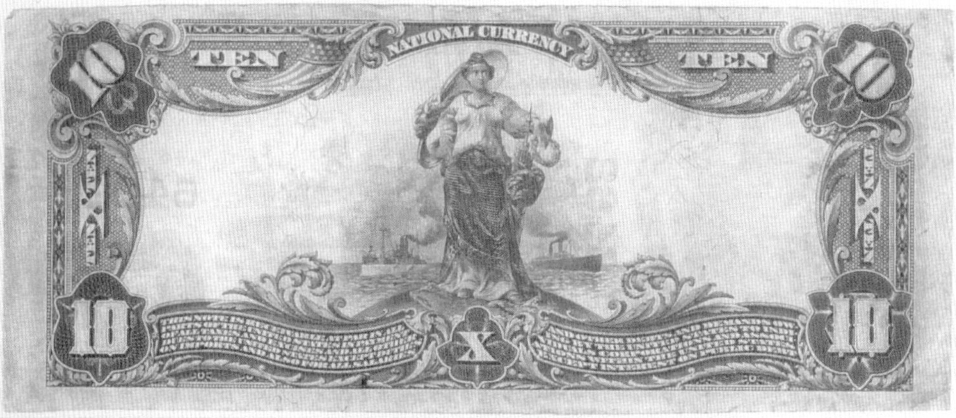

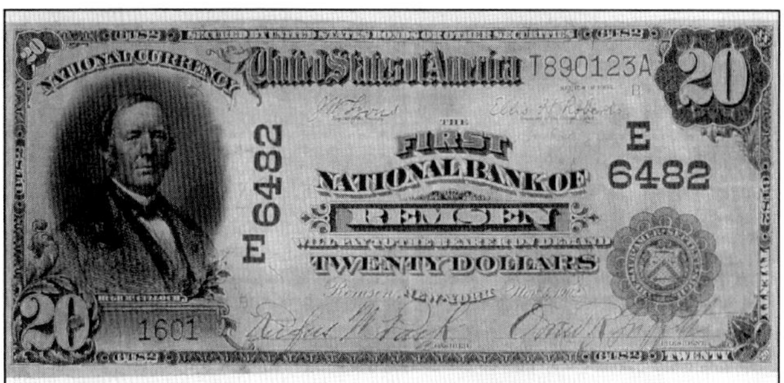

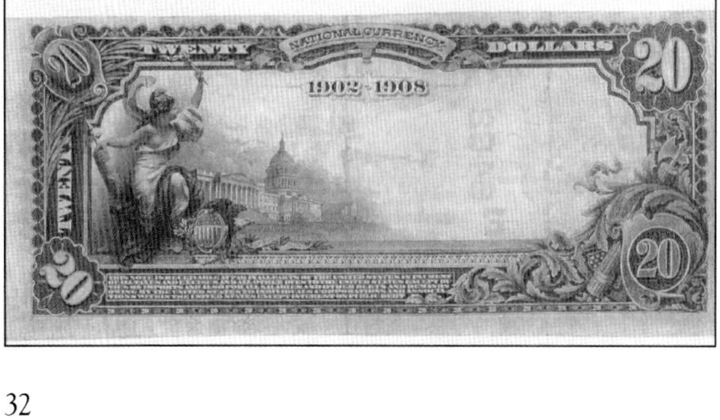

These First National Bank of Remsen notes were legal tender, signed by Rufus M. Parks, who worked as both bank manager and president. The $10 bill bears the likeness of William McKinley, the 25th president of the United States, who was assassinated in 1901. The $20 bill bears the likeness of Hugh McCulloch, the first comptroller of the currency. Selected for this position by Secretary of the Treasury Salmon Chase and Pres. Abraham Lincoln, McCulloch served 22 months. He later served as the secretary of the treasury, first under Lincoln and later under both Pres. Andrew Johnson and Pres. Chester Arthur. (Both, courtesy of Jeanette Walter.)

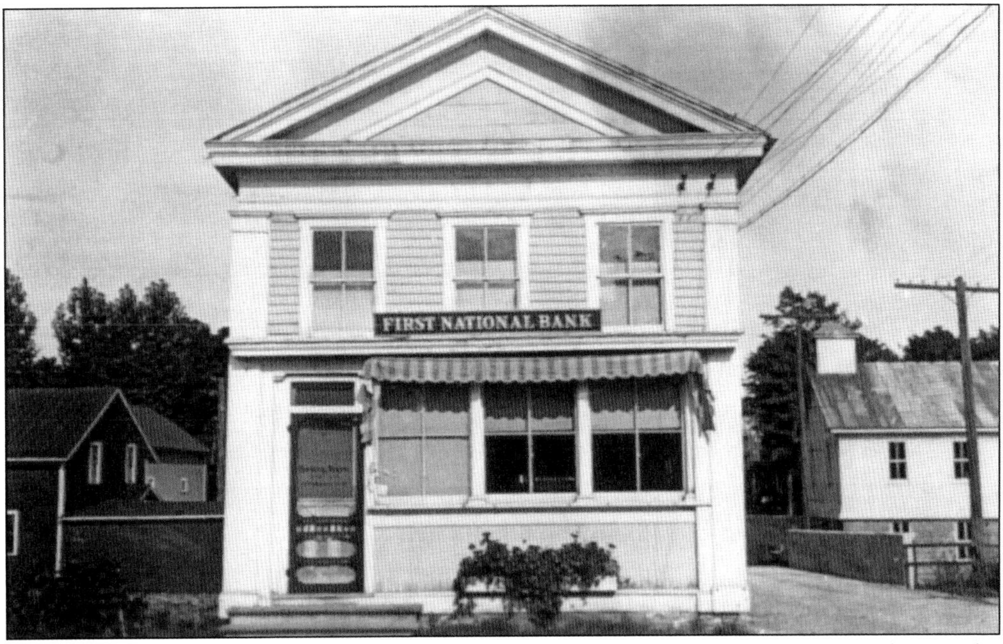

Pictured is the First National Bank of Remsen. At one point in the late 1800s, before the building was used as a bank, it was a general store operated by merchant Richard Richards. The First National Bank of Remsen was organized in November 1902. The first day of business was November 10 of that year. One hundred years later, the last bank to operate in Remsen was Fleet Bank, which left town in 2002. (Courtesy of Jeanette Walter.)

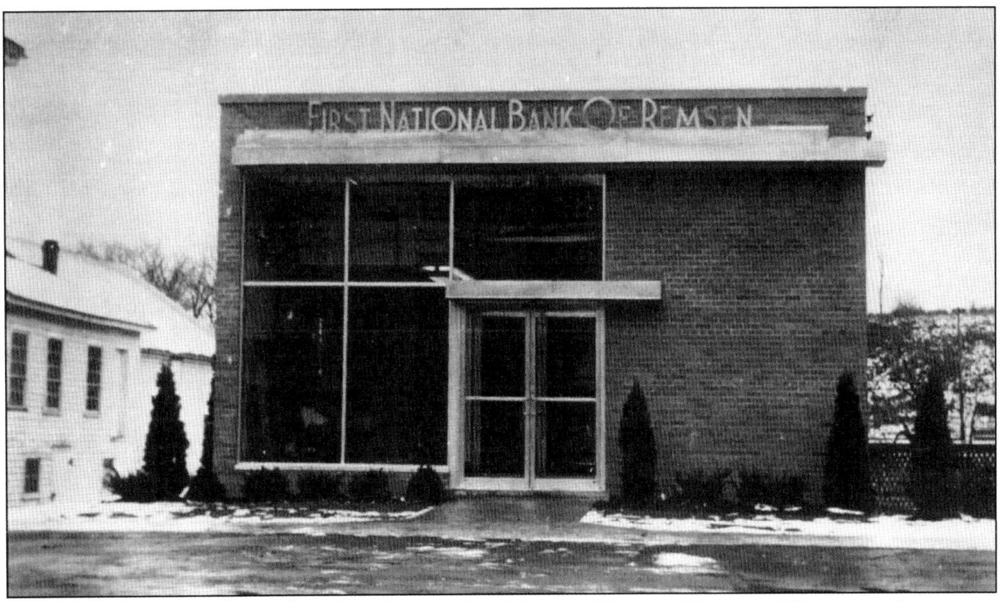

This smaller brick building also served as the First National Bank of Remsen. This was in later years and on the other side of the street, bordering the town park. This building is currently the home of the family-owned and -operated Smith Insurance Company. (Courtesy of Jeanette Walter.)

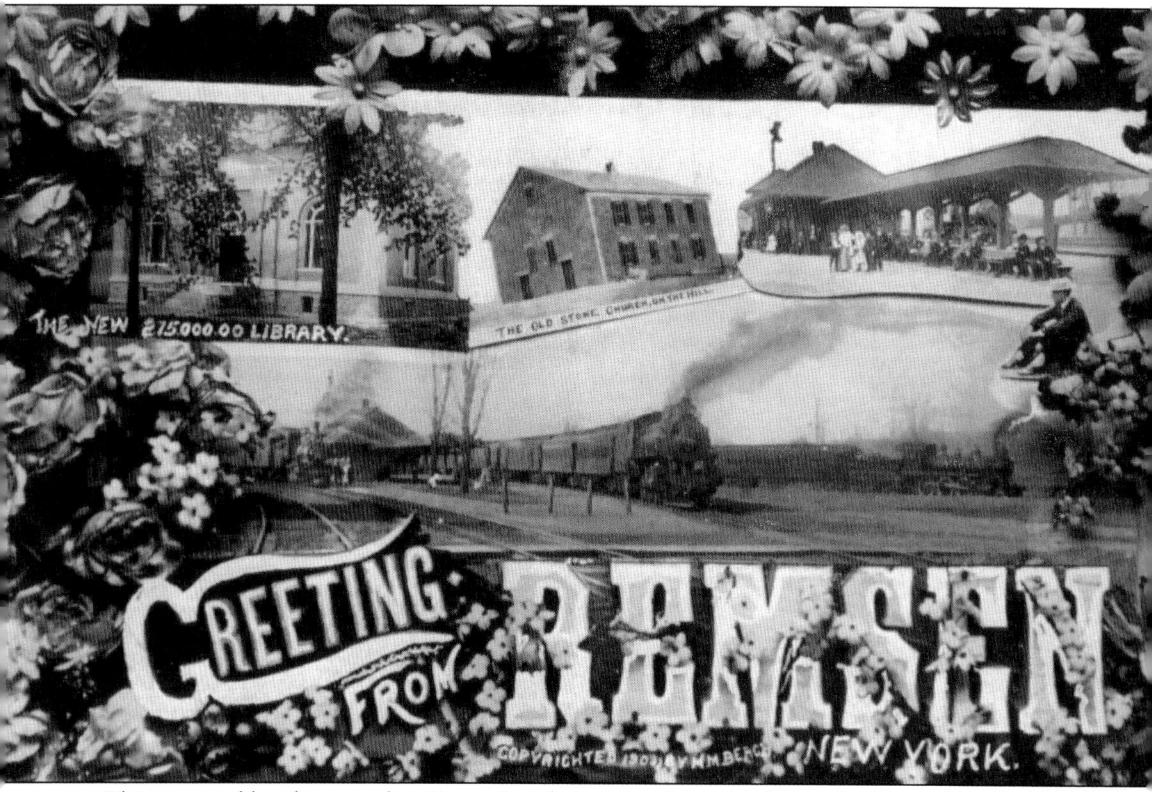

This postcard by photographer Henry Beach features the train depot, the Stone Church (Capel Cerrig), and the Didymus Thomas Library. A well-known photographer who documented life in the Western Adirondack region during the early 20th century, Beach (1863–1943) had a home at the end of Pleasant Avenue. Before coming to Remsen, he lived in Lowville. Beach produced and sold thousands of postcards along with his photographs. In addition to standard-view cards, he produced montages and advertising postcards. Much of his work, which documents life during a time of transition, was sold as souvenirs to tourists. He focused on landmarks, schools, churches, work camps, hunting and fishing, industrial mills, train stations, and roads and transportation. His images capture the decline of the horse and buggy era and continue through the era of the early automobile. (Courtesy of Jeanette Walter.)

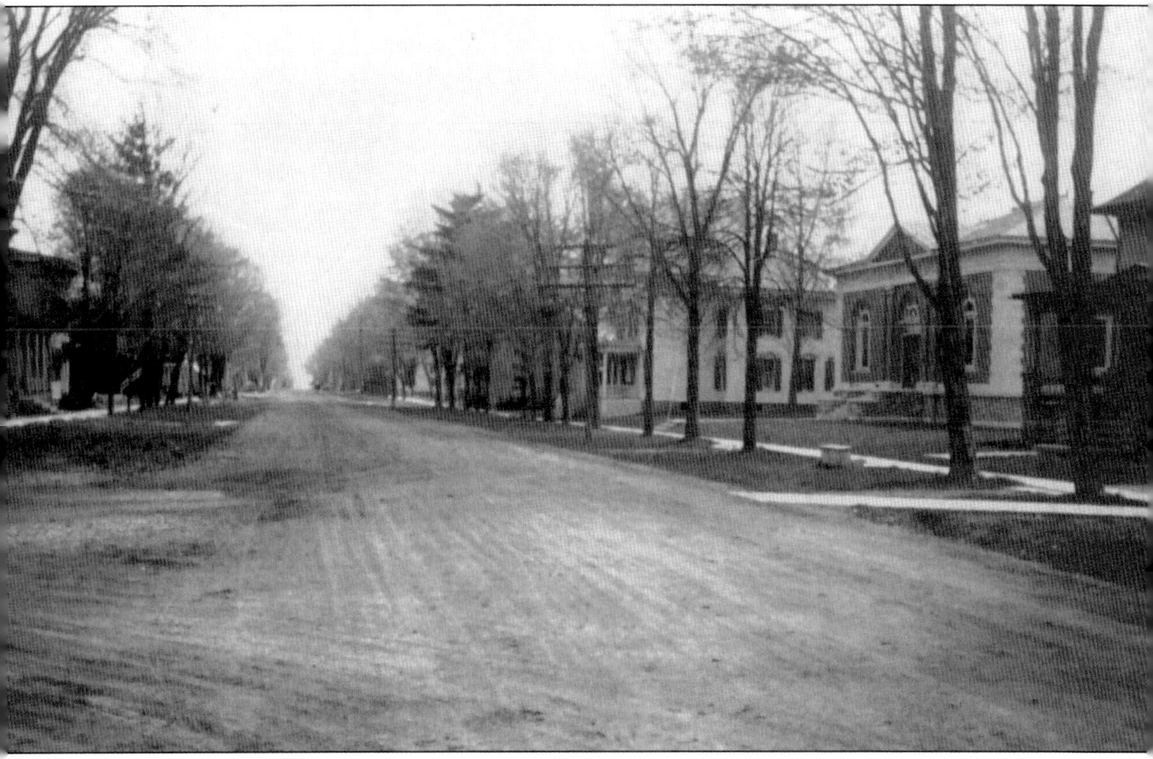

The Didymus Thomas Library can be seen on the right side of Main Street. The library's namesake, Didymus Thomas (whose name means "twin" in Greek), was born in Steuben on May 24, 1812, to Thomas Thomas and his wife, Mary Hughes Thomas. Both were natives of Wales. The couple immigrated to the United States in 1800 and settled in the village of Steuben in 1804. Thomas attended school in Steuben and worked on farms growing up. As a young man, he worked as a schoolteacher, and he later settled into a career as a merchandiser. He was married in 1835 to Lydia Pierce, with whom he had one daughter. Since 1908, the library has been at this location in the middle of the village, but before that, it was on the upper floor of the E.G. Williams drugstore, located in the southern portion of town. Marion Francis, the daughter of Didymus and Lydia Thomas, left money to provide a building for the library. The exterior is pressed brick and marble. The interior is finished oak. (Courtesy of Jeanette Walter.)

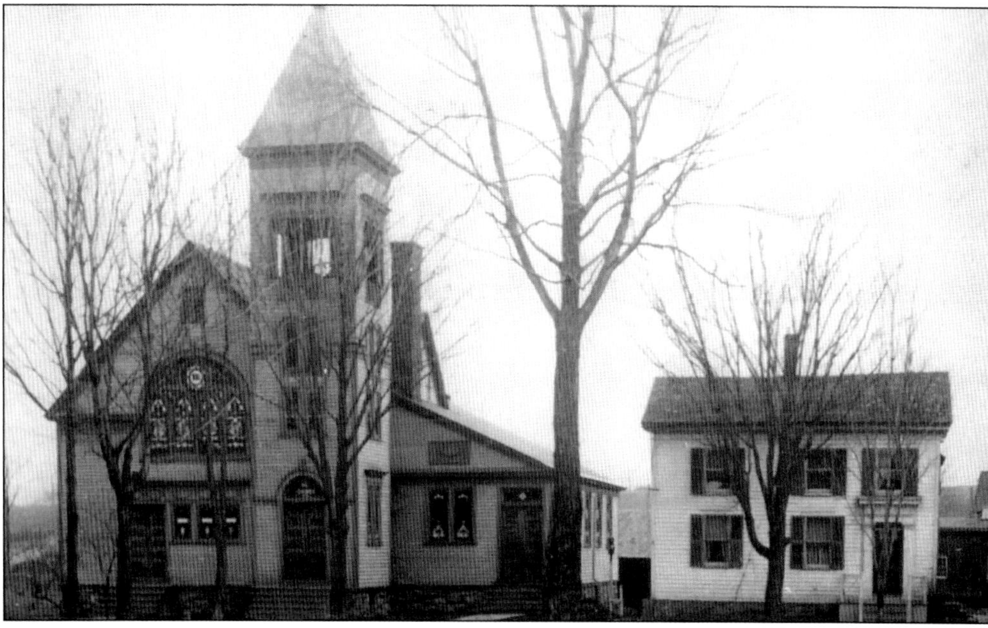

The Remsen Methodist Church was built in 1892. It is the last remaining functioning church in Remsen. The parsonage is shown to the right of the church. (Courtesy of Jeanette Walter.)

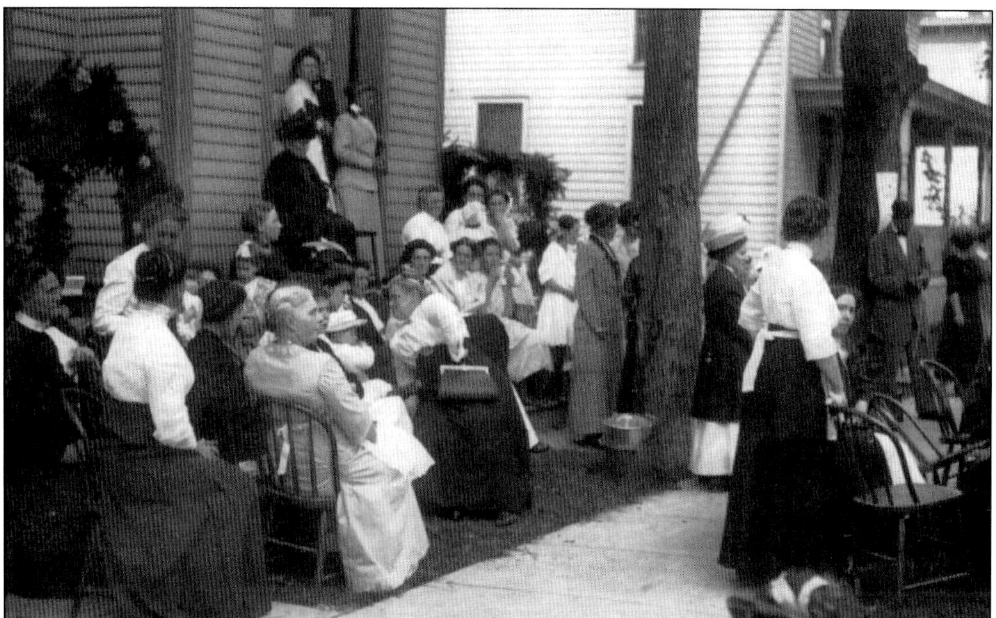

A crowd comprised of members of the Epworth League gathers on Main Street at the Methodist church for the Lawn Fête on July 31, 1912. Some of the ladies wear pretty hats, probably purchased from the millinery at the southern end of the village. (Courtesy of Jeanette Walter.)

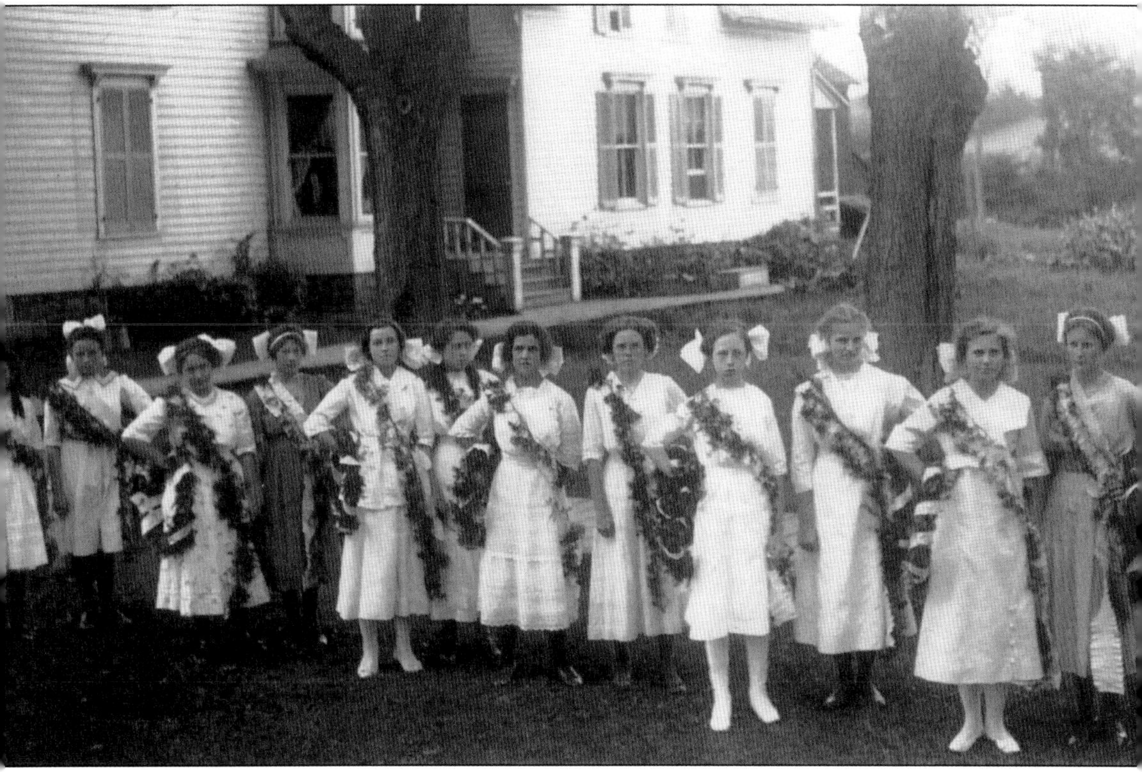

These girls are participating in a drill during the July 1912 Lawn Fête at the Remsen Methodist Church. A lawn fête was a community gathering, sometimes a fundraiser, commonly hosted by the church and included food, games, fellowship, and entertainment. These often provided a courting opportunity for young adults coming of age under the watchful eye of elders. (Courtesy of Jeanette Walter.)

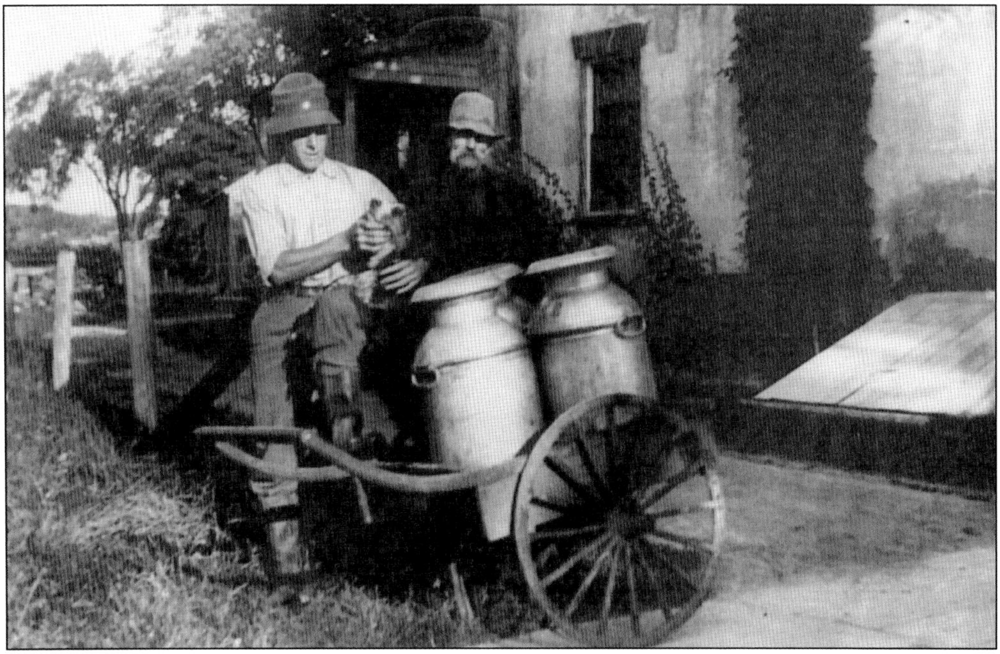

Roger Brant and Hugh Hughes (nicknamed "Hugh Flat") pose before bringing milk from Brant's stone house (the tannery building on Main Street) to the B.K. Brown Cold Storage Plant, located near the railroad crossing on Prospect Street, between Maple Avenue and the Cincinnati Creek. The office for the plant is abandoned but still stands at the railroad crossing. (Courtesy of Jeanette Walter.)

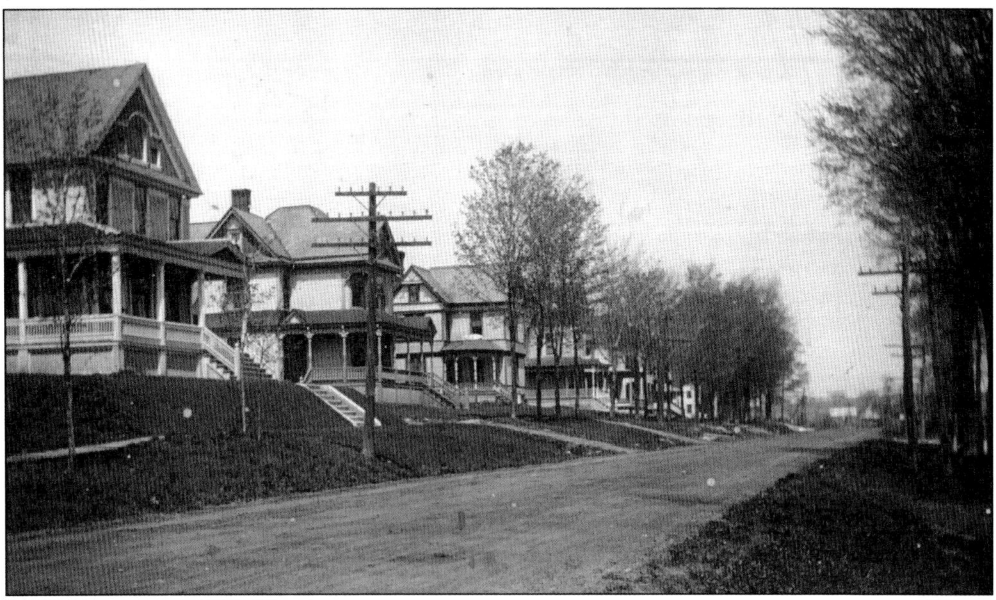

Many of the houses shown in this view looking north in a residential section of Main Street are still similar to the way they appear in this 1923 image by photographer LeRoy Thomas. He should not be confused with local author and historian Howard Thomas, whose work covered most of the Adirondack Foothills region. Howard lived in nearby Prospect. (Photograph by LeRoy Thomas, courtesy of Jeanette Walter.)

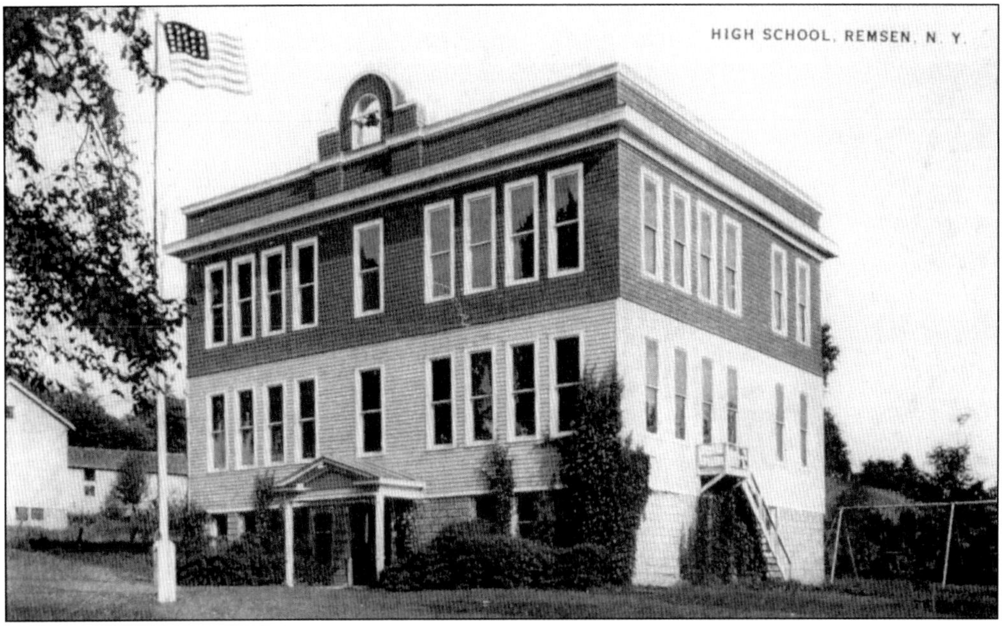

The Remsen High School is pictured early in the 20th century. It was built on Steuben Street, where the post office stands today. Posing in a May 1926 school picture are, from left to right, (first row) Elizabeth Robert (Jones), Elenor Mortice, Erma Salmon (Countryman), Margaret Evans (Oliver), Anne Roberts, Grace Schott (Hall), and Mildred Norris; (second row) Margaret Fanning, Catherine Dickinson (Fanning), Jane Evans (Putman), Margaret Manley (Coleman), Elizabeth Morris (Carrier), Gladys Pugh (Davies), Florence Shaw (Barnerd), Beulah Dailey (Beagle), Francess Williams (Williams), Ahnes Zacek (Fisher), Roy Pugh, and Joe Manley; (third row) Genevieve Jones (Milgate), Lorna Dickinson (Kent), Mary Davis (Williams), Marion Ingersoll (Cole), Myrtle Clemons (Thomas), Gardner Griffith, John Slusarczyk, Russell Thomas, Ed Buckley, Erwin Salmon, and teacher Mr. Dotter; (fourth row) L.J. Kirk, Reg Parks, Ed Roberts, Milton Cole, Bill Durlee, Lyle Walter, Wally Thomas, Roy Spall, Lancing Bardwell, Hank Dodds, Gardner Broadbent, and Lawrence Beagle. (Both, courtesy of Jeanette Walter.)

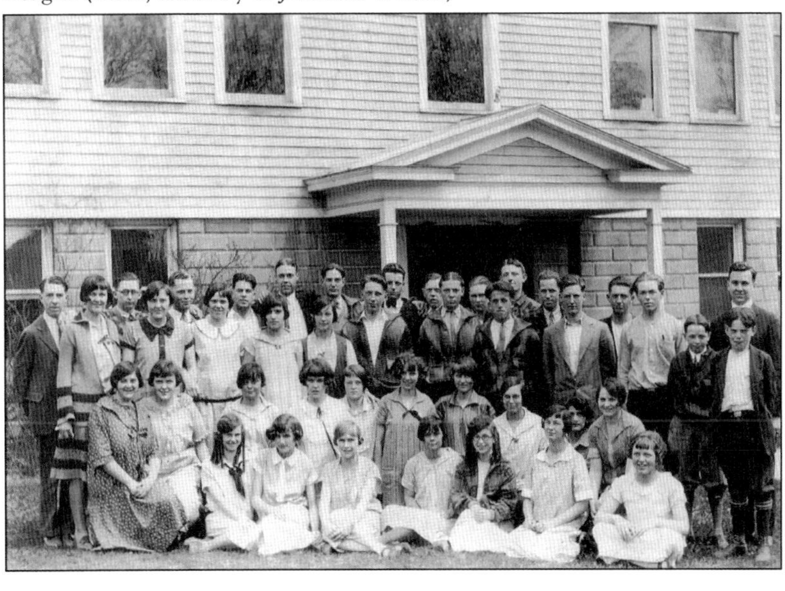

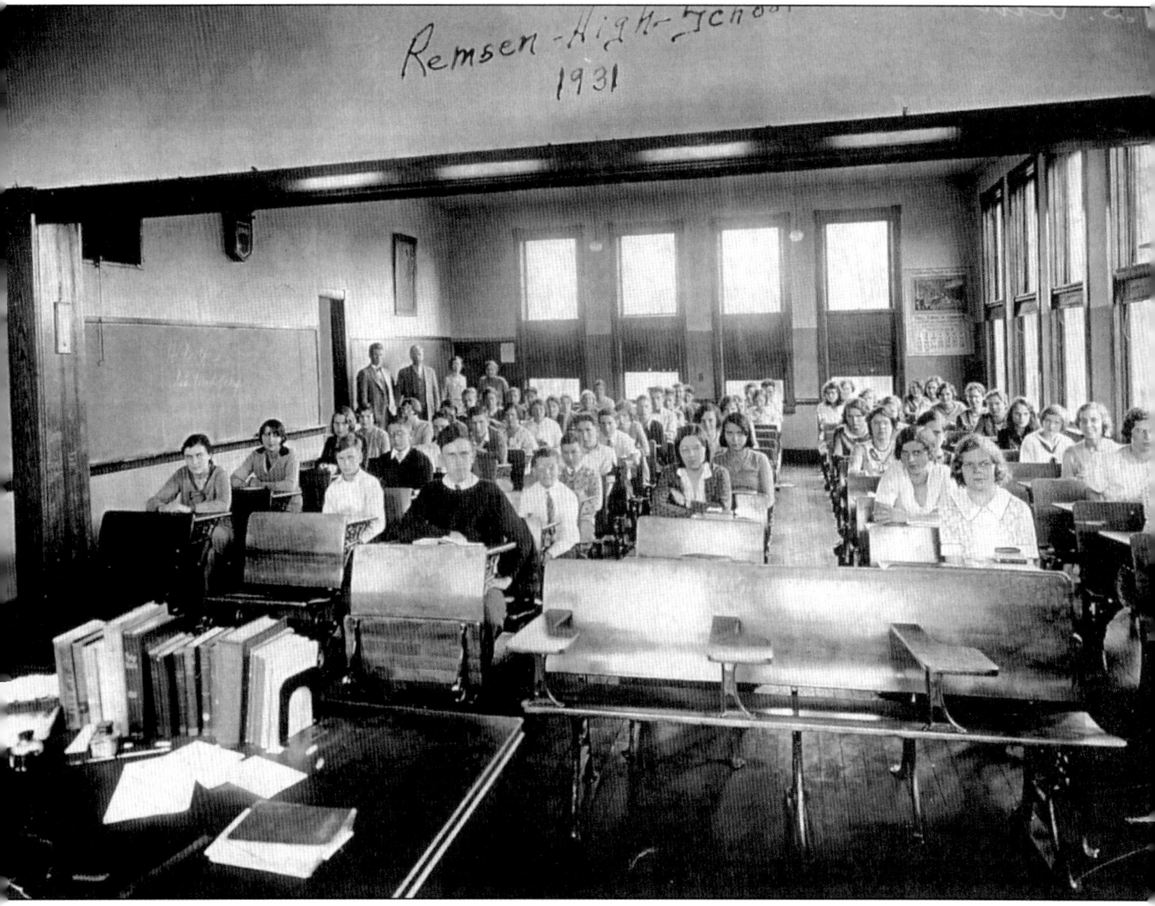

This photograph, taken in 1931, shows the students at the Remsen School. They include Evelyn Williams, Mary Pishko, Maude Pugh, Mildred Pugh, Edna Tanney, Elizabeth Williams, Robert "Bob" Anderson, William "Bill" Dutcher, Steve Dubinski, Doc Pugh, Mike Walter, Fat Williams, Robert "Bob" Williams, Trevor Williams, Mildred Ingersoll, Mildred Brant, Francis Delkewitz, Florence Davis, Anna Dubinski, Mary Brant, James "Jim" Francis, William "Bill" Griffith, Charles Hughes, Hank Hughes, Clarence Ingersoll, Julia Manley, Frank Miles, Merwin Pugh, Joseph "Joe" Saiviki, Alexander Senchyna, Willard Smith, Beatrice Pugh, Katherine Roberts, Mary Francis Roberts, Flora Tanney, Betty Thomas, Olga Worby, Al Clemons, Lewis Davis, Charlotte Ellithorpe, Elizabeth Franis, Alta James, Charlotte Johnson, Betty Jones, James "Jim" Jones, Adalide Miles, Setta Monesterski, Katherine Pishko, Francis Arthur, Arvilla Annis, Estelle Anderson, Lucille Bowen, Helen Carlosh, Alberta Carter, Fredreka Carter, Eva Countryman, Helen Daley, and Lylith Dickerson. (Courtesy of Jeanette Walter.)

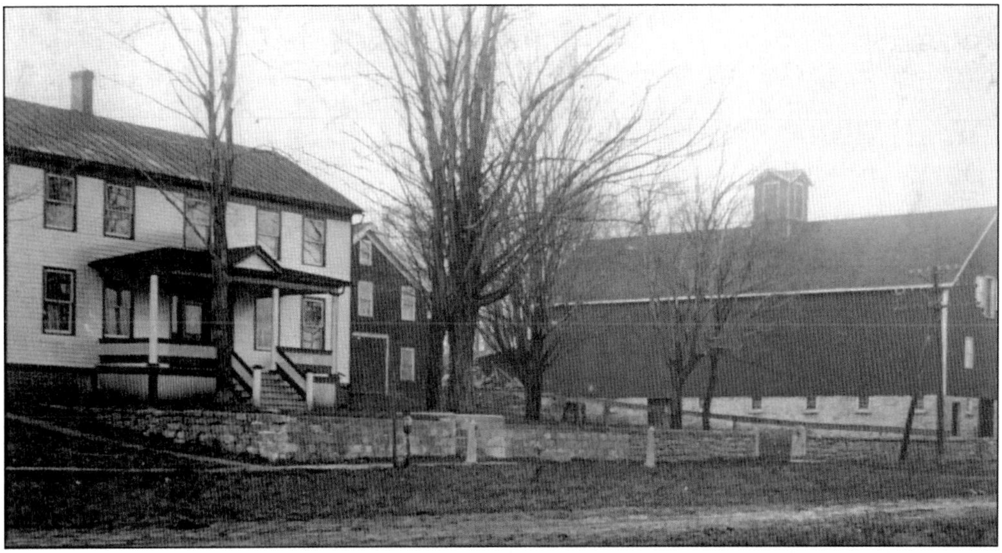

The Harley Williams house and its barn are pictured in 1911. The area where the barn stood became school property, and the barn was removed. The house and stone wall in front remained. The wall then became a gathering place for generations of students to converge on when school let out for the day. (Courtesy of Jeanette Walter.)

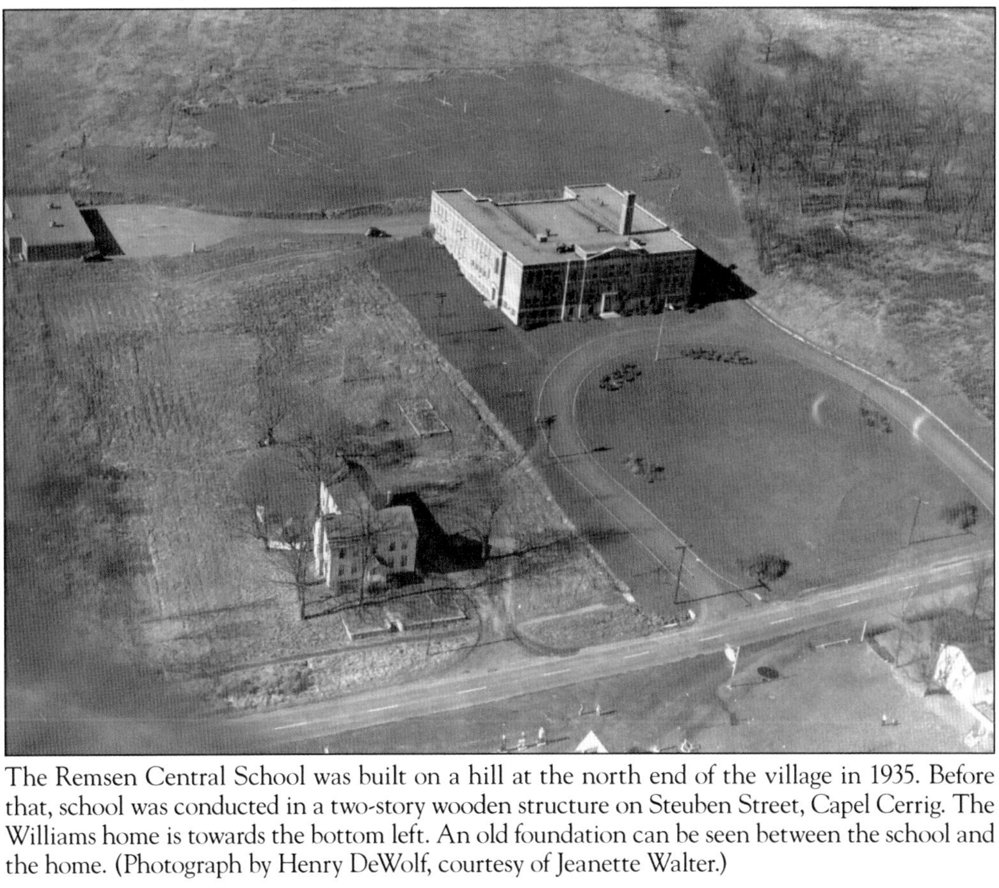

The Remsen Central School was built on a hill at the north end of the village in 1935. Before that, school was conducted in a two-story wooden structure on Steuben Street, Capel Cerrig. The Williams home is towards the bottom left. An old foundation can be seen between the school and the home. (Photograph by Henry DeWolf, courtesy of Jeanette Walter.)

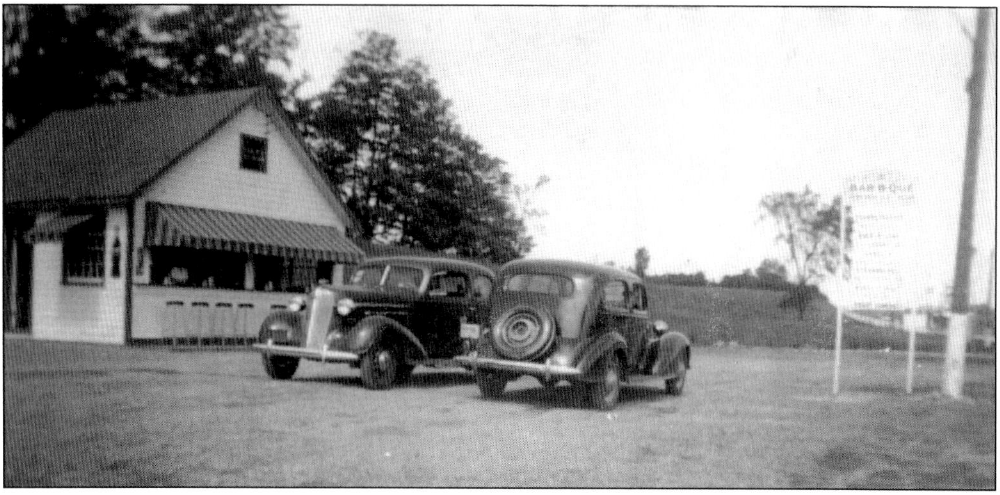

Griswold's Diner, known to many as "Jack and Harley's," was a local favorite for many years. The operator was John "Jack" Griswold. He grew up in nearby Prospect, but spent most of his adult years in Remsen. This photograph was taken in 1938 at the first Remsen Griswold's Diner location near the former Williams Oil business on Main Street. For a short time, Griswold also operated a diner in Lowville, about an hour north of Remsen. In the 1950s, Griswold ran a diner at a new location on Route 12. This new building was constructed in the mid-1950s. The business has been sold many times throughout the decades. Cindy's Diner now operates from the former Griswold's location on Route 12. (Both, courtesy of Jeanette Walter.)

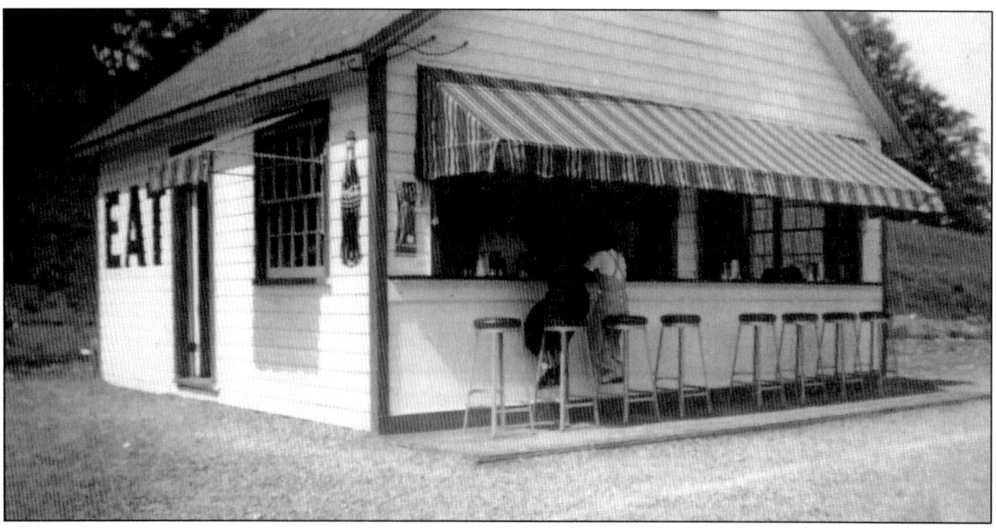

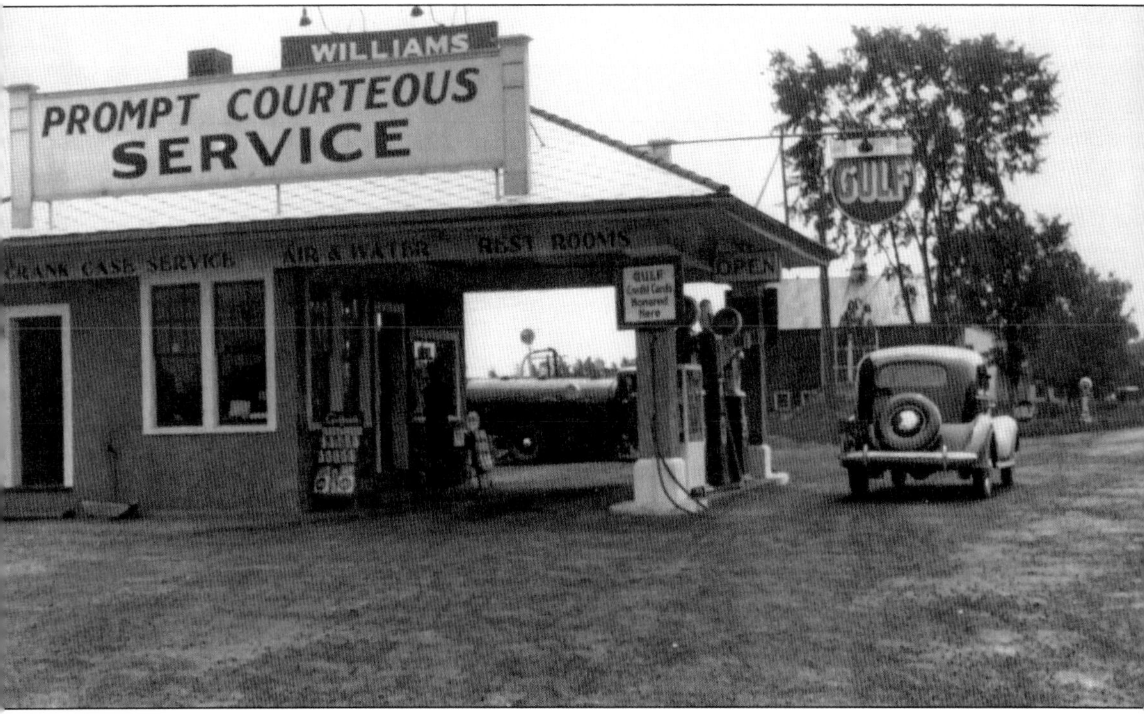

The Williams family operated Williams Oil Company on the north end of Main Street for generations starting in 1929. The company provided home heating oil to residences, kerosene, diesel fuel, and gasoline to service stations. It also sold bulk lubricating oil in 55-gallon drums. At one time, Williams Oil Company owned at least five service stations, located in Alder Creek, Barneveld, Holland Patent, Rome, and Utica. It also owned the Remsen NAPA store. The family had a strong focus on customer service, and customers remained loyal to the oil company for years. It was sold to Mohawk Valley Oil in the 1990s. This loss of local jobs was devastating to many in the community. The Williams family not only had a keen business sense but also an interest in community service. The family helped found the Munson Williams Proctor Arts Institute. (Courtesy of Jeanette Walter.)

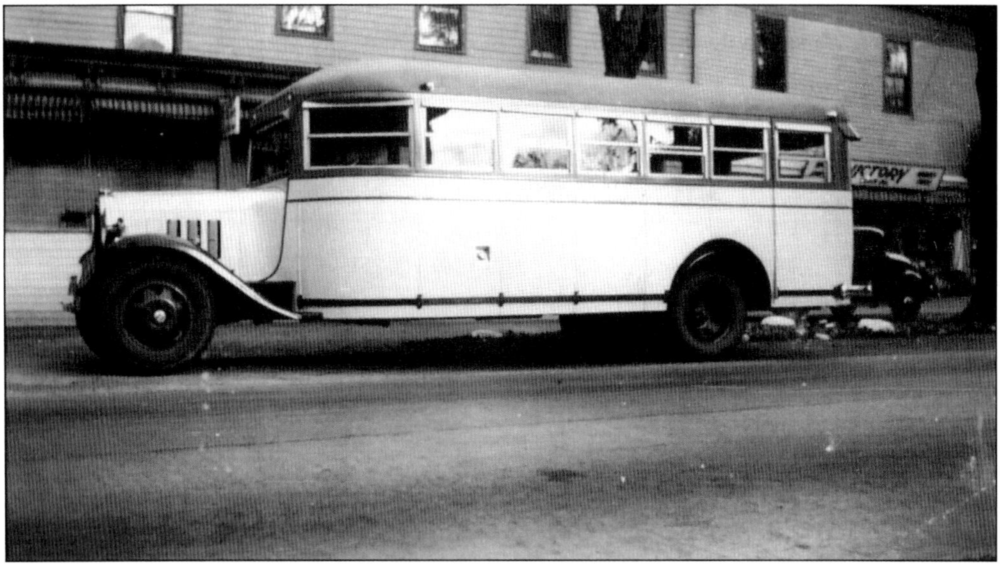

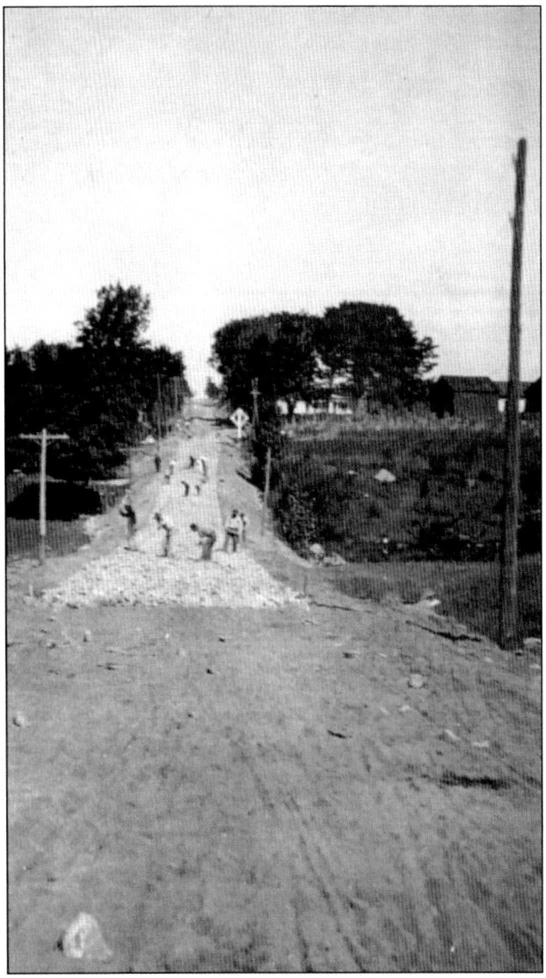

Remsen Central School's first school bus is parked in front of the Victory Store, located in the Bristol House on Main Street. The bus driver owned the Bristol House. Many businesses operated in rented offices from this location. A stage and dance hall were upstairs. (Courtesy of Jeanette Walter.)

Prospect Street connects the Remsen village to the Prospect village (now hamlet), a distance of about three miles. The village of Prospect was founded in 1803. Starting in 1855, Prospect was the jumping-off place for travelers headed to the Adirondacks via the Black River & Utica Railroad. (Courtesy of Jeanette Walter.)

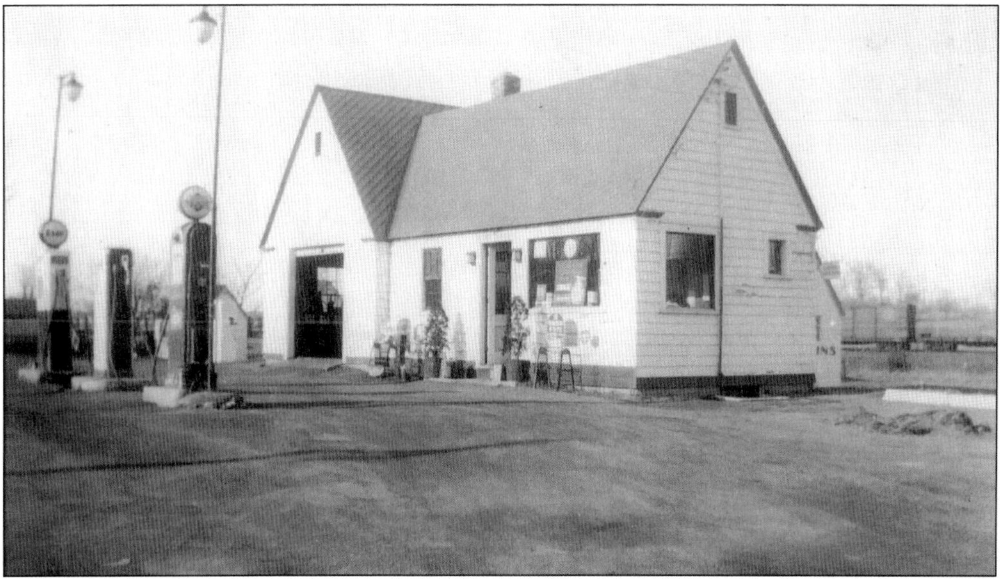

This gas station was operated by Steve Davis on the north end of the village, across from the Williams homestead. It was closed in the 1950s due to slow traffic. (Courtesy of Jeanette Walter.)

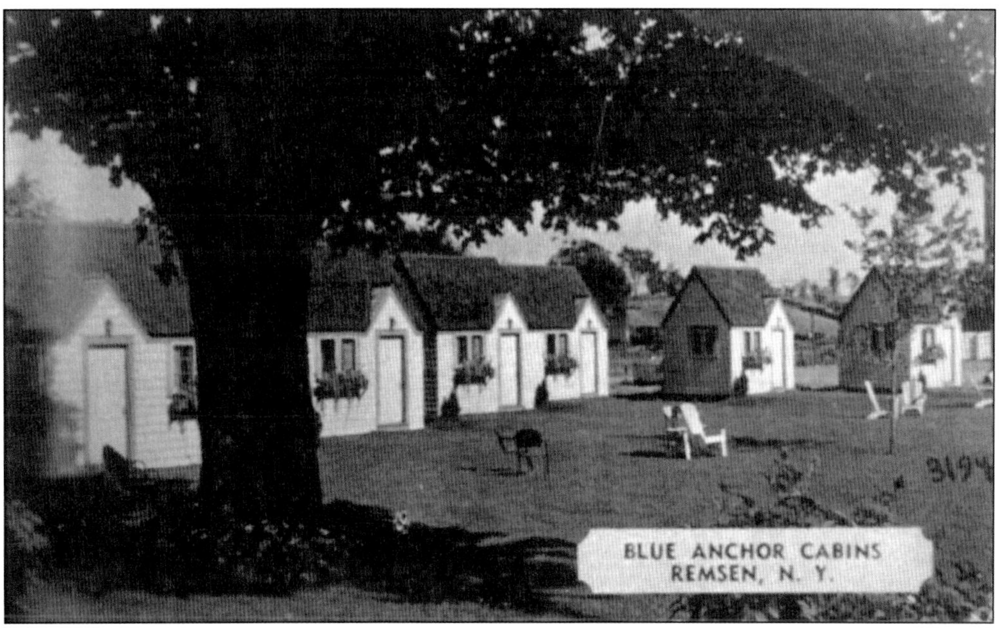

Blue Anchor Cabins and Restaurant has become a staple of the nearby Poland community, but it started in Remsen. Owner Steve Davis built multiple sleeper cabins for rental in Remsen in 1951. Business was slow, so the family business relocated to Poland, on the banks of the West Canada Creek, in the mid-1950s. Opening a diner there proved to be a solid business strategy for the Blue Anchor Cabins. (Courtesy of Jeanette Walter.)

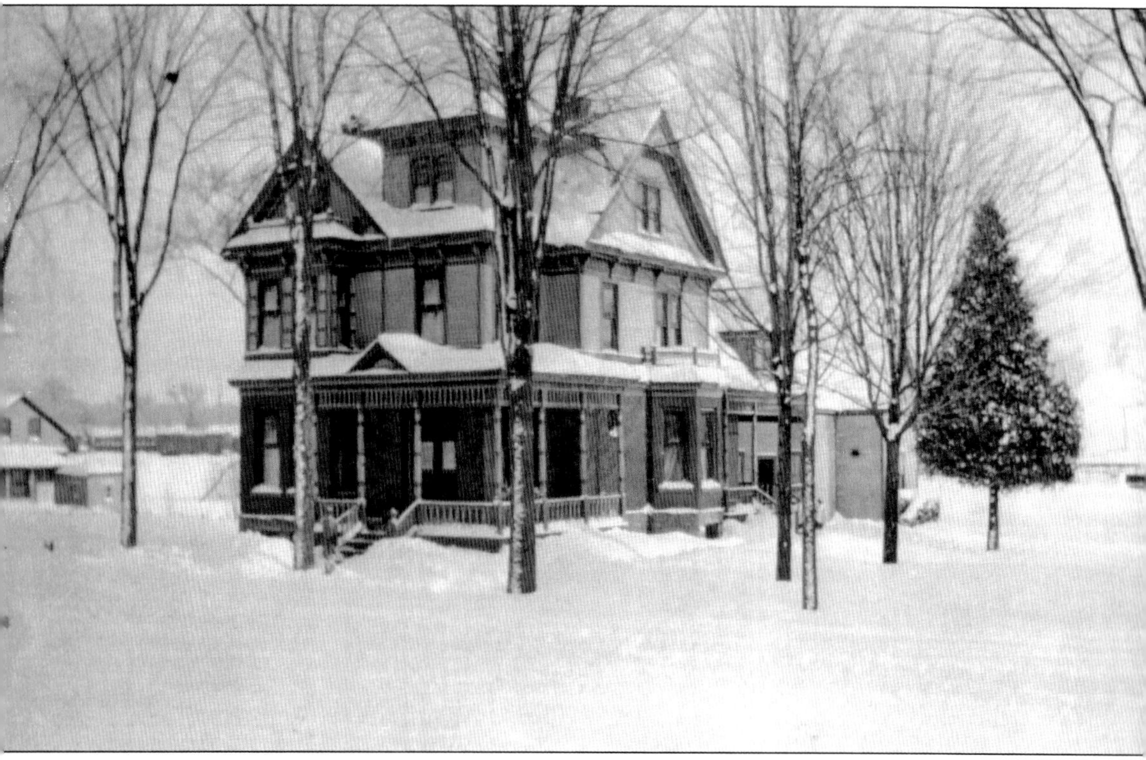

The brick house on the upper end of Main Street was known as the George Williams Home. It was built by carpenter John Pritchard. The home is still standing and, other than wear and tear, looks much like it did when it was first constructed. (Courtesy of Jeanette Walter.)

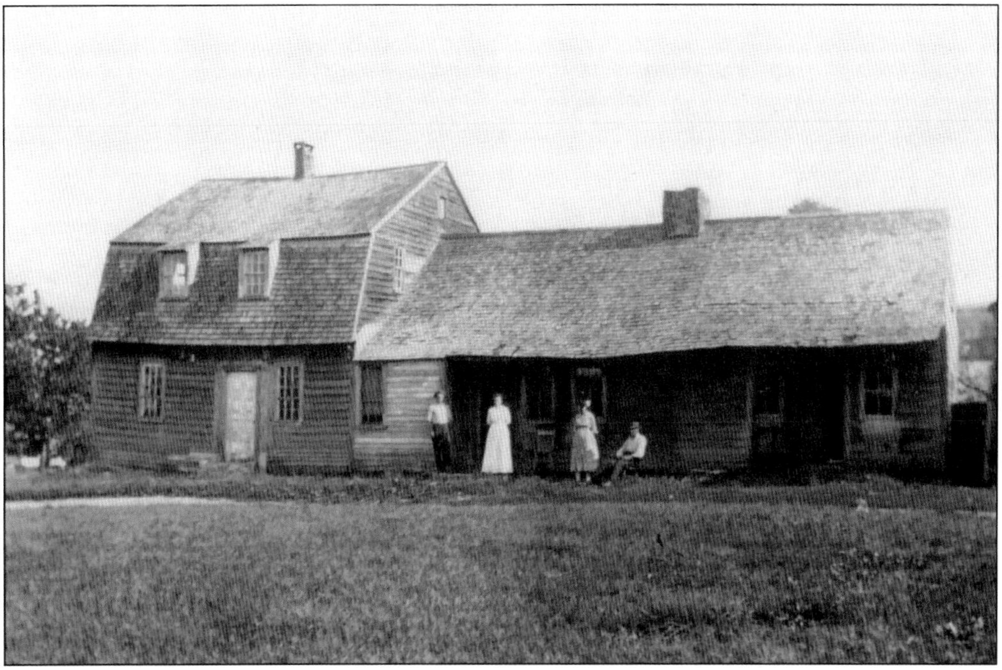

This gambrel-roofed home was located at the southern tip of the Remsen village. From left to right are owners Mr. and Mrs. Louis Humphrey, Louvern Humphrey, and Louis Jones (seated). The Humphreys were known for always welcoming travelers into their home. The home has been replaced by a stuccoed residence. (Courtesy of Jeanette Walter.)

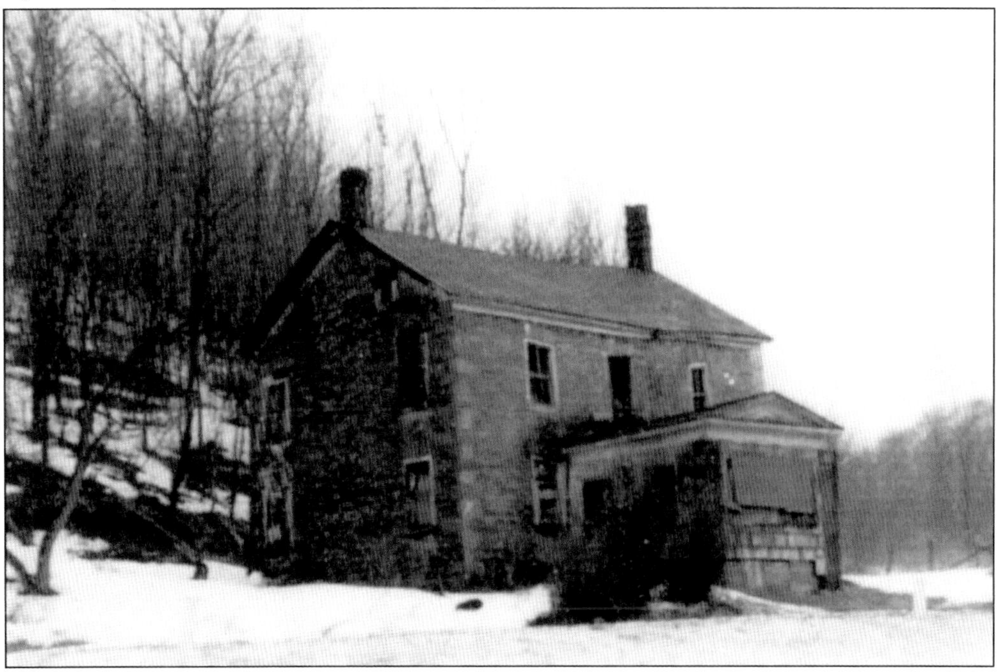

This stone house was located at the junction of Old State Route 12 (before it turns into Main Street) and Plank Road, where the railroad tracks cross over Plank Road. The house is gone, and the only thing that remains is a crumbling foundation. (Courtesy of Jeanette Walter.)

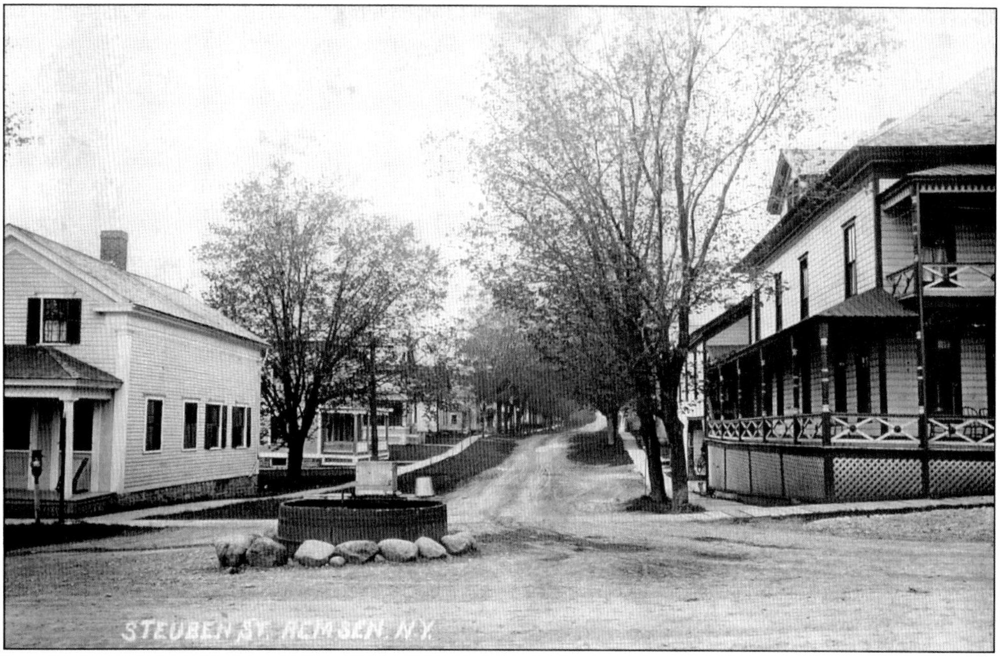

This public village watering hole was in the street at the corner of Main Street and Steuben Street in front of the Milgate House. At one time, this was a busy village corner with a traffic light at the intersection. It is a residential section today. (Courtesy of Jeanette Walter.)

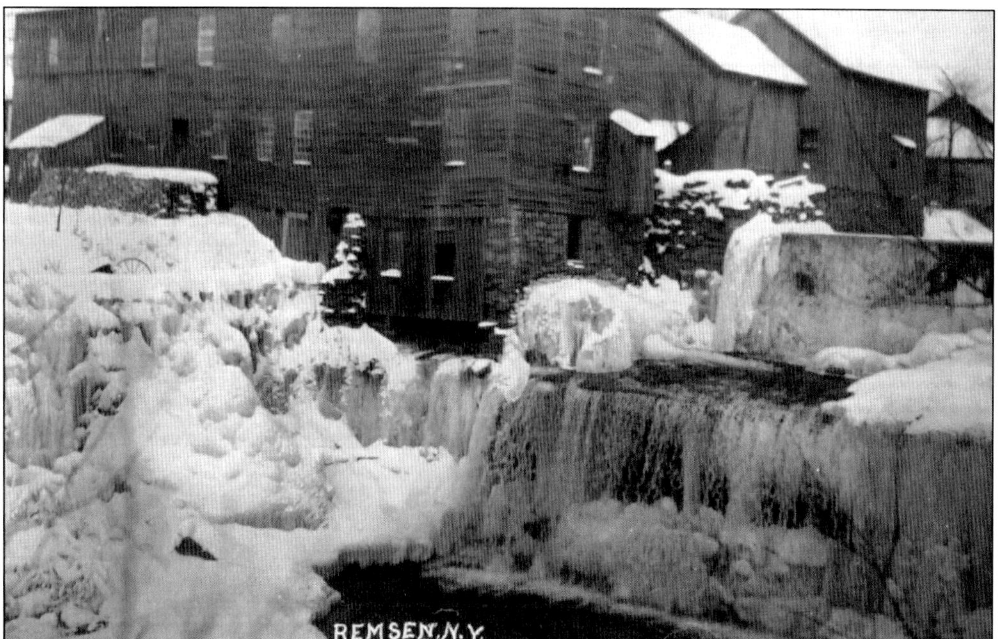

The Remsen Falls were a popular subject for photographers. Many postcards were produced depicting the falls and nearby mills. The mill that can be seen in the photograph was a gristmill sometimes known as the Remsen Mills. It was built around 1852. (Courtesy of Jeanette Walter.)

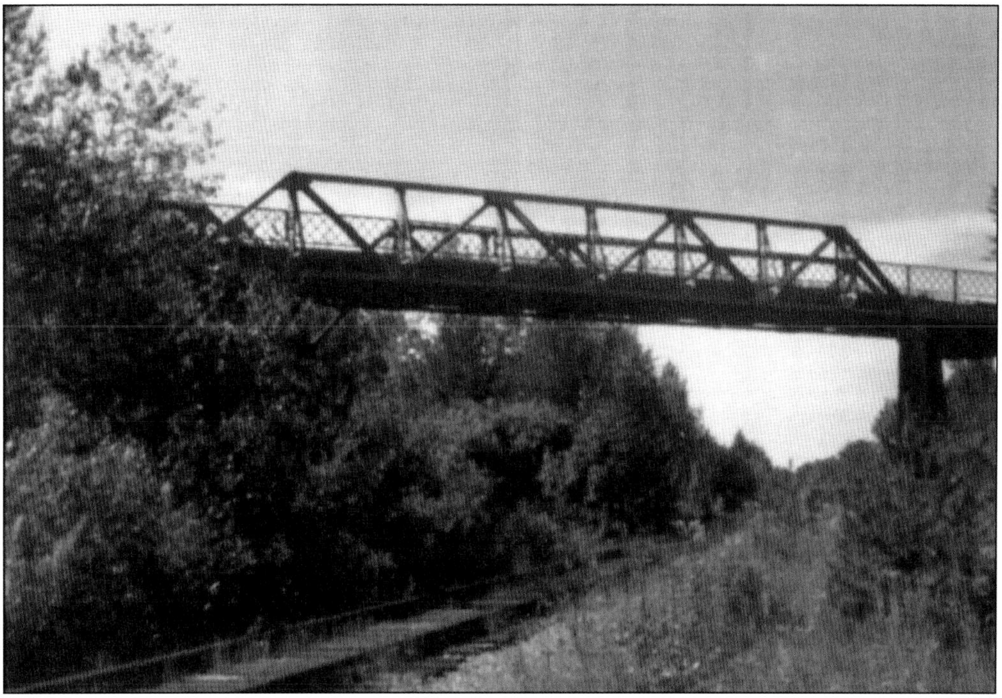

The overpass that spanned the railroad tracks connected Old Route 12 to Pritchard Road just north of the village limits north of the school. It was dismantled and used to repair Harvey Bridge in the town of Ohio. The raised land abutments from the overpass still remain. (Courtesy of Jeanette Walter.)

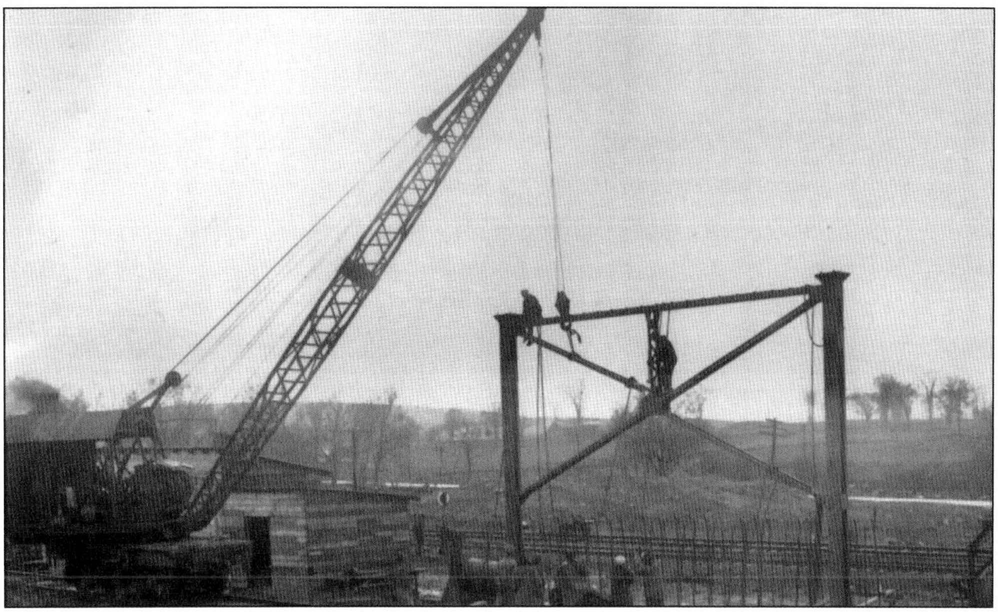

This photograph shows the construction of the Remsen railroad track overpass. The town of Remsen forms the northeast corner of the county. The terrain is hills and ridges broken by open meadows. The Black River, West Canada Creek, and the Cincinnati Creek all run through portions of the town. (Photograph by LeRoy Thomas, courtesy of Jeanette Walter.)

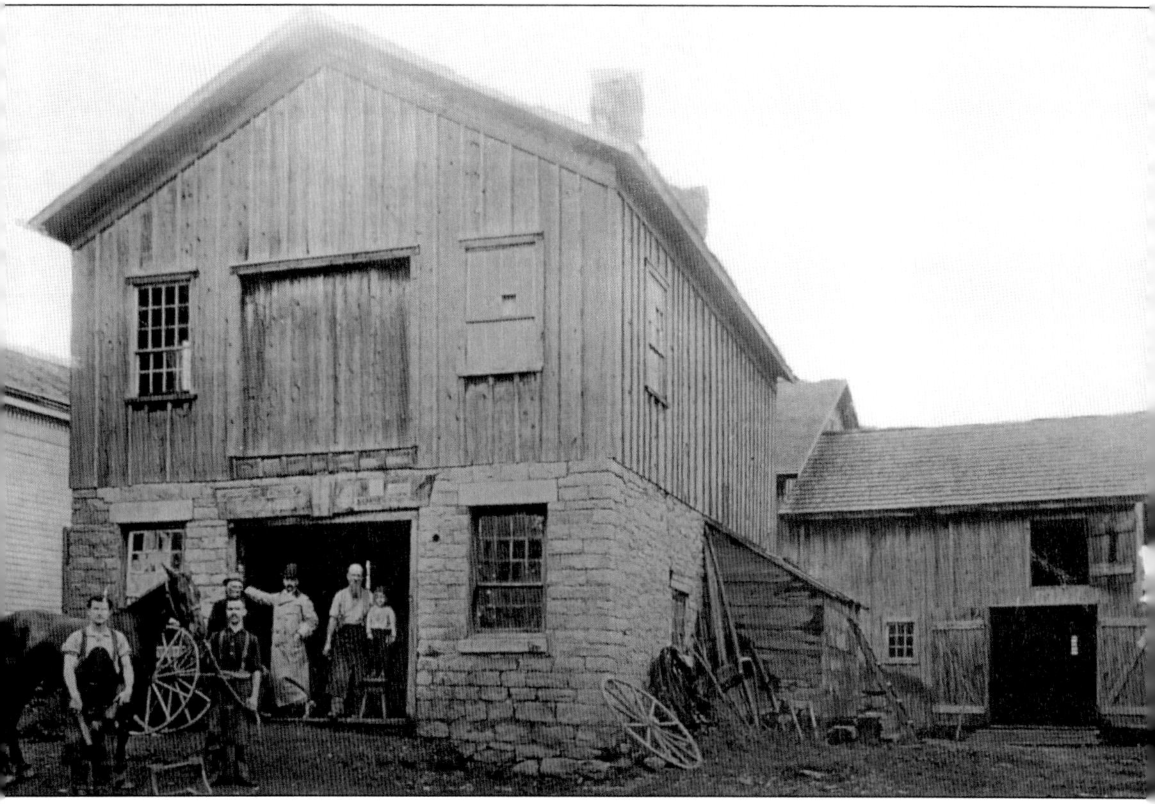

By 1800, gristmill, sawmill, and blacksmith shops were operating adjacent to the high falls at the south end of the village. The photograph depicts the Thomas Blacksmith Shop, located across from the junction of Main and Steuben Streets. It was built in 1802. In 1848, it was destroyed by fire and promptly rebuilt by Hugh Thomas. The new blacksmith shop was built on the original foundation. It still stands. It operated for three generations within the Thomas family. (Courtesy of Jeanette Walter.)

Two

No Law East of Ninety Five Hill

The Rambling Countryside and Surrounding Communities

While the village was a place of industry and business, the surrounding countryside was a place of dairying and agriculture. Food was grown at home, and meat was harvested locally. Children attended nearby one-room schoolhouses. All of the grades were taught by one teacher. The students had to walk to school every day, which could be a distance of a few miles. Schoolhouses could be found in all corners of Remsen and Steuben, the very first being at Fairchild. The land was donated by Ezekial Fairchild, and he served as the schoolhouse's first teacher. The settlements around Remsen and Steuben included Bardwell Mills, Kayuta Lake, Alder Creek, Hinckley (Gang Mills), Grant, Prospect, Ninety Six Corners, Northwood, and Wheelertown. Many families lived in the settlements or the greater area for generations. The inhabitants of these rural areas were accustomed to a hard day's work. The workday often started before the sunrise, and every member of the family had to do his or her share of the tasks. Some of the tasks might include cutting, splitting, or carrying firewood for the stove or fireplace, tending to the farm animals, sewing clothes for the family, carrying water to the house, putting up or repairing fencing, working in the gardens, hunting, trapping, fishing, cooking, milking cows or goats, collecting eggs, churning butter, making breads and cheeses, preserving foods, cleaning, doing laundry, making candles, caring for the youngest members of the family, and helping the elderly family members. Like their village-dwelling counterparts, the men, women, and children who made a life in these rural areas were tough, skilled, and hearty. Each settlement had its own sense of character. Certain areas seemed to have clusters of rowdier, rugged types. In nearby Forestport, a town known for its high density of outlaws, the saying was "no law north of Remsen." In Remsen, however, the saying was "no law east of Ninety Five Hill."

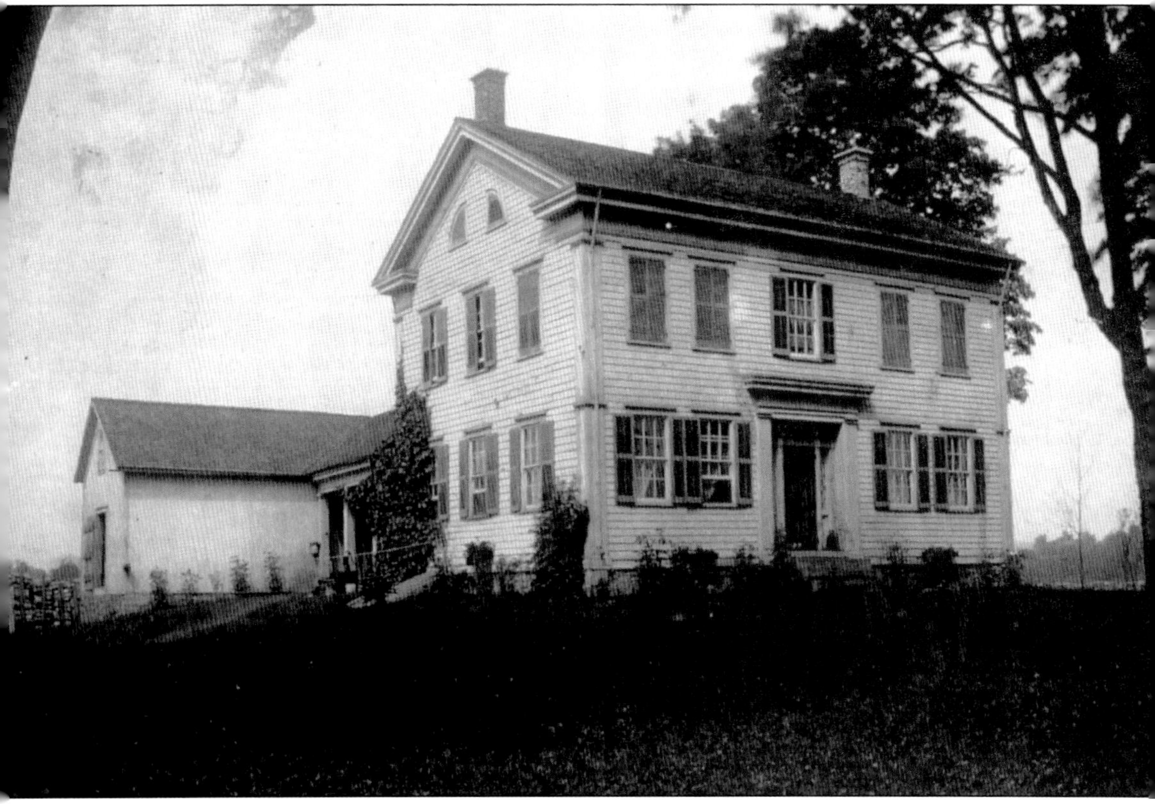

The Stephen Hutchinson House, located about a half mile north of the Remsen village across from Fairchild Road, served as Remsen's first post office. Hutchinson served as the first postmaster of Remsen. The home was built in 1809 by the carpenter Ellis Pritchard. He and his son Richard built many of Remsen's early houses. There used to be a cow barn across the street from the Hutchinson house. It was referred to as the "Long Barn." The first documented religious service in Remsen occurred in that barn, delivered by an itinerant preacher. Later on, the home was known as the "Price Place." The barn was destroyed by fire in the 1960s. (Courtesy of Jeanette Walter.)

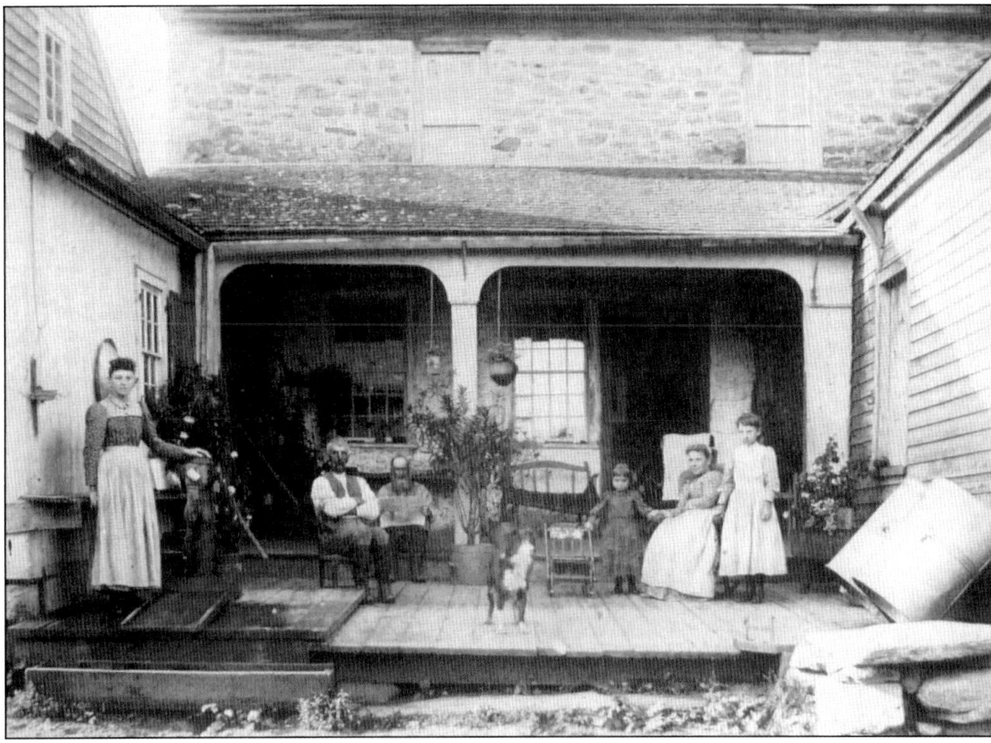

The Sheldon House on Commons Road was the home of James Sheldon, one of the pioneer citizens of Remsen. He worked as a land agent for the John Brown Tract, owned by John Brown, a former governor of Rhode Island who acquired 210,000 acres in the northern New York wilderness in the northern part of Oneida, Herkimer, and Hamilton Counties, as well as the eastern portion of Lewis County. Sheldon is credited with bringing many settlers to the region and was responsible for clearing the land, building passable roads, and building sawmills to make the area desirable for settlers. A onetime town of Remsen supervisor, Sheldon built his limestone house in 1809 on what was then the State Road, which stretched from Johnstown to Sackets Harbor. A main throughway between the Mohawk Valley and Black River Valley areas, this was a busy road with many inns to shelter weary travelers. The Sheldon House was one of those inns. Sheldon died in 1819. His wife, Mary, died in 1845. The property was sold many times after that. Some of the later proprietors were William L. Williams, George W. Williams, Frank Gainsway, John E. and David T. Evans, and Lucy Cobb Coventry. (Both, courtesy of Jeanette Walter.)

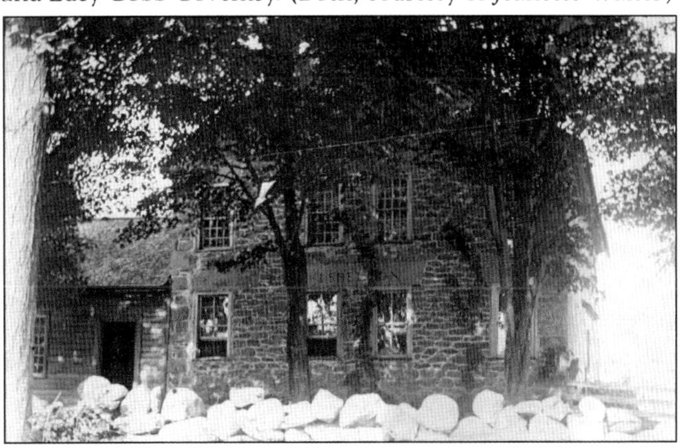

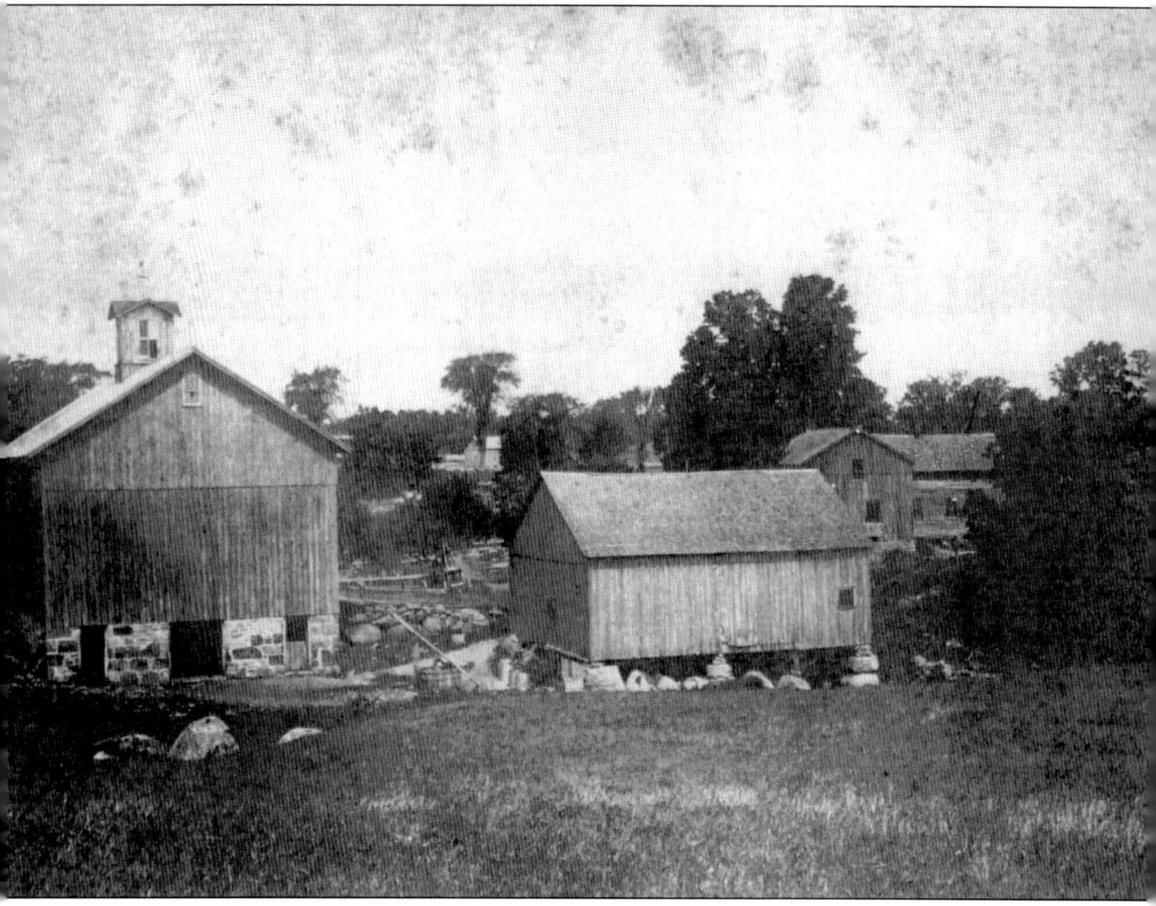

This photograph shows the James Ingersoll farm, on Commons Road where the Remsen City Airport is now located. The barn on the left has been renovated and remains today. There was also a sawmill run by the Ingersoll family at this location. (Courtesy of Jeanette Walter.)

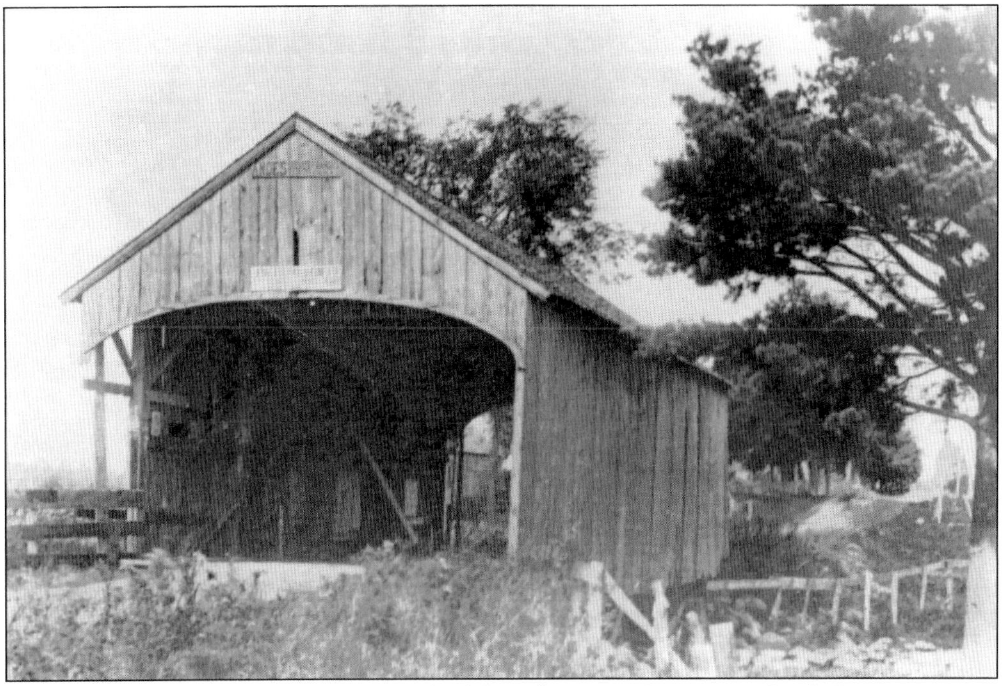

This covered bridge was located just north of the village over Cincinnati Creek. It was in service in the 1800s. Those who passed through at a speed faster than a walk could face a fine of $5. (Courtesy of Jeanette Walter.)

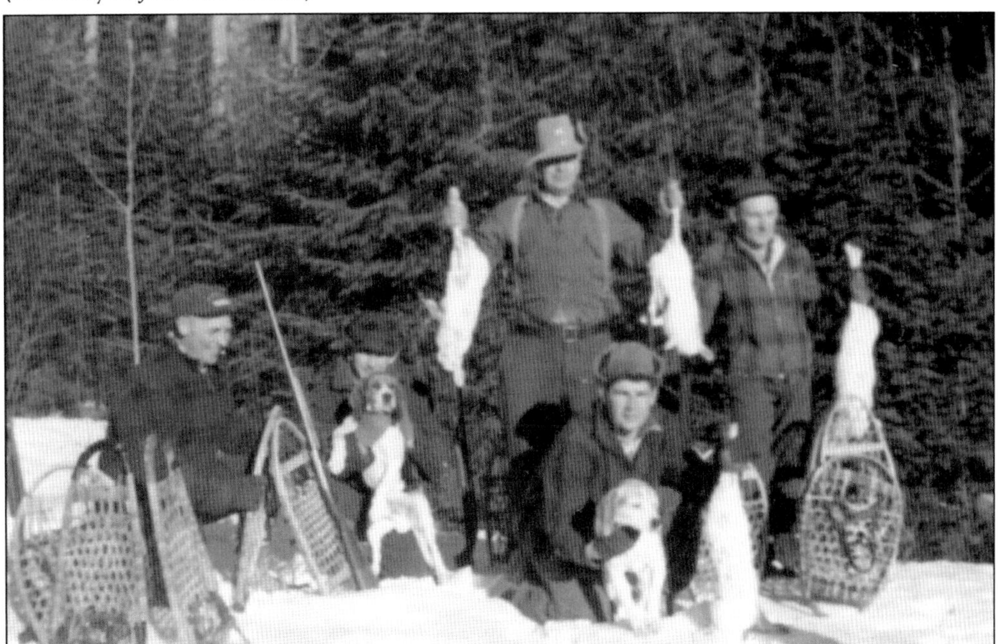

Rabbit hunting with beagles is a popular pastime in Remsen and many rural areas. Beagles were bred for hunting and had been used in England as far back as the 14th century. This early-1950s image shows a productive day's spoils. From left to right are Henry Krupa, Skip Manning, Philip "Bill" Plete, Bernard "Bill" Plete, and Herb Manning. (Author's collection.)

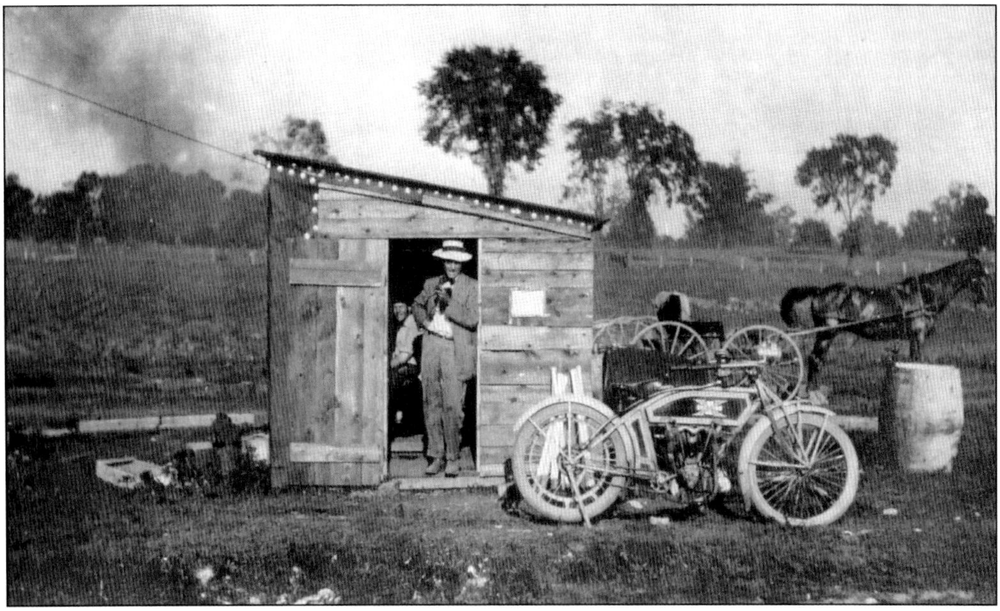

In the early 1900s, many of the Remsen area's main roadways were built. The photograph above shows a construction office built for supervisors along the Trenton-Remsen-Prospect state road. The image below shows a construction crew on the original Route 12. Old State Route 12 used to be a main roadway running north-south through New York State. In 1908, the New York State Legislature declared it and many other routes to be legislative routes. Over time, this route has been realigned, bypassing many of the small communities on its route. The Remsen section was built between 1910 and 1912. The first bypass constructed in Oneida County was around Remsen in the 1950s. (Both, courtesy of Jeanette Walter.)

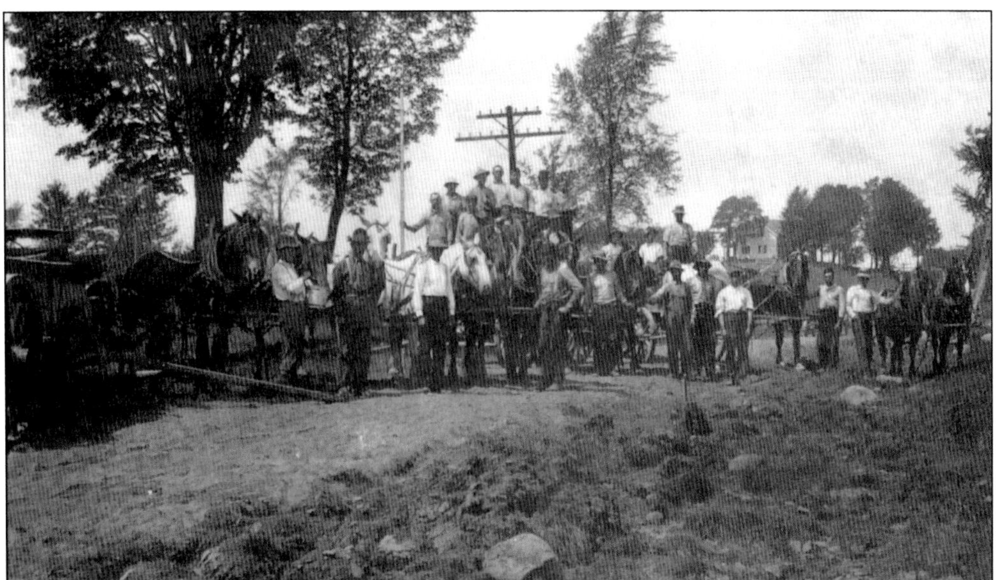

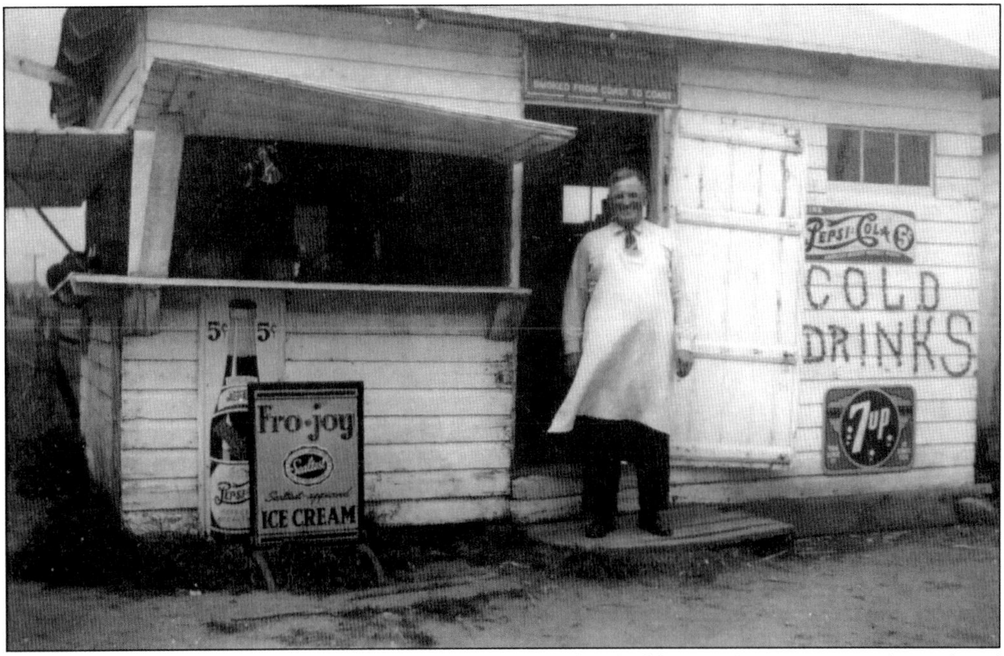

George Huther operated a hot dog stand on the east side of Old State Route 12 near the railroad crossing. Huther served hot dogs, snacks, ice cream, and cold drinks. Notice the hill in the background in the photograph below. This served as an opportune location for a business when this was the main route. It was a popular spot to stop, as, from left to right, Beatrice Kelly Williams, Mary Whitlock Evans, Paul Griffin, and Kenneth Roberts have done in 1943. The words "cold drinks" on the stand are spelled out with bottle caps. When the new Route 12 bypass was built, traffic was routed around Remsen and the hot dog shack. (Both, courtesy of Jeanette Walter.)

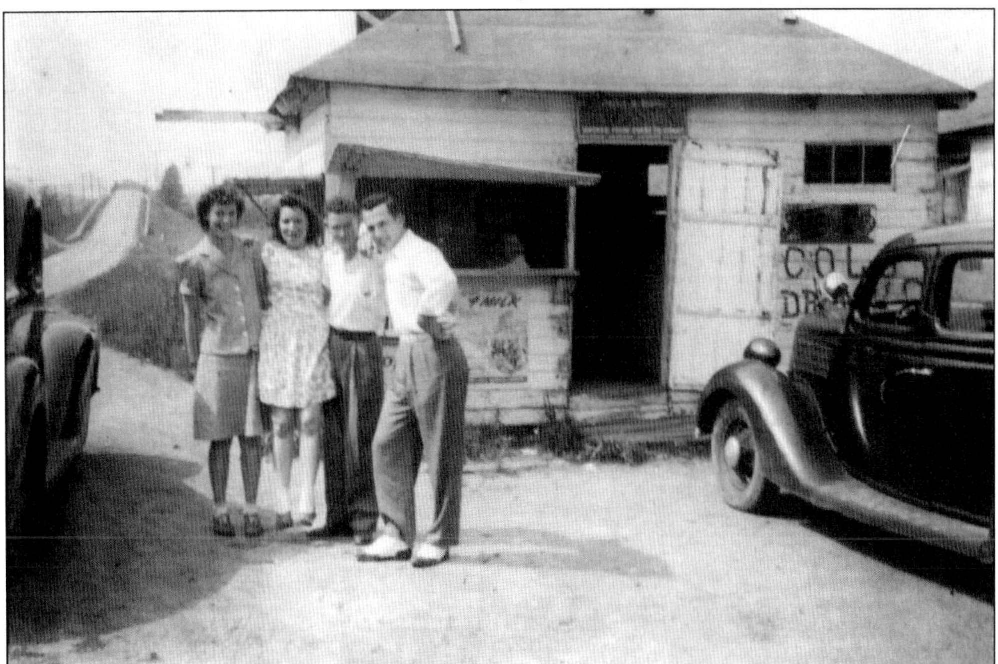

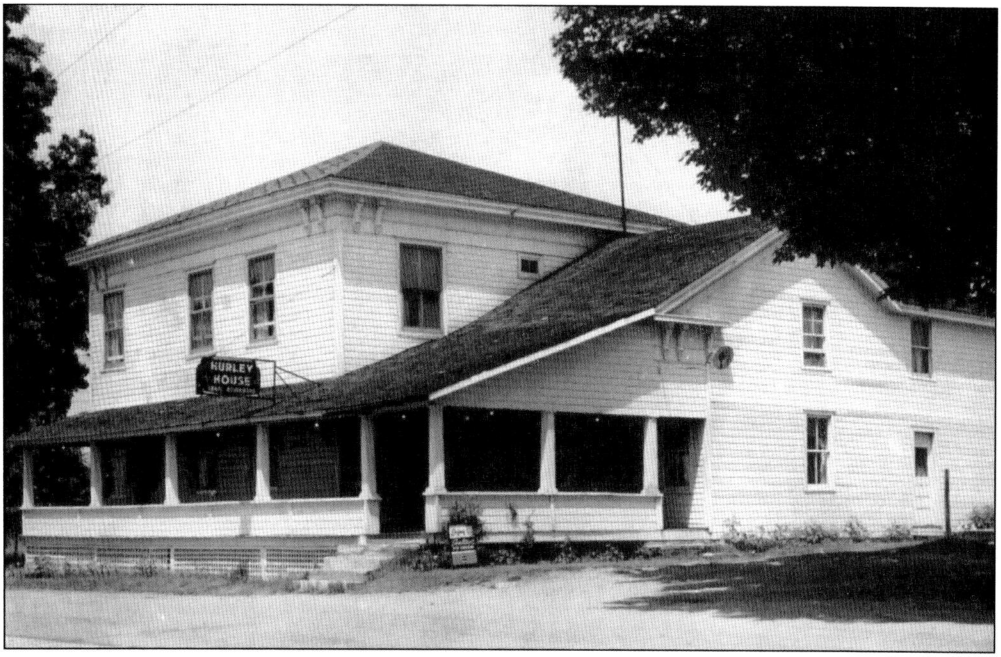

The Hurley House, located on New York State Route 12 just before Joslyn Road, was operated as a barroom and inn. In the 1860s, Remsen included the town of Forestport and town meetings were often held here because of its central location. It was then known as Higby's Tavern. (Courtesy of Jeanette Walter.)

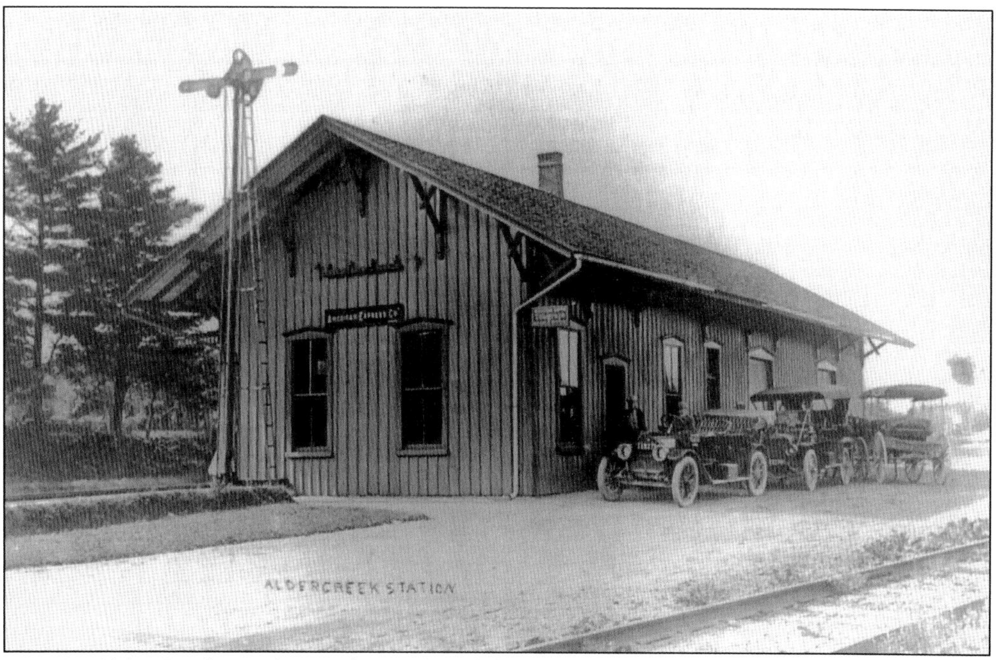

In 1862, Alder Creek, on the northern edge of the town of Remsen and the southern end of the town of Boonville, had two churches (Presbyterian and Baptist), two hotels, a tannery, and about 20 houses. In this photograph is the Alder Creek train station. (Courtesy of Jeanette Walter.)

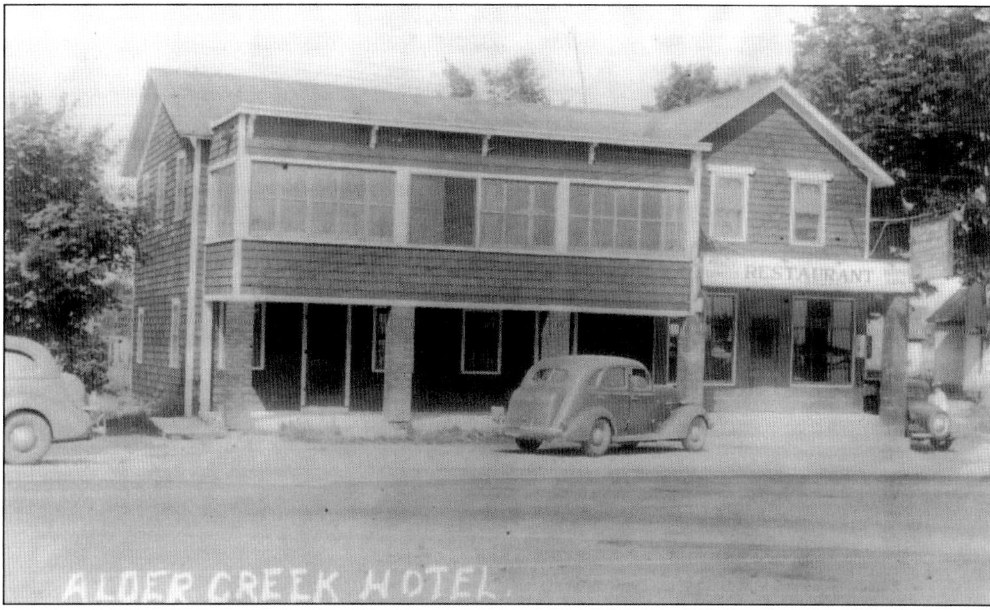

The Alder Creek Hotel (shown above and below) welcomed travelers passing through via New York State Route 12. The hotel was located at a convenient branch in the road where travelers could continue north to Boonville or head east to Forestport and the Adirondacks. Around 1832, Calvin Allen came from Remsen and built a butter tub factory on Alder Creek. He was soon disappointed with this location, because the creek could not provide an adequate supply of water to run his facility. He moved his plant to Forestport, which was then still in the Remsen township. While constructing his house in Forestport, he cut his leg, leaving him crippled. In 1854, Allen underwent an amputation, but he died of complications four days later. (Both, courtesy of Jeanette Walter.)

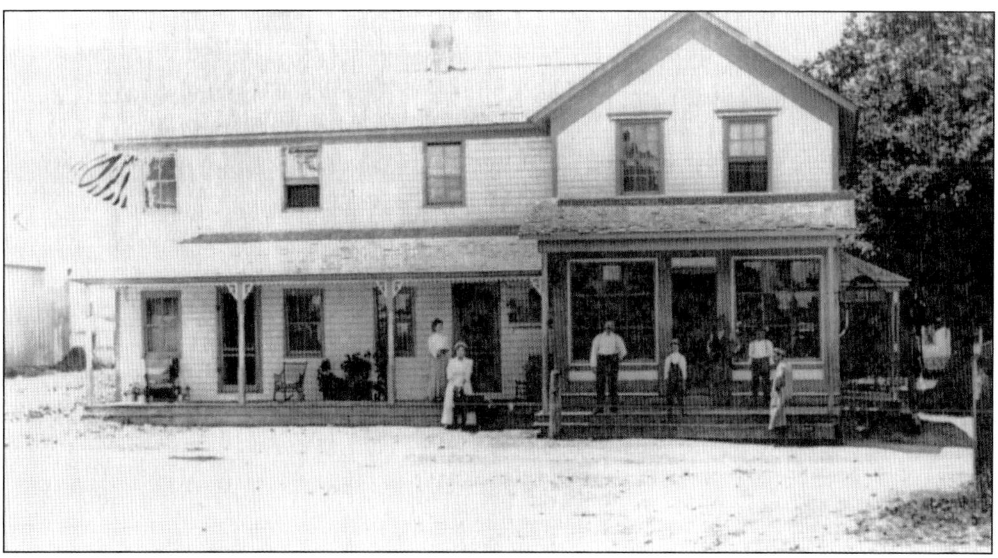

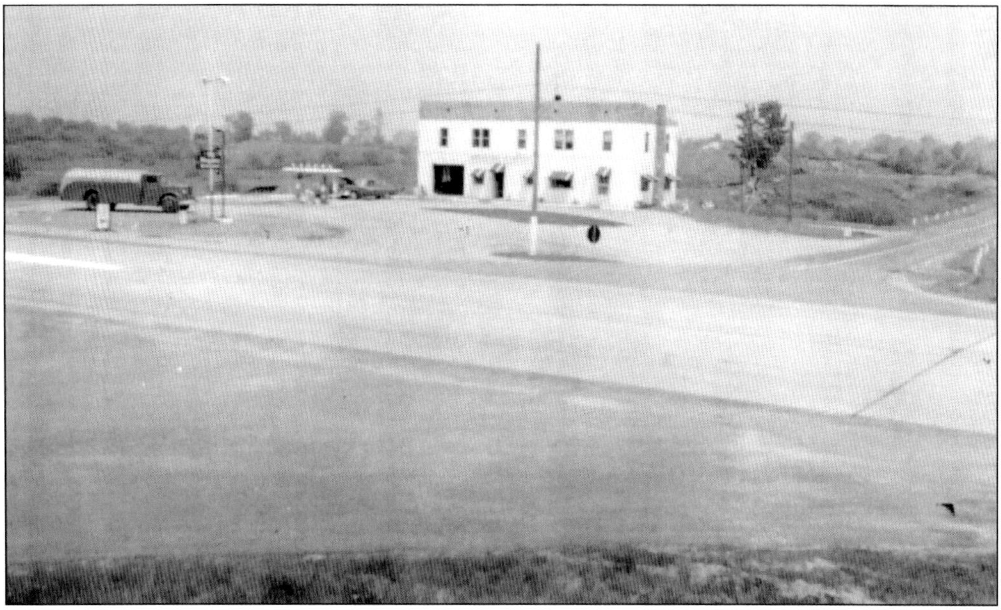

Originally the Just-Keys gas station and restaurant, the Fireplace Restaurant (pictured) was located at what is now the site of Evans Equipment on the corner of Dayton Road and New York State Route 12. Prior to this, Evans Equipment had a location on Main Street in the village of Remsen. Evans Equipment has been family-owned and -operated since 1945. (Courtesy of Jeanette Walter.)

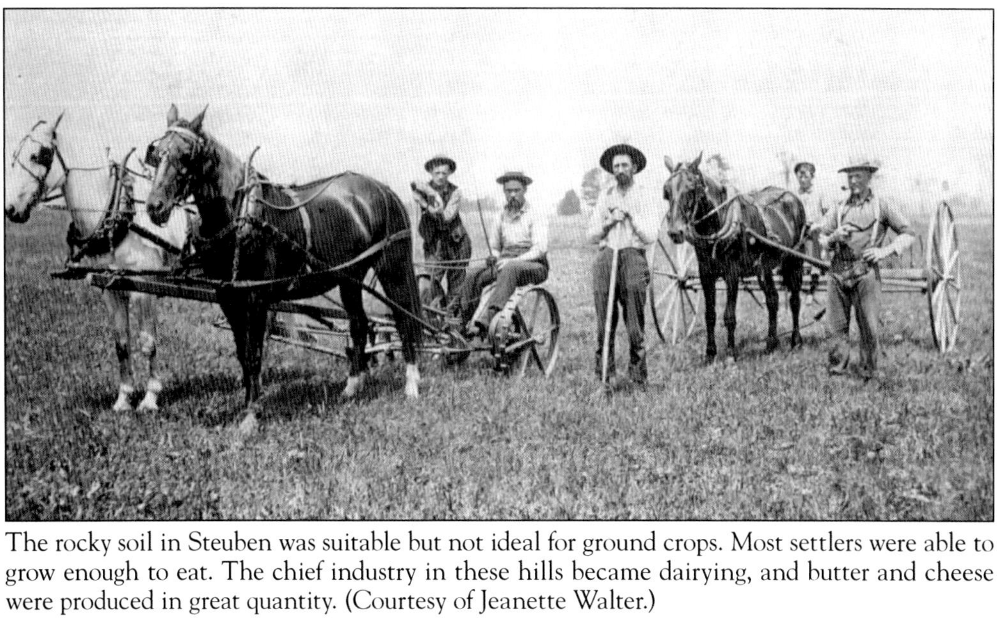

The rocky soil in Steuben was suitable but not ideal for ground crops. Most settlers were able to grow enough to eat. The chief industry in these hills became dairying, and butter and cheese were produced in great quantity. (Courtesy of Jeanette Walter.)

Snowshoeing was more than a hobby in the early 20th century. Winters in Upstate New York were harsh, and snow often accumulated as high as the rooftops. Many people used snowshoes to walk in the wintertime on the snow. The man in the photograph is Nelson Folts. (Author's collection.)

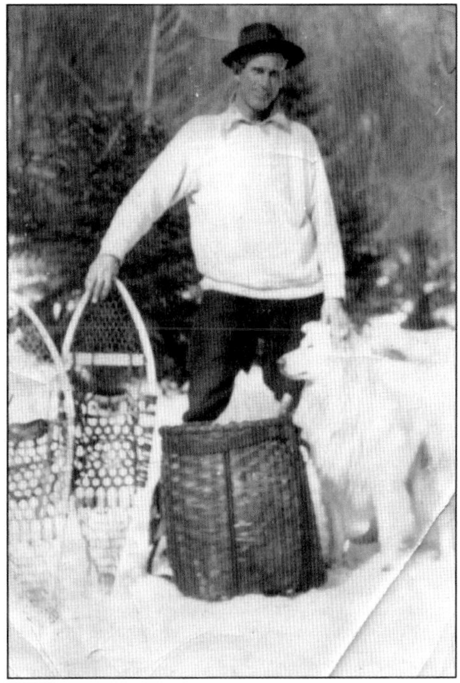

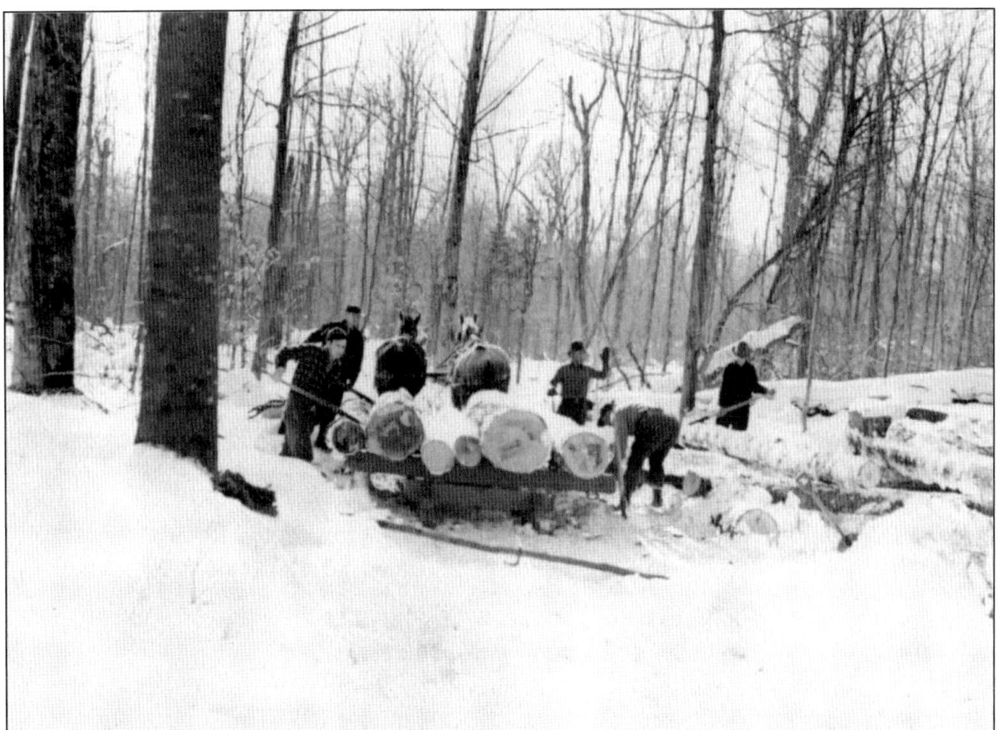

Logs were skidded out of the forest using teams of horses during the 19th and early 20th centuries. Logging in the Adirondack Foothills was a busy industry. This photograph was taken north of the Remsen area. (Author's collection.)

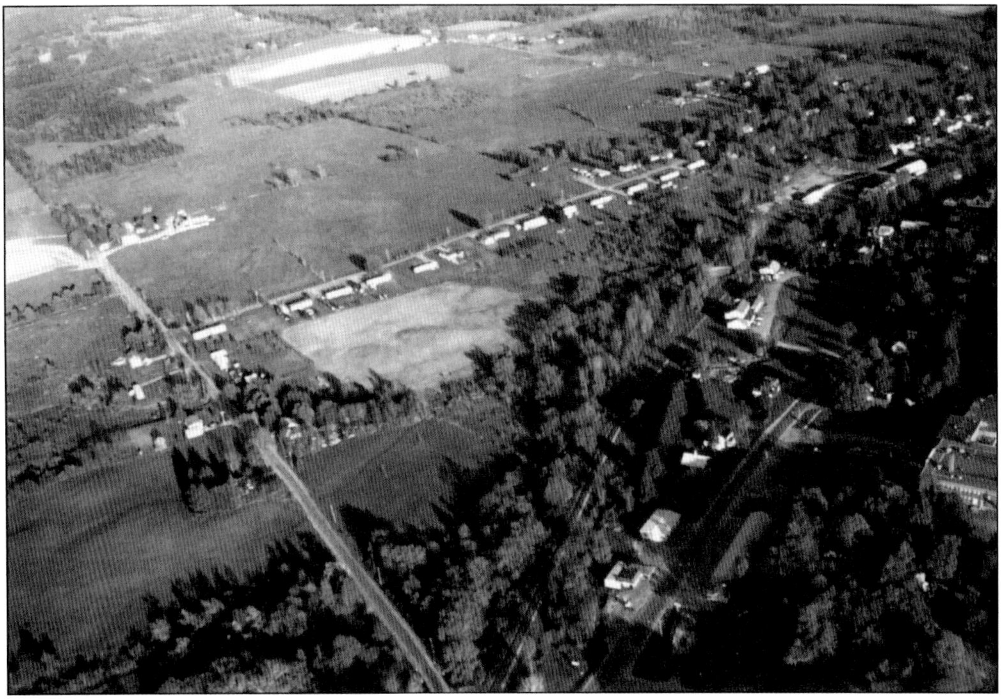

Remsen was named for early patentee Henry Remsen. He had inherited the Remsenburgh patent, which contained approximately 48,000 acres in Oneida and Herkimer Counties. The Remsenburgh patent was granted in 1766 to Remsen and four other New York merchants. Remsen, a New York City merchant and owner of Henry Remsen Jr. & Company, was the descendant of some of the earliest Dutch settlers of New Amsterdam. His earliest ancestors to live in America were Rem Jansen Van Der Beeck and his wife, Janetie, who married in 1652. The family eventually dropped the Van Der Beeck and took the name Remsen. These aerial views show the landscape of Remsen. (Both, courtesy of Jeanette Walter.)

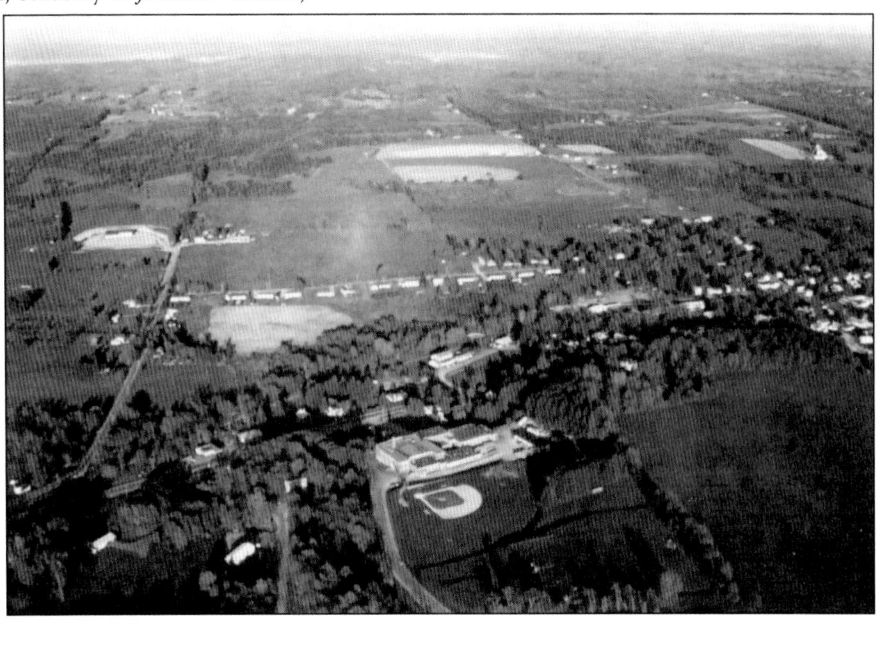

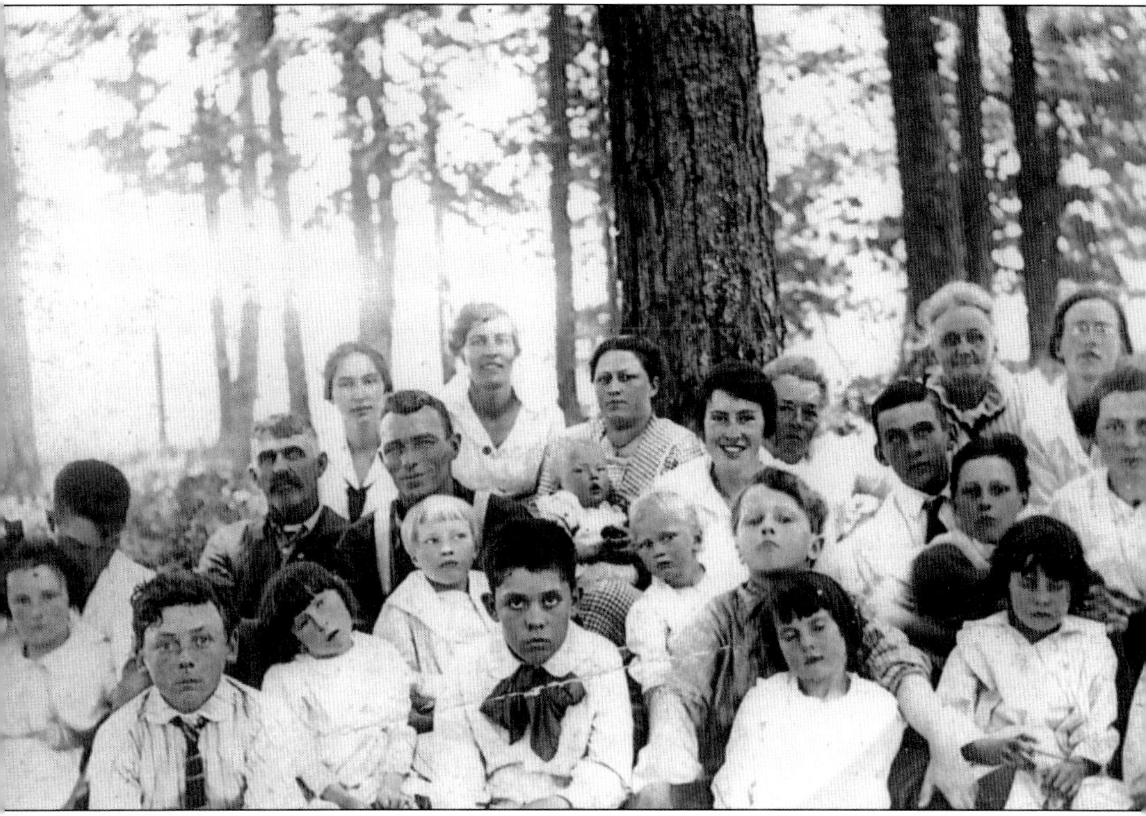

There were schoolhouses scattered in all corners of the Remsen, Steuben, and surrounding areas. The Enlli (No. 6) Schoolhouse was located on Black Hollow Road in Remsen, near the Banner Dairy Farm. The Jones family farm was also nearby, on Lake Julia Road. The first recorded murder in Remsen's history occurred on Black Hollow Road. This photograph most likely depicts a school and community picnic. Among those in the photograph are a Ms. Parker (teacher), Kelly Hughes Ingersoll, Burlie Brant Jones, Ella Francis, Mary Francis (mother of Sam and Gib), Sara Hughes, Karl Kelly, Dick Francis, William Jones, Bill Jones, Lillian Kelly, Joe Smith, Ethyl Griffith, Violet Rowlands, Erma Jones, Howard Francis, Winifred Jones, Walter Jones, Oliver Jones, Evelyn Rowlands, and Mary Rowlands. The schoolhouse is now empty but still stands, although it had been previously converted into a home. (Courtesy of Jeanette Walter.)

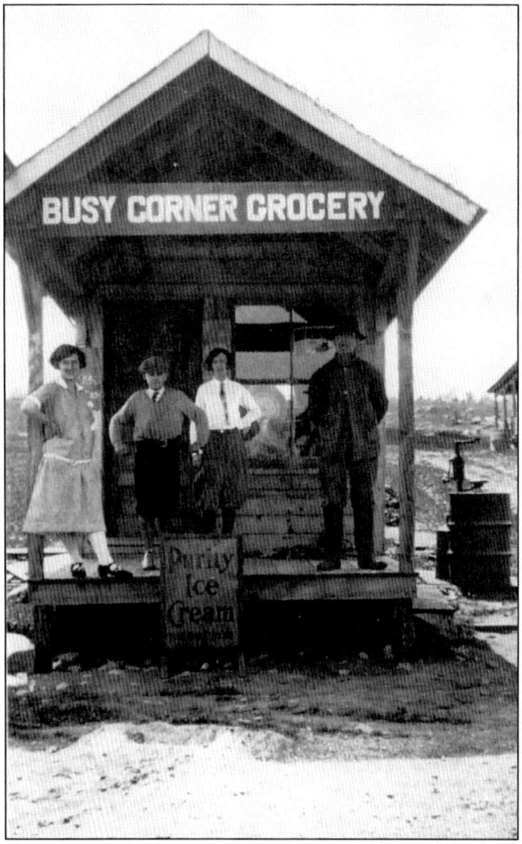

The Busy Corner Grocery was also known as the Edwin Thomas store. It was located at the Bardwell Mills corner near the Brown Tract Road. From left to right are Annie Williams Thomas, Sandy Housten, Janet Housten, and Edwin Thomas Jr. (Courtesy of Jeanette Walter.)

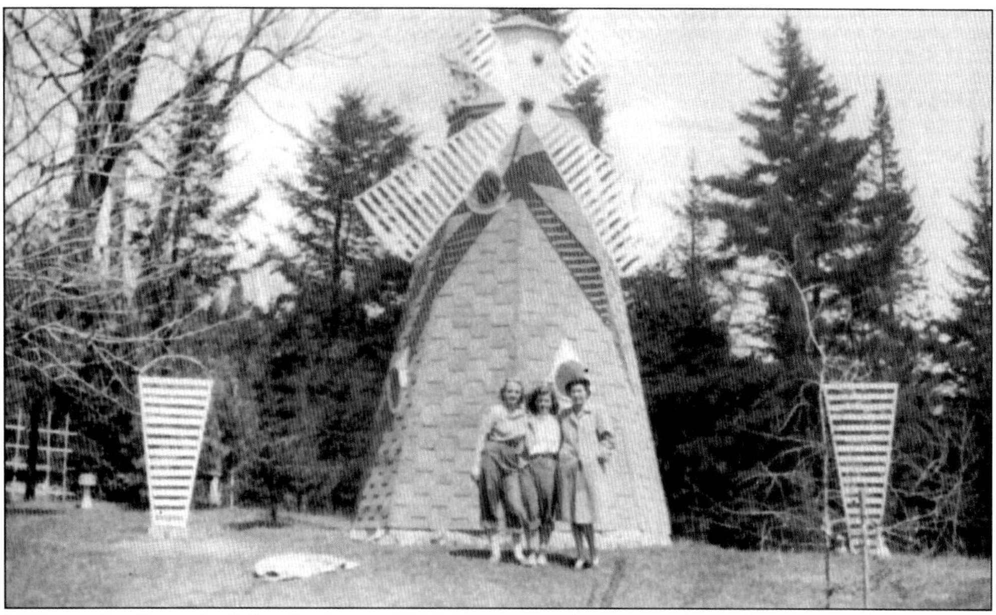

This windmill was built by the Setzer brothers—Joe, John, Al, and Otto—in the Bardwell Mills district of Remsen. From left to right are Mimi Setzer Worden, Betty Francis, and Hanna Setzer. (Courtesy of Jeanette Walter.)

A group of children poses for a photograph in the doorway of the Enlli church on Fairchild Road at the base of Ninety Five Hill. Enlli has been well preserved. Among those in the photograph are Garrie Jones, Liz Jones, Nancy Roberts, Jeanette Ingersoll, Donna Williams, Shirley Williams, Marleen Pugh, Bev Pritchard, Bob Pugh, and Joanne Pugh. (Courtesy of Jeanette Walter.)

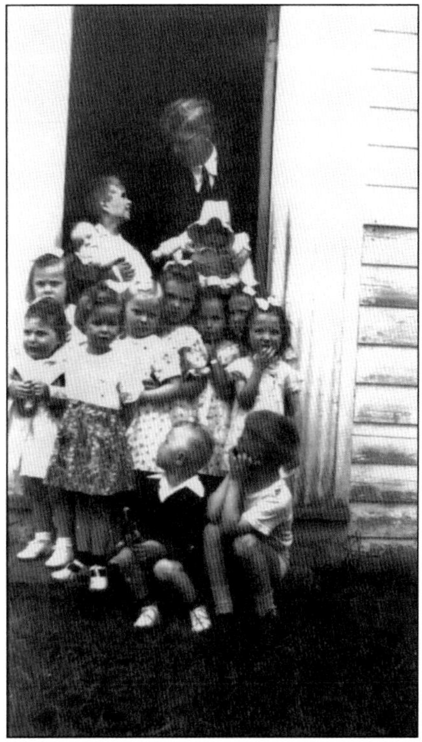

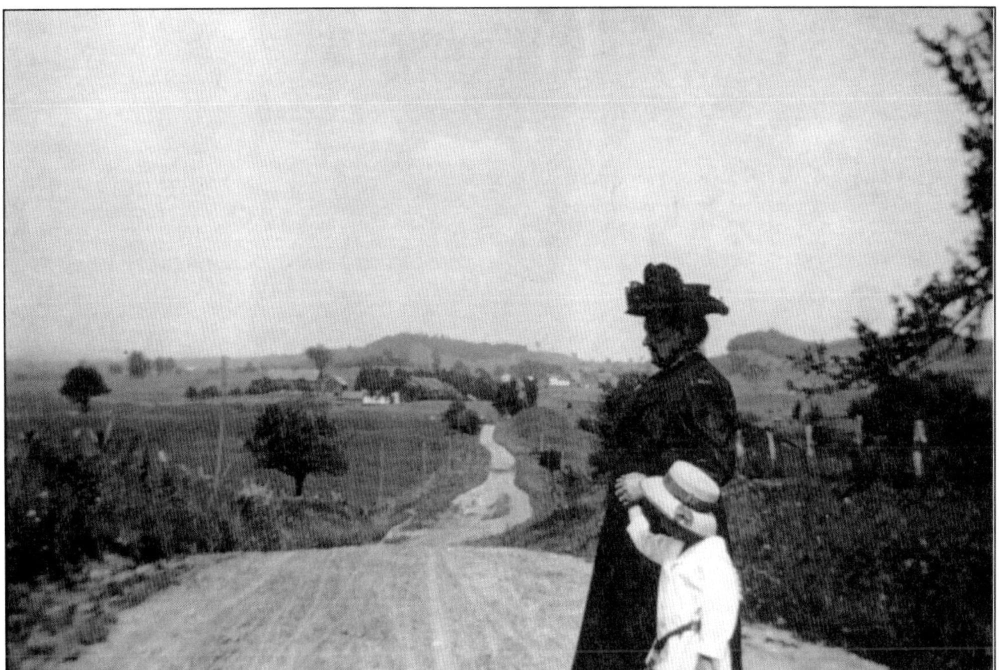

This photograph shows an early Fairchild Road, before pavement, in a view looking east from Welsh District Road towards Ninety Five Hill. Many of the structures in this photograph still stand. The area has become thickly forested. The woman and child are unidentified. (Courtesy of Jeanette Walter.)

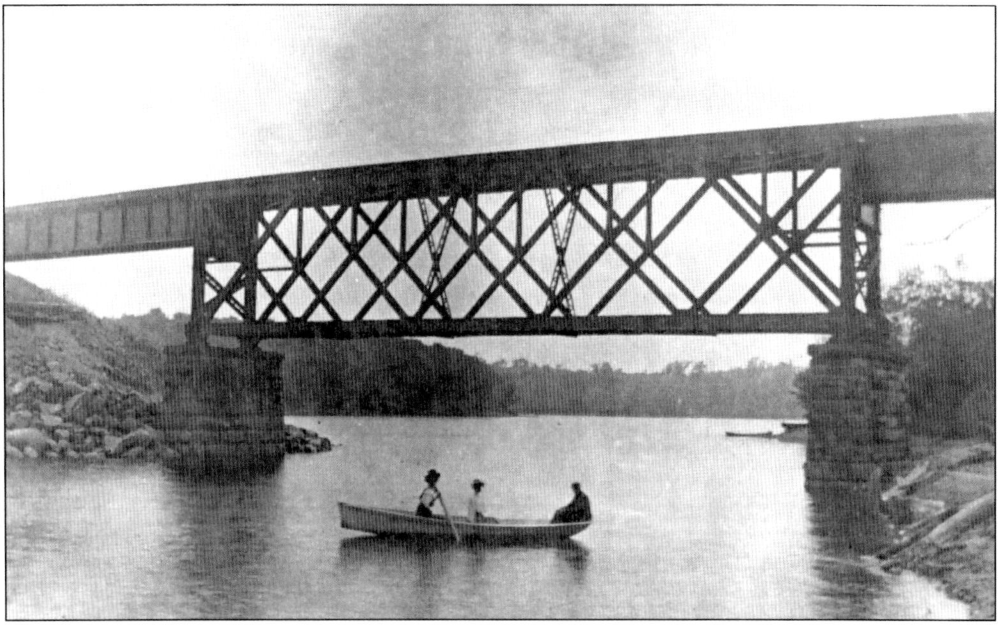

Tourism was a profitable industry in the Forestport area even after the forest was stripped and logging slowed. Local guides led travelers into the wilderness for hunting, fishing, and camping. Many people came to Forestport for the clear Adirondack air. This image shows the Kayuta Lake trestle. (Courtesy of Jeanette Walter.)

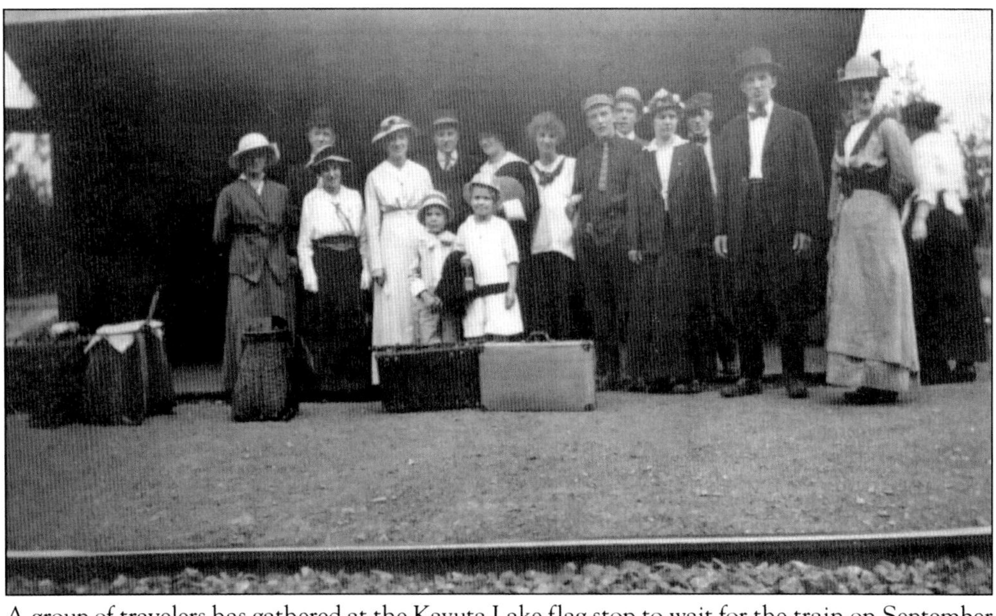

A group of travelers has gathered at the Kayuta Lake flag stop to wait for the train on September 6, 1915. Among the people in the photograph are Bessie Bauer, Anna Mae Lockwood, Lelia Jones, Earl Jones, and Gert Jones. Notice the fishing creels in the left front corner. (Courtesy of Jeanette Walter.)

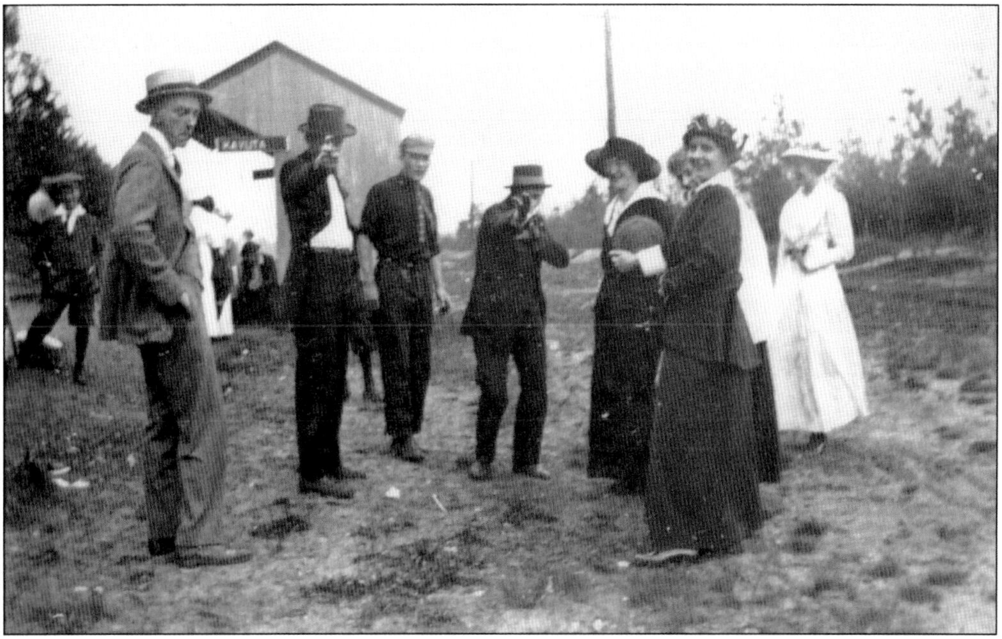

In this 1915 photograph, a small crowd is waiting for the train at the Kayuta Lake flag stop. The building of the railway in 1913 spurred commerce and tourism for Forestport. The area around Kayuta Lake, however, did not see much development until 1949. (Courtesy of Jeanette Walter.)

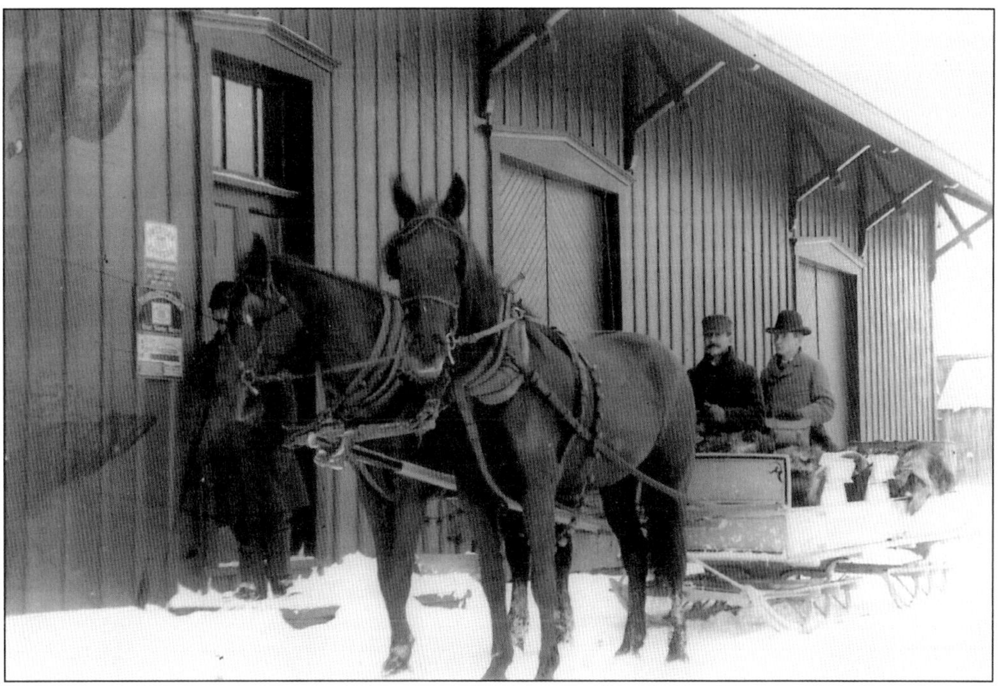

The village of Forestport became a hamlet in 1937, the same year that Route 28 was built, bypassing the community. Logging had begun to slow in the early 1900s. The last logs floated down Adirondack waterways in 1945. (Courtesy of Jeanette Walter.)

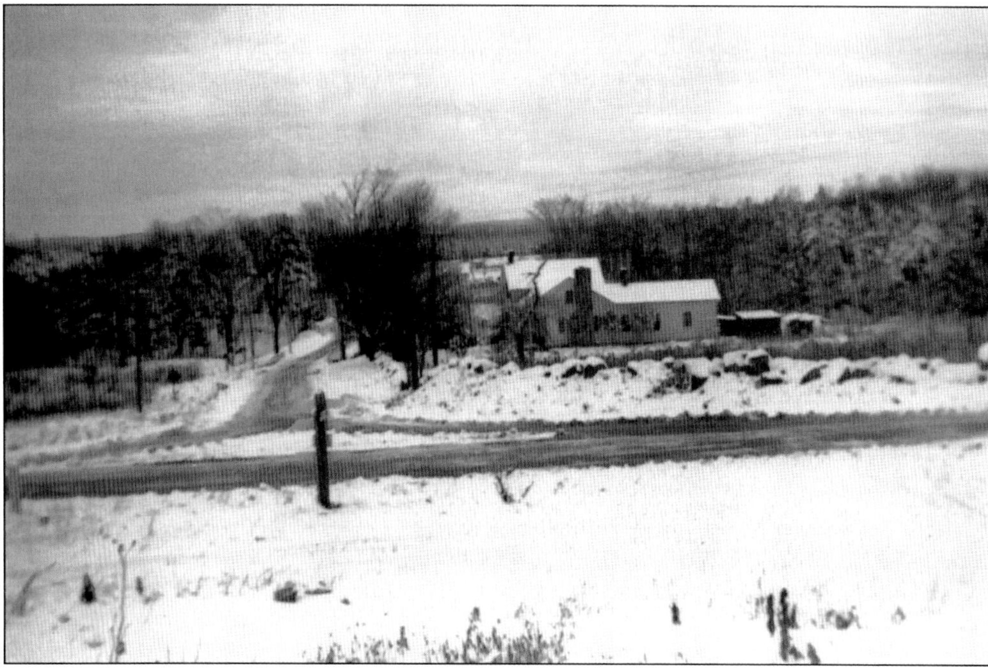

This photograph shows a wintry view looking out on the Bardwell Mills corner from the location where the Busy Corner Grocery once stood. Notice the rock wall partially covered with snow at the edge of the road. (Courtesy of Jeanette Walter.)

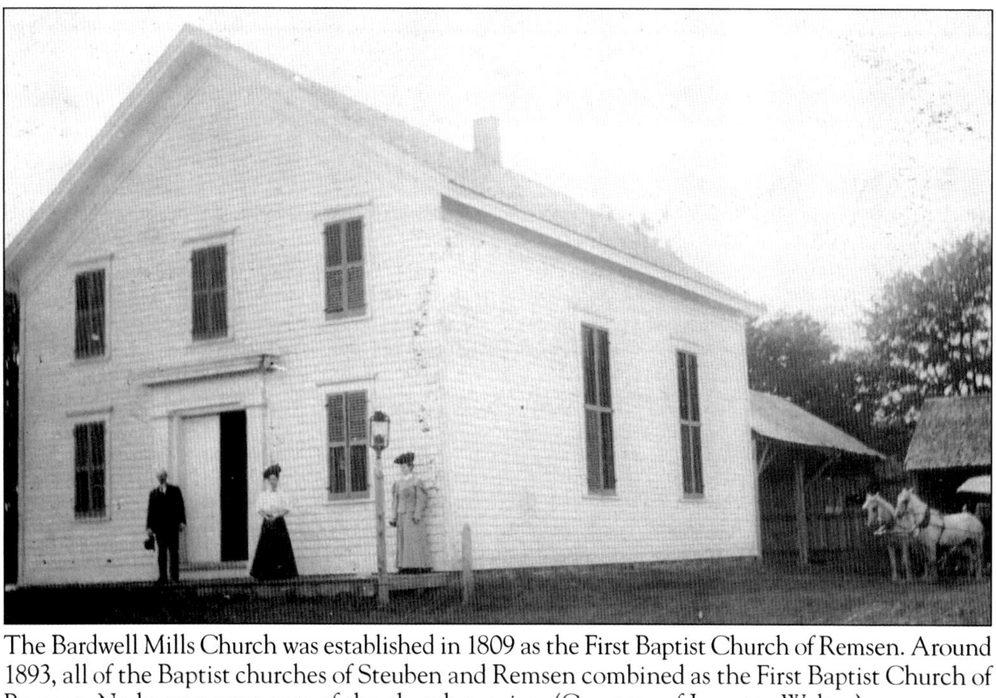

The Bardwell Mills Church was established in 1809 as the First Baptist Church of Remsen. Around 1893, all of the Baptist churches of Steuben and Remsen combined as the First Baptist Church of Remsen. No known remnants of the church survive. (Courtesy of Jeanette Walter.)

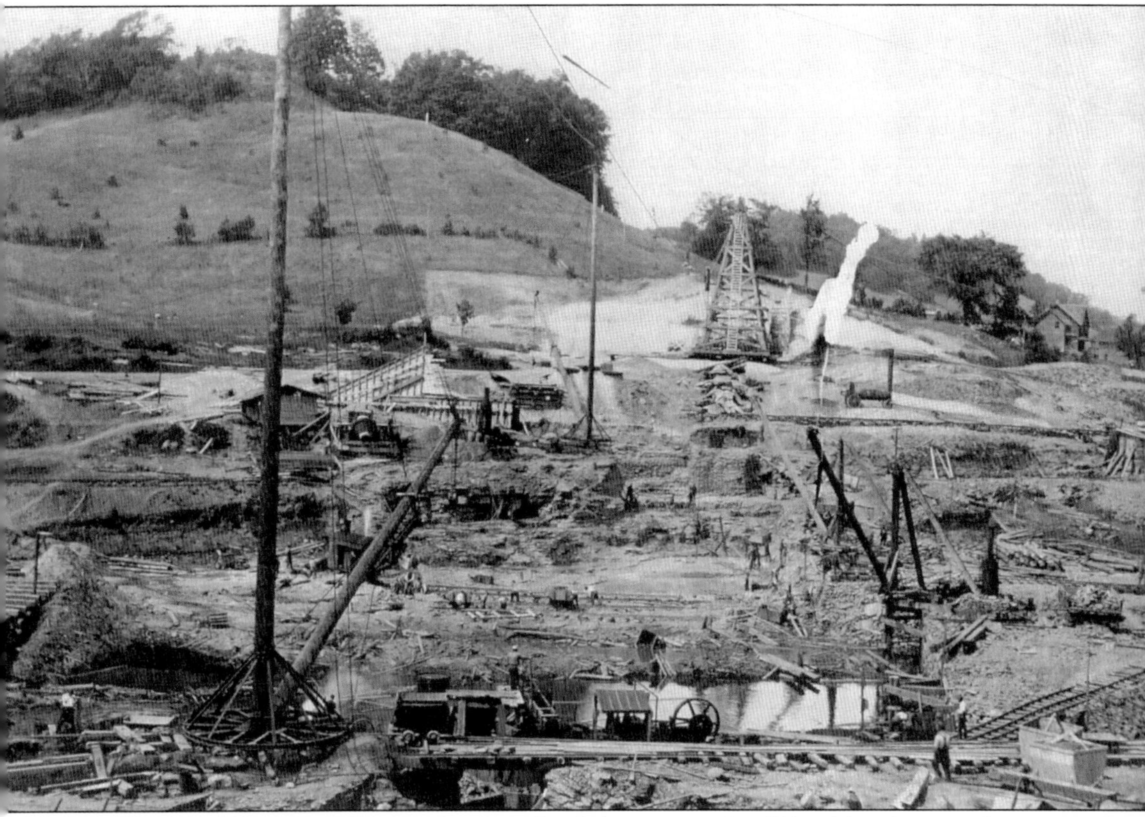

The damming of the West Canada Creek to flood the area north of Hinckley eliminated many roads. Roads from Grant and Ohio crossed the creek at Northwood Bridge in Northwood. These were destroyed when Hinckley Reservoir was flooded in 1915. Also underwater are Bousfield Road and part of Twin Rock Road. Today, the remaining section of Twin Rock Road, opposite Fairchild Road on Route 365, is blocked and posted at the lake end. On the north end of the reservoir on Route 365 stood the Northwood Post Office and Inn. It was built around 1900, making the building (which still stands) older than the reservoir. The Northwood Post Office overlooked Finch Bay, which was created by the flooding of the Hinckley Reservoir. The landscape has changed over time. It has become denser, with thicker surrounding forest area. The detested loyalist Walter Butler, who spread terror throughout the Mohawk Valley during the American Revolution, was killed about three and a half miles north of this location in 1781. (Courtesy of Jeanette Walter.)

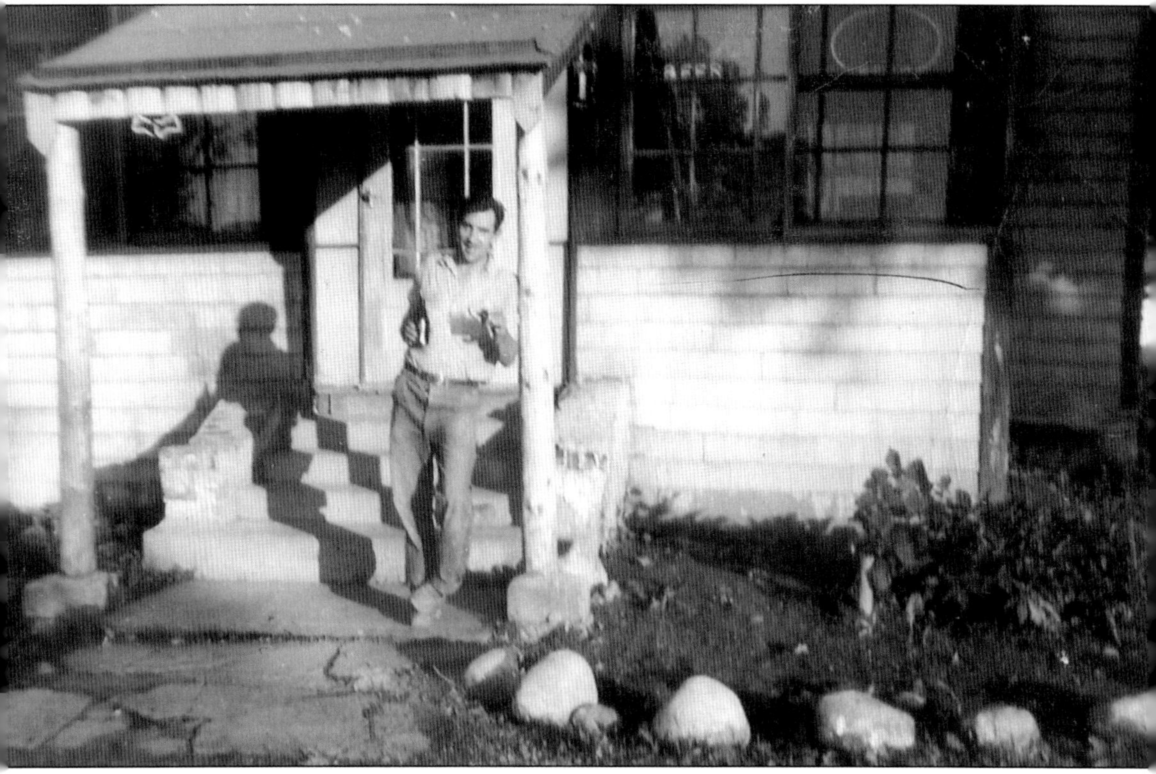

Greenwood Court was owned by Albert Schoen in the 1930s and early 1940s. From the later 1940s through the 1960s, it was owned by Angelo Santucci and wife, Anna. It was located on New York State Route 365 shortly past the intersection of Twin Rock Road and Fairchild Road. The structure still stands and is currently a residence. This photograph shows Joseph "Joe" Wilcox taking a smoke break at the exterior door of the barroom. Before Hinckley Reservoir was flooded, people traveled via Twin Rock Road and crossed the bridge that spanned the West Canada Creek to Dan McCarthy's cheese factory. Farmers who delivered milk to McCarthy often held on to his checks for years without cashing them, knowing that he kept a large balance. When the construction of the Hinckley Dam began, McCarthy paid his last check, closed the factory, and relocated. (Courtesy of Helen Griswold.)

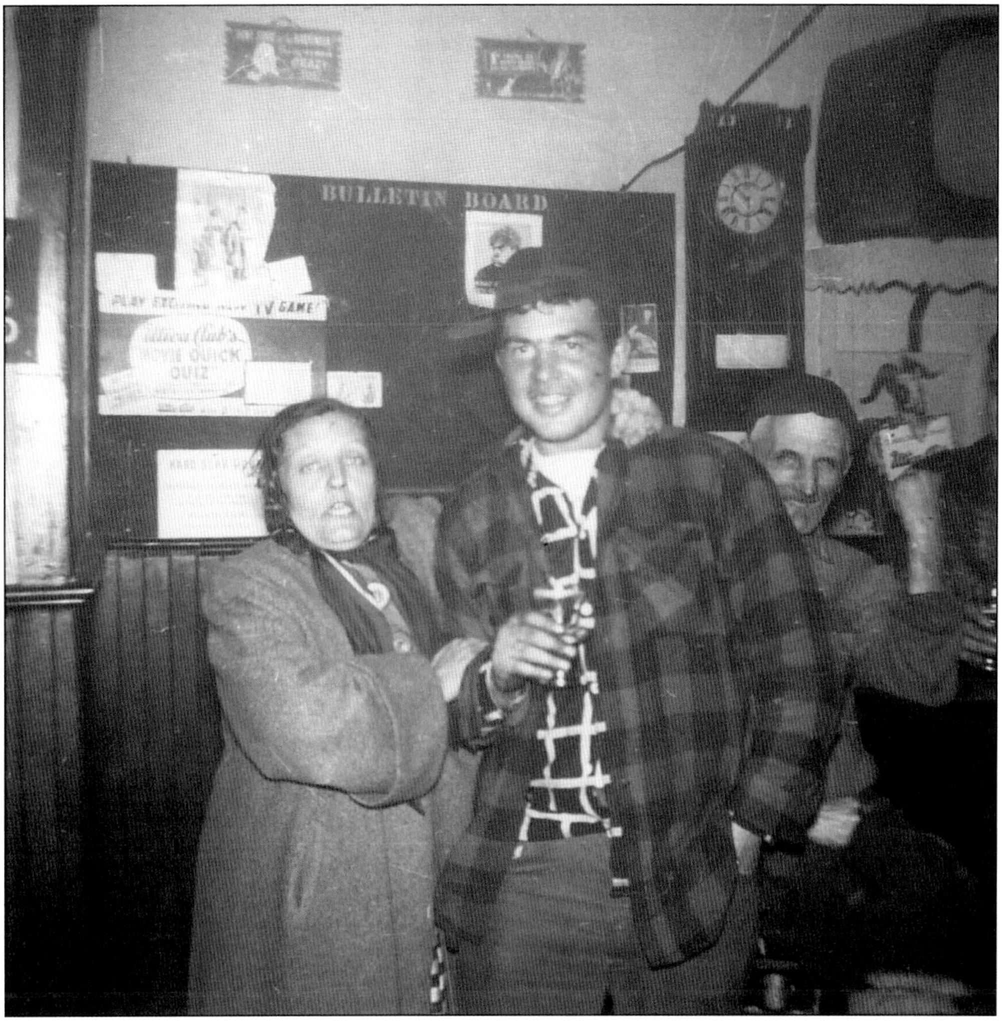

Toots Wandover and John "Jack" Wilcox are pictured here in the Greenwood Court barroom. Wandover was the daughter (one of 13 children) of the famous Adirondack guide George Wendover. The family name has been spelled alternately with both an *e* and an *a*. George guided in the North Lake region, east of Forestport. Men who came to the Adirondacks from the cities were called sports or greenhorns. These sports depended on men like Wendover to navigate them through the woods. Wendover had the reputation of being one of the Black River area's most respected guides. He enjoyed gathering with other local guides at taverns in Forestport to drink whiskey and tell great tales. The guides told colorful stories of their adventures. Wendover died at age 96 in 1945. He is buried in Wheelertown Cemetery. (Courtesy of Helen Griswold.)

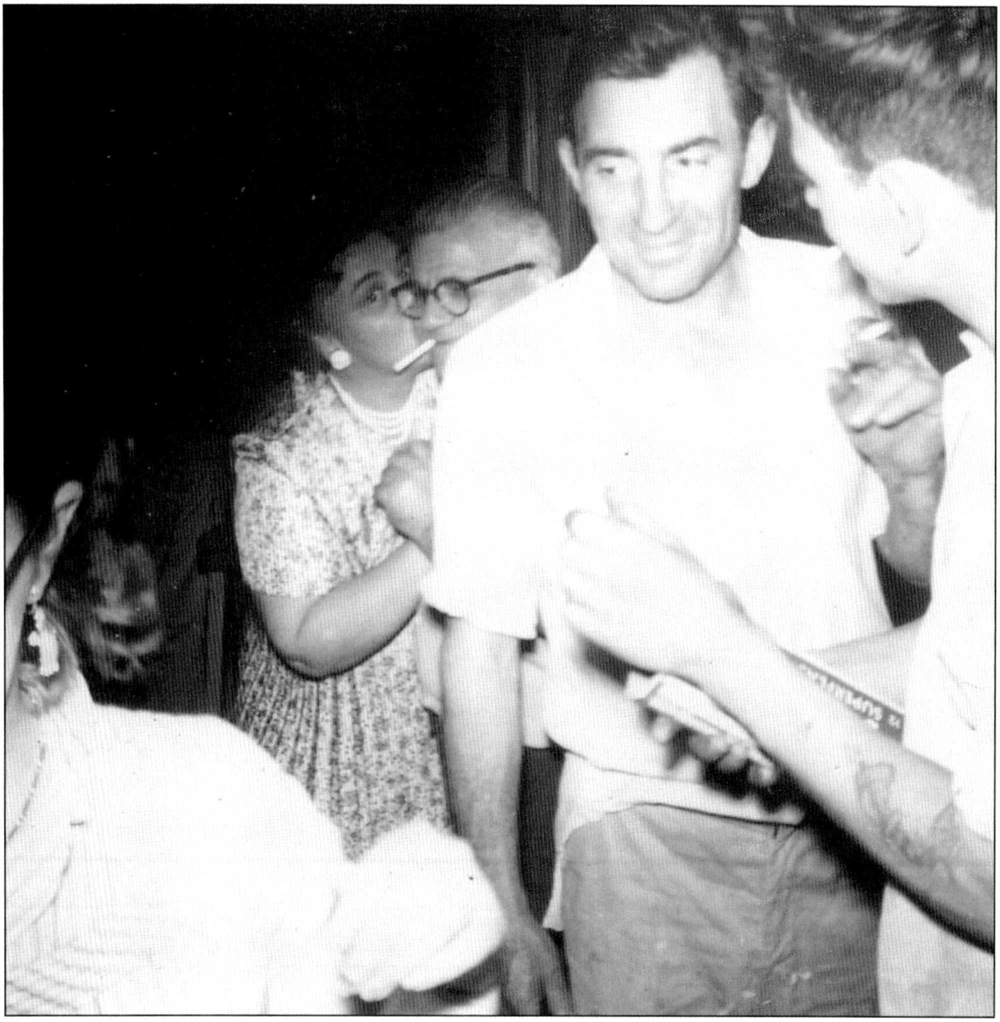

Greenwood Court was located on Route 365 in the Northwood area near Hinckley Reservoir. The owner of Greenwood Court in the 1950s, Angelo Santucci is shown with a cigarette in his mouth. Greenwood Court was a popular gathering place for many who dwelled in Northwood. It is now a residence. (Courtesy of Helen Griswold.)

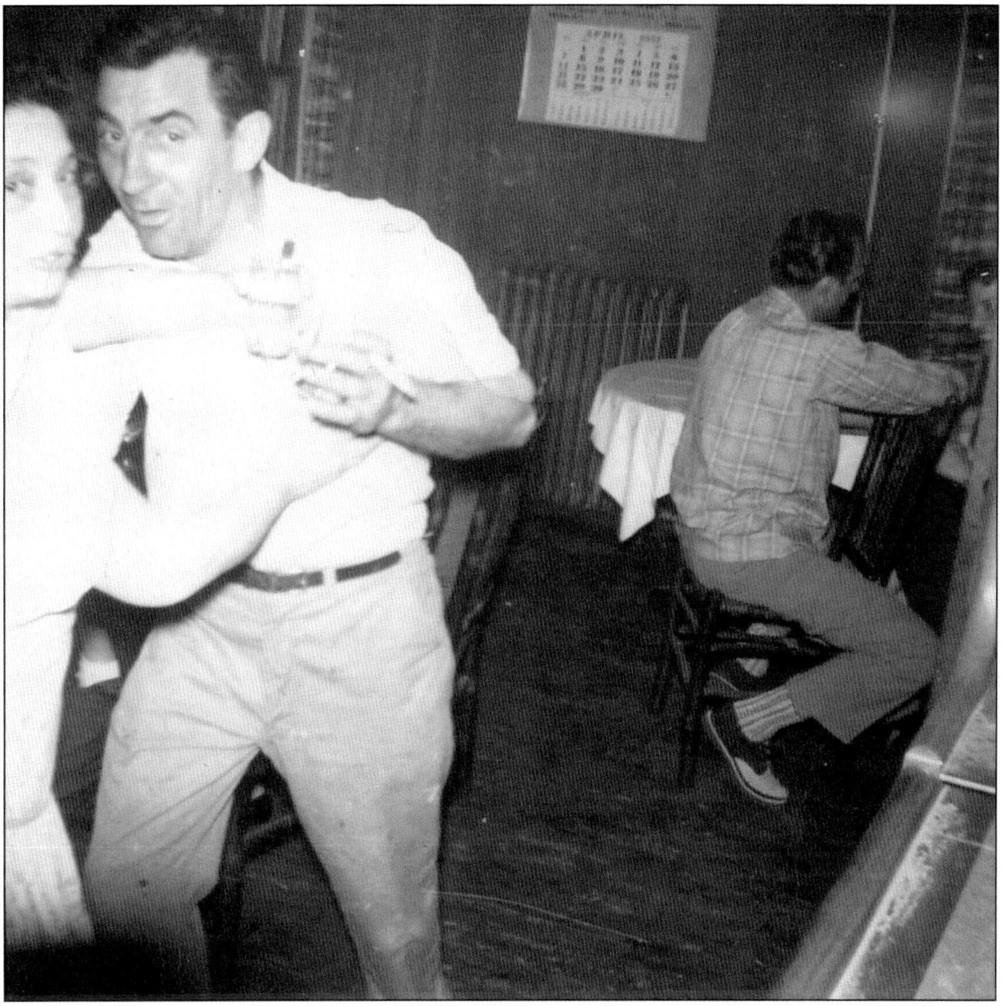

This photograph shows a celebration at Greenwood Court. Joseph Wilcox, shown front left, lived in Northwood. Wilcox served in the Navy during World War II and was at Pearl Harbor. He and his wife, Mary, had 10 children—John "Jack," James "Jim," Joseph, Elizabeth, Helen, Margaret, Jerome, William, Patrick, and Ann. (Courtesy of Helen Griswold.)

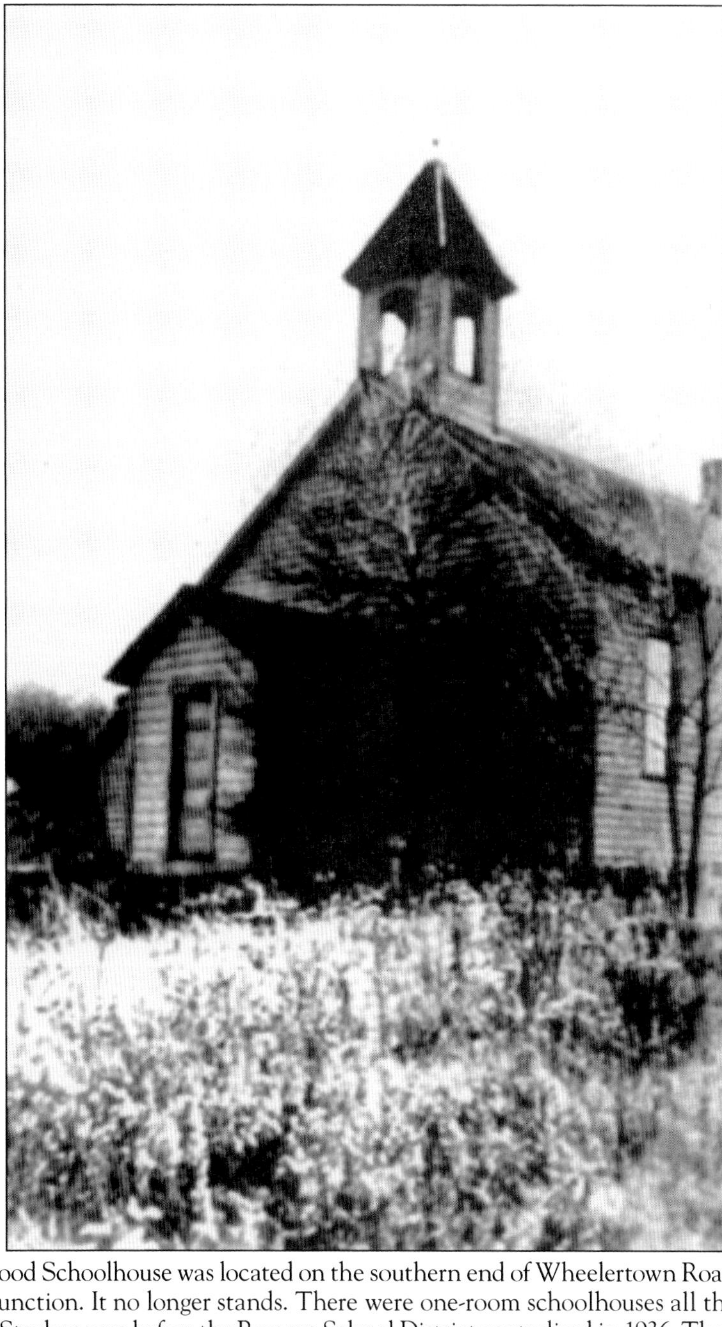

The Northwood Schoolhouse was located on the southern end of Wheelertown Road, close to the Spall Road junction. It no longer stands. There were one-room schoolhouses all throughout the Remsen and Steuben area before the Remsen School District centralized in 1936. The schoolhouses in the district also included Steuben Corners School, Maple Mountain School (Boody Hill), Beaver Meadow School, Fink Hollow School, Penn Mountain School, Starr Hill School, Pugh District School, Wolfenden School, French Road School, Sixty School, Fuller District School, Bethel School, Covered Bridge School, Pirnie District School (Plank Road), Honnedaga Keat District School (Dayton Road), Fairchild School, Bardwell School, Welsh District School, Hall District School (Lake Julia Road), Enlli School, and Ninety Six School. The present Remsen Central School was built in 1935. (Courtesy of Jeanette Walter.)

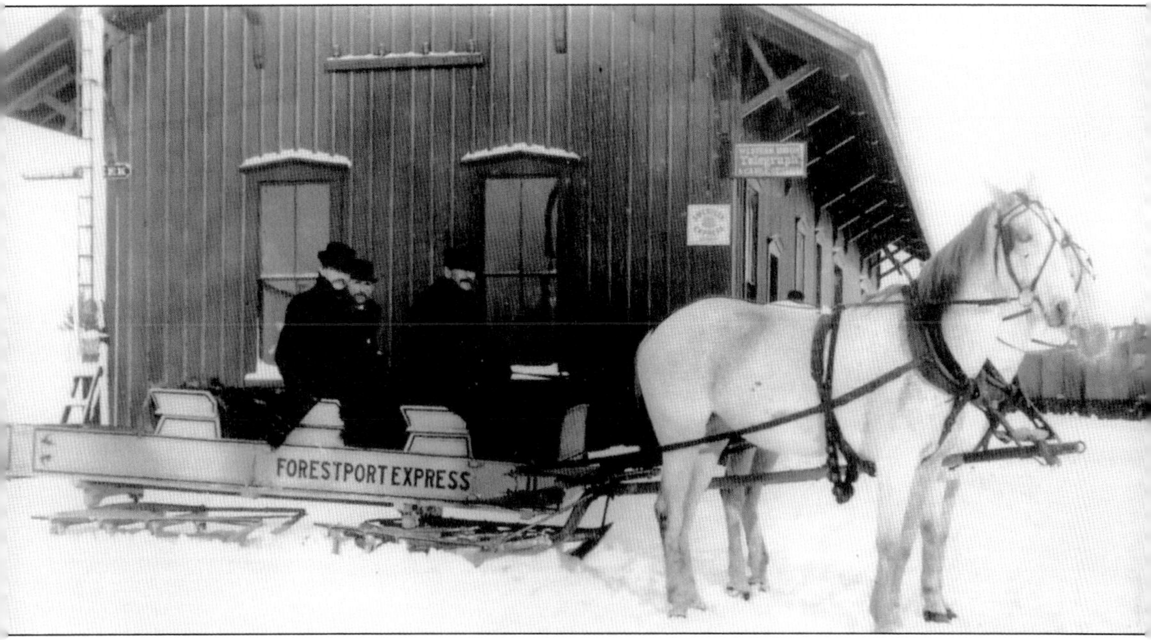

The Forestport Express is parked in front of the Alder Creek train station. In its early days, Forestport had a few different names. The first was Smith's Mill, due to an early sawmill on the west side of the Black River. Later, Platt Williams built a large home on the Alder Creek Road and the settlement became known as Williamsville. Forestport was also known as Punkeyville because of the biting insects known punkies or no-see-ums. (Courtesy of Jeanette Walter.)

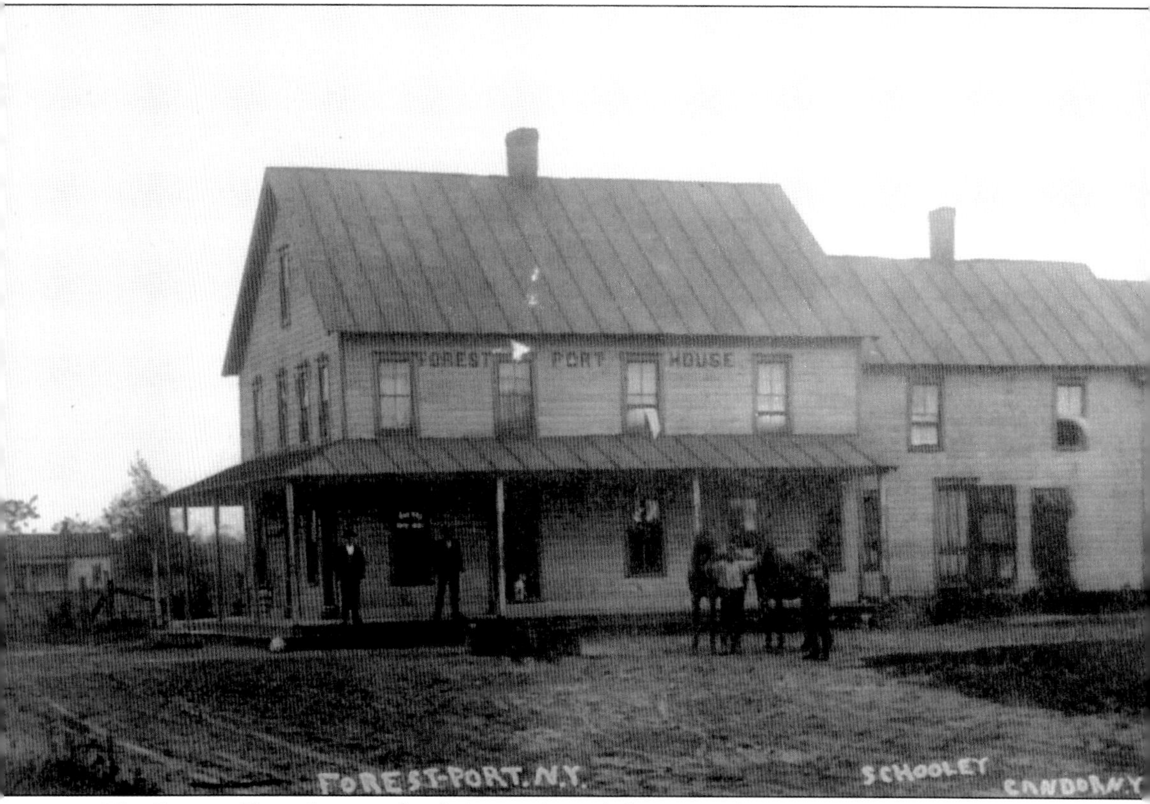

The Remsen Township was divided in 1869, and the town of Forestport was formed out of the township on November 24 of that year. Forestport was a lumbering town on the banks of the Black River feeder canal and the setting of the infamous canal breaks. This image shows the Forestport House. (Courtesy of Jeanette Walter.)

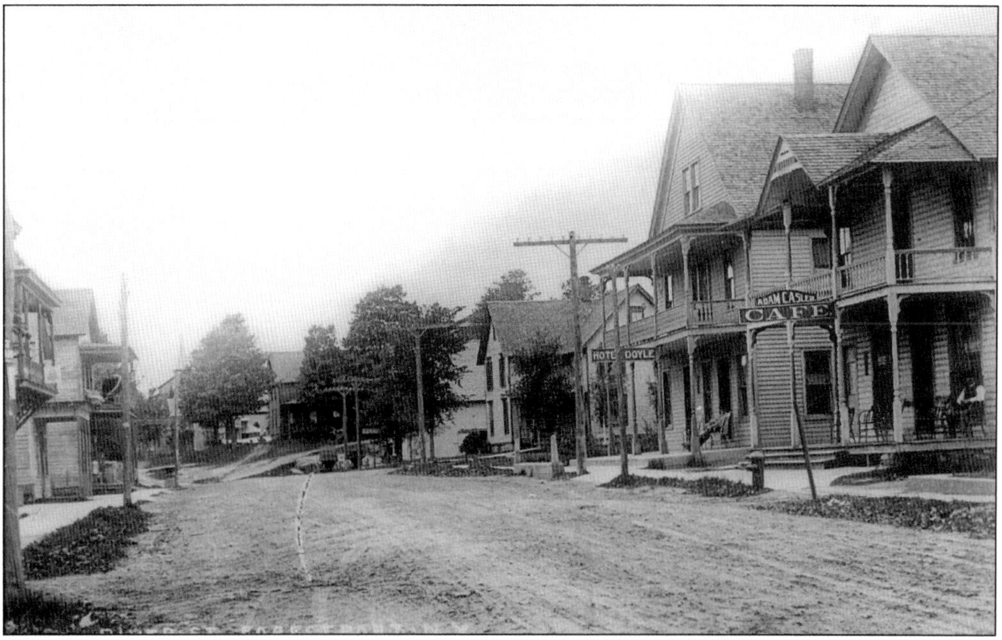

At the end of the 19th century, a number of Forestport residents were found to be involved in a conspiracy to divert funds set aside for canal repair for the Black River Canal. Sections of the Black River Canal were dynamited so as to profit from repair work, infamously known as the "Forestport Breaks." The Pinkerton National Detective Agency, appointed to investigate by Gov. Theodore Roosevelt, found what one lawman called one of the most gigantic conspiracies ever hatched in New York. The photograph above shows River Street in Forestport in a view looking north, and the photograph below shows a view looking south. Hotel Doyle (present-day Scooters) is visible in both images. (Both, courtesy of Jeanette Walter.)

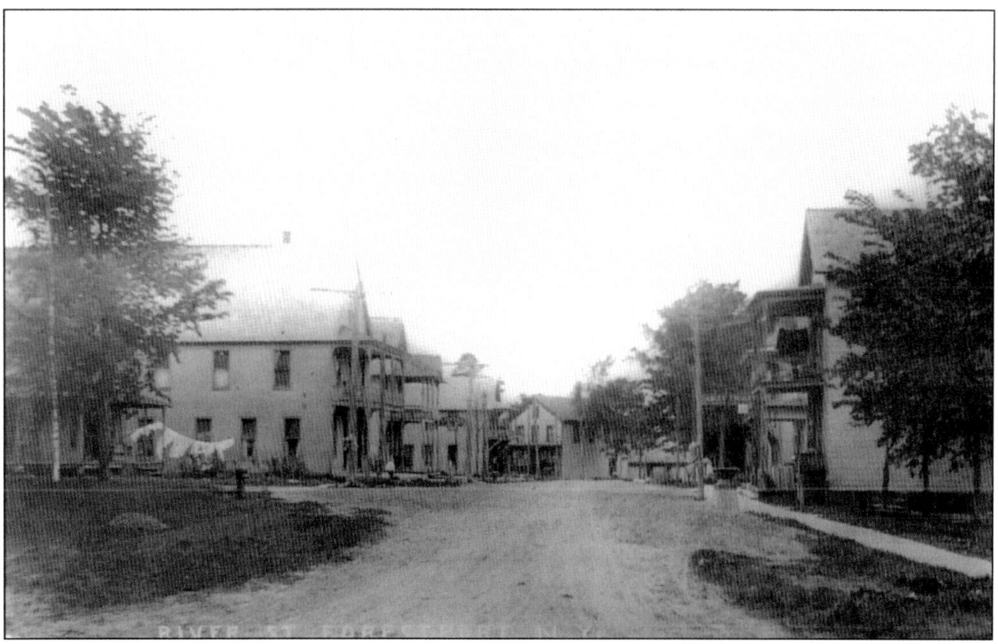

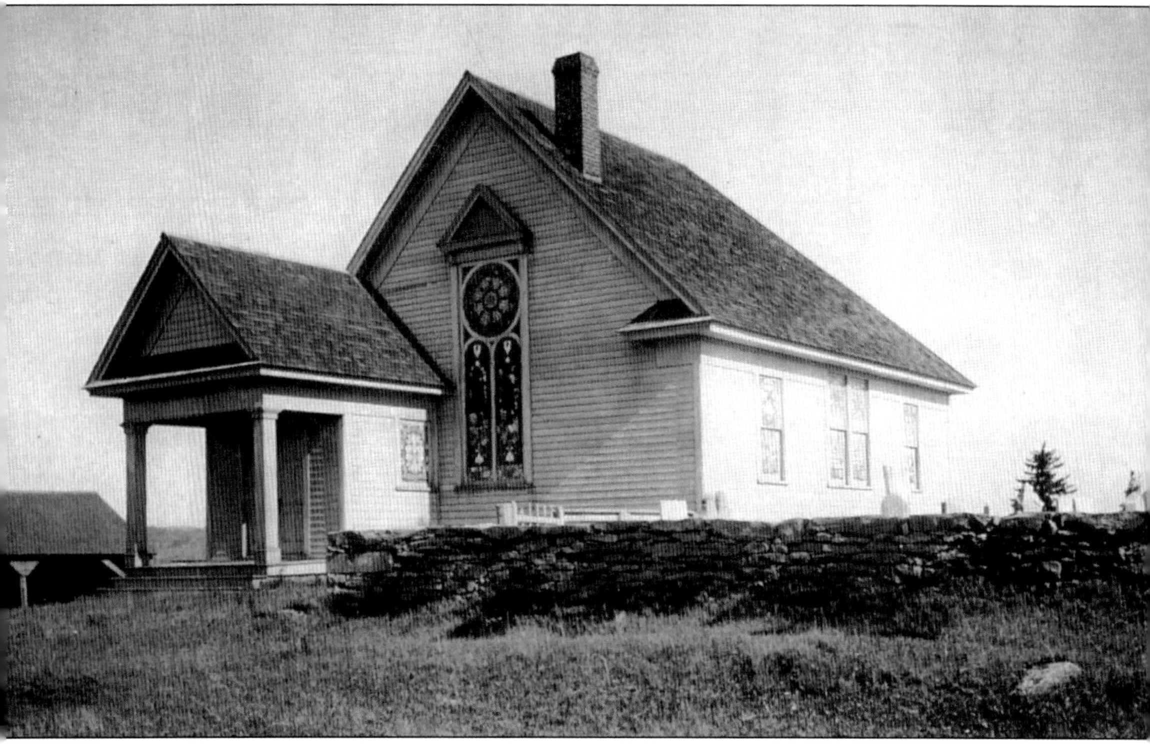

Capel Ucha, built in 1804, was located on Starr Hill Road approximately a half mile from the village of Remsen. The most notable pastor of Capel Ucha was Rev. Robert Everett, who came to Steuben in 1830. Everett was an educated man who had received training at Wrexham Seminary in Wales and later received an honorary doctor of divinity degree from Hamilton College. During his years in Steuben, Everett preached at Capel Ucha and also established Pen Y Mynydd, another Welsh Congregational church on Pen Mount (Penn Mountain). Everett formed temperance societies in both Remsen and Steuben. He was involved with abolitionist activities, and his home was rumored to be a stop on the Underground Railroad. In 1853, Everett and his son translated Harriet Beecher Stowe's best seller *Uncle Tom's Cabin* into Welsh to make it available to the native speakers living in the hills of Steuben, Remsen, and surrounding area. This translation has been credited for the enthusiasm of the Welsh, usually a pacifistic group, towards the Civil War. There were some who opposed Everett's humanistic work. He was harassed, and at one point, the tail and mane of his horse were cut off in ridicule. (Courtesy of Jeanette Walter.)

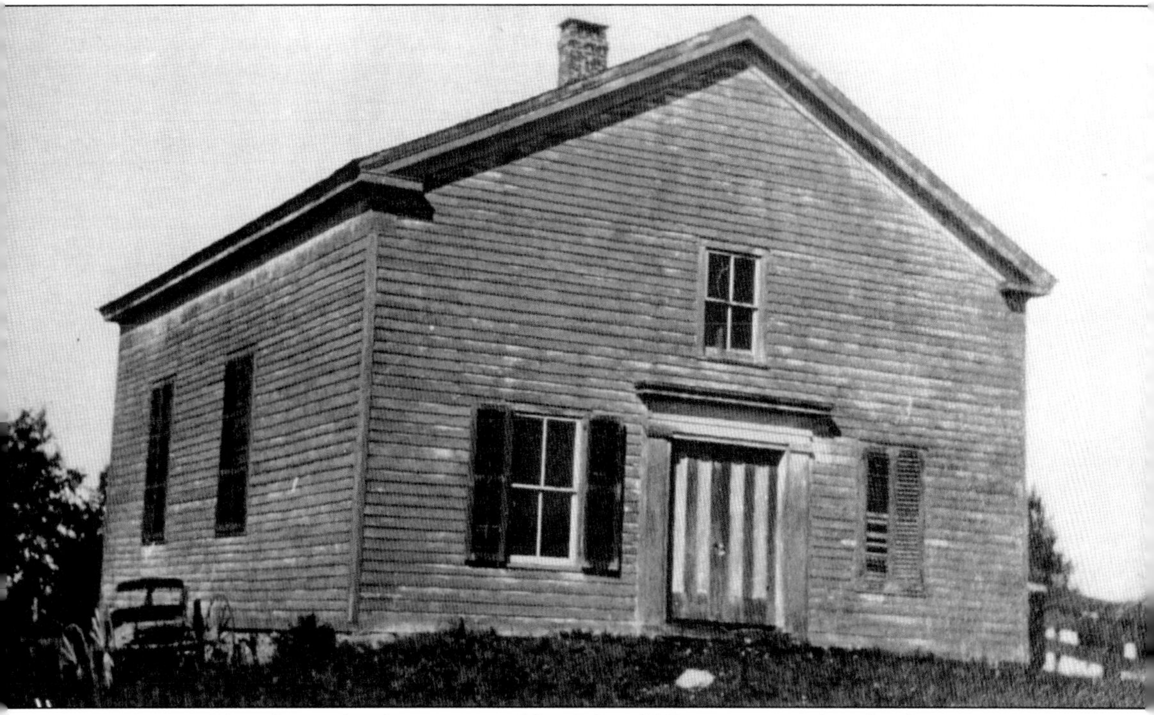

Pen-y-Caerau Church may be the most notable of the old Remsen area churches because it was the first Calvinistic Methodist church in the United States. It was located on the corner of James Road and Francis Road, about two miles east of the village of Remsen. There remains now only a marker along with a cemetery enclosed by a wooden fence. The Calvinistic Methodists of Wales came to Steuben in 1800 and worshipped at the Union Church of Capel Ucha until they organized as a congregational society. Pen-y-Caerau was built in August 1824. Some notables who left the Capel Ucha for Pen-y-Caerau were James Owen, Owen Owens, Hugh Owens, Lewis Lewis, and Moses Jones. James served as a church elder at Pen-y-Caerau for 54 years and played an active role in its endeavors during that time. The first sermon in Pen-y-Caerau was delivered by the pastor of Capel Ucha, William Pierce. The Reverend Benjamin Davis was the first ordained minister of the Calvinistic Methodist denomination in America. He helped to establish three Calvinistic Methodist churches in the town of Steuben in 1828 and a Moriah Calvinistic church in Utica in 1830. Membership outgrew the original church, and in 1852, a larger church was built. The original church was removed to a nearby farm. (Courtesy of Jeanette Walter.)

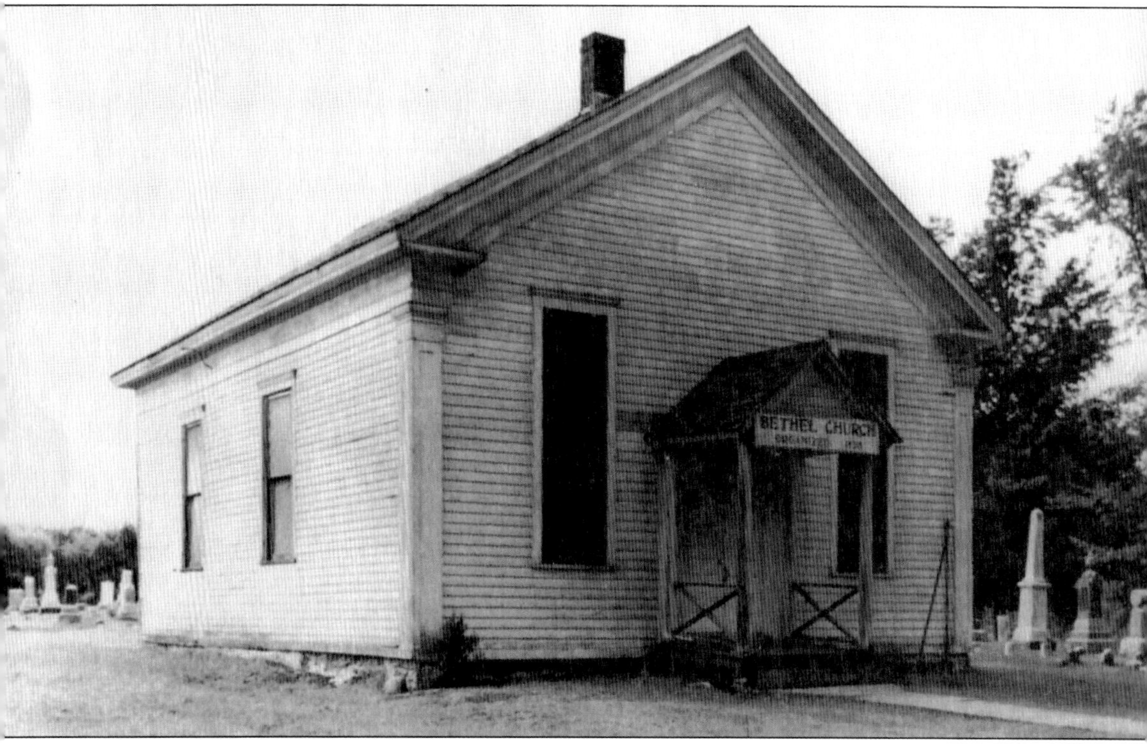

The Bethel Church, on the corner of Bethel Road and State Route 12, was built in 1839 by the Second Congregational Church Society. Before the church was constructed, the society had been holding services in homes and schoolhouses. Soon after the Bethel Church was erected, Remsen experienced a religious revival and membership increased quickly. The young and robust Rev. Morris Roberts, then age 39, served as the first pastor. The building was incorporated in September 1842. By 1859, the congregation had outgrown the original Bethel Church building, so it was rebuilt and enlarged. At that time, five regular services were held every week. Many influential people in the area were members of the Bethel Church. Reverend Roberts led the church until 1872. He was succeeded by Rev. Trogwy Evans. During Reverend Evans's time, the maple trees were planted out in front of the church in 1874. He was succeeded in the 1890s by Rev. Edward Davies. (Courtesy of Jeanette Walter.)

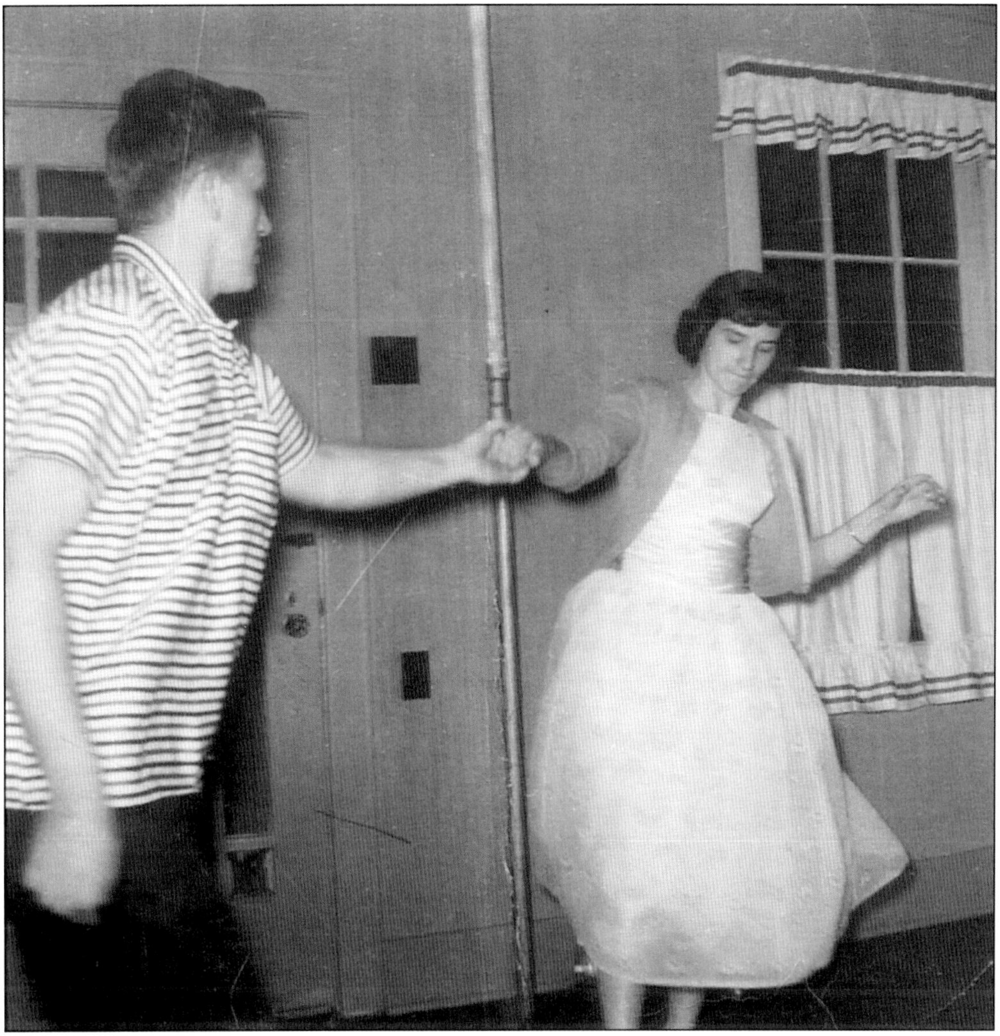

Helen Wilcox celebrates her graduation from Remsen Central School with a dance. She is pictured with her brother Joseph "Joe" Wilcox at Greenwood Court. Barn dances and square dancing were popular among Central New York youth in the 1940s, 1950s, and 1960s. One of the most popular barn dances in the area was hosted by the Jones family on Black Hollow Road in Remsen. Other local barn dances were held in Steuben Valley, Frenchville, and Boonville. Wilcox later married John "Jack" Griswold. He was the proprietor of Griswold's Diner in Remsen. They had five children—Theresa, Joseph "Joe," Ann Margaret "Maggie," Patricia "Trish," and Michelle. (Courtesy of Helen Griswold.)

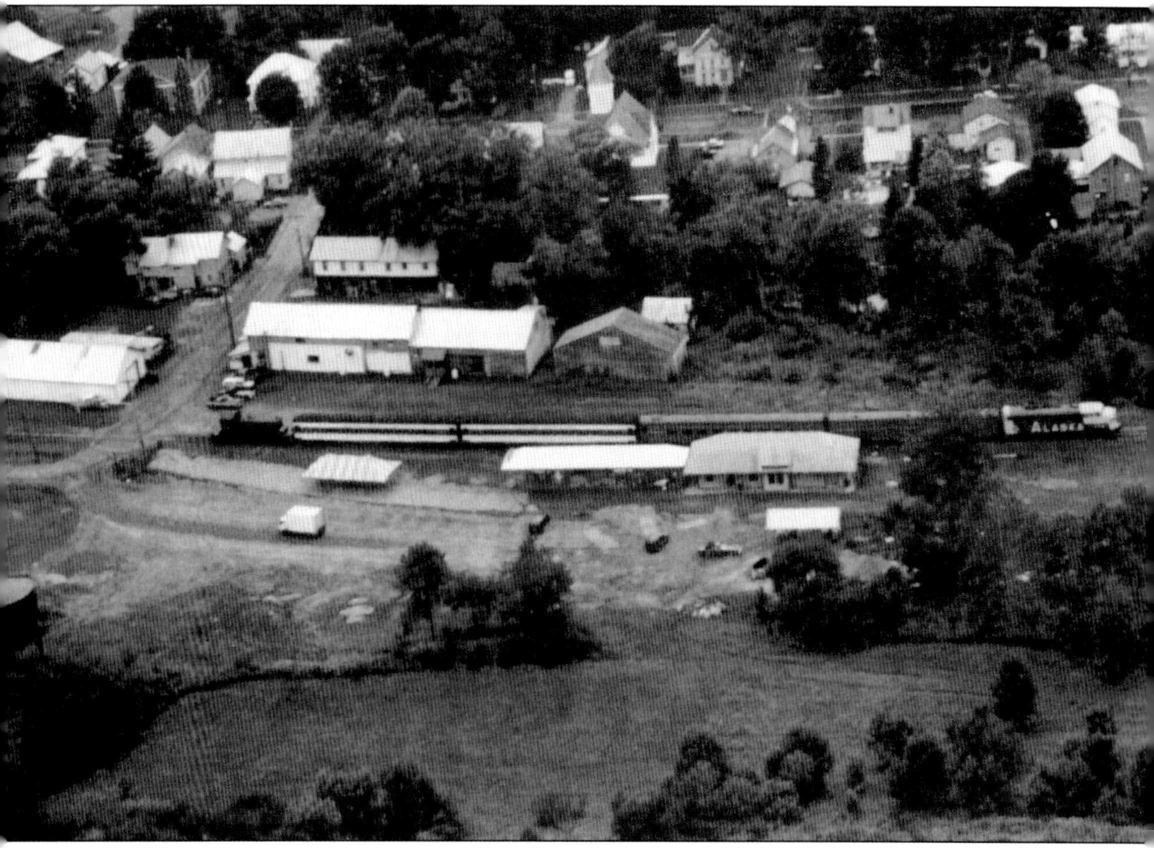

This aerial view is of the Remsen Depot and surrounding structures. An expert quoted in Margaret P. Davis's *Honey Out of the Rafters* describes the nostalgia of Remsen's early years: "It was a period of thrift and saving and making do in any way possible. We saved fat to make soap. We saved potato water to make bread, and we saved matches by making lucifers or lighters. We had not come to the time when everyone spent all the money they could get hold of. . . . What changes have taken place! The population of Steuben is but a fraction of what it was in 1830. The farms of Steuben that were once cleared and inhabited have been abandoned and are rapidly returning to look like Steuben in the 1790s. Remsen, which was more fortunately situated, as to railroads, than perhaps any village in this section of the state, finds itself almost completely without rail transportation." (Courtesy of Jeanette Walter.)

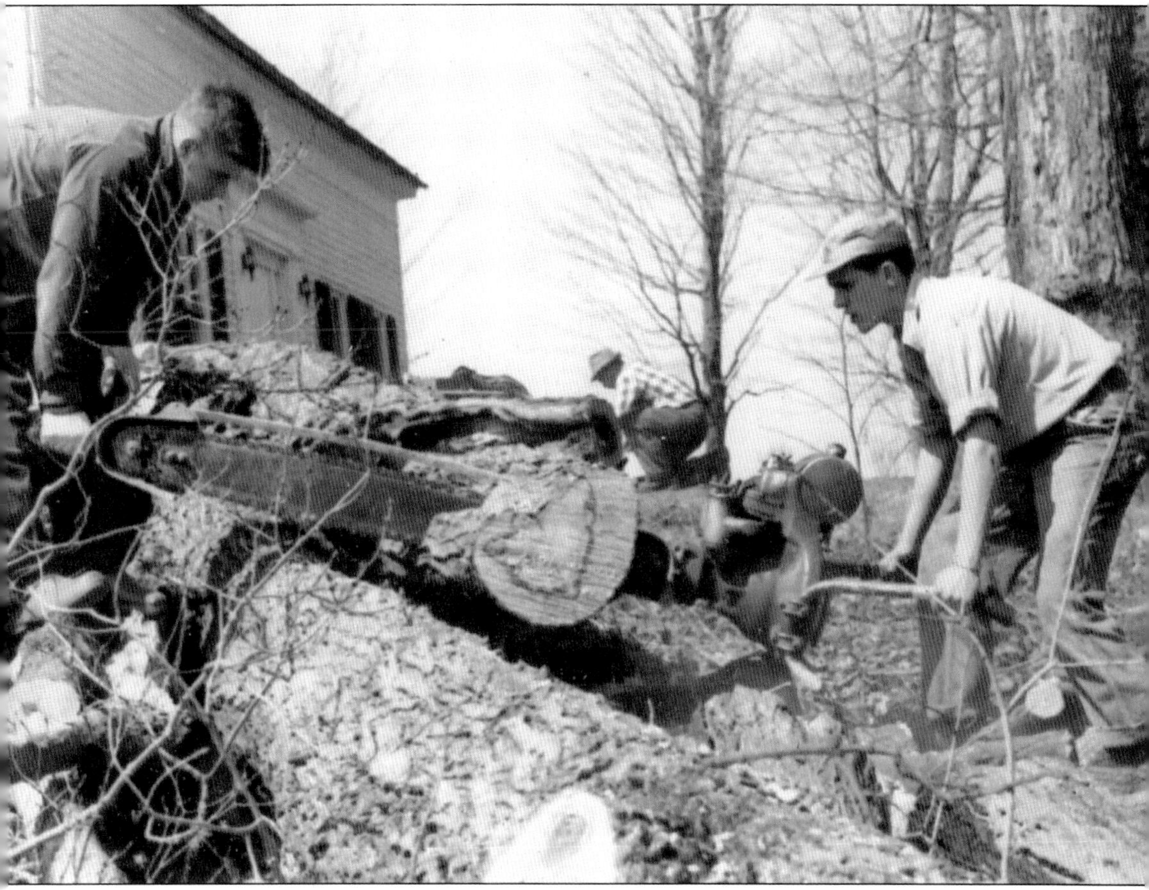

In this photograph, two young men use a two-person saw to cut through a large log. The first motorized chain saws were developed in the 1920s. Early chain saw models were heavy, two-person devices with long bars. The first two-person gas chain saw was patented by German engineer Andreas Stihl and weighed 139 pounds. World War II interrupted the supply of German chain saws to North America. This allowed new domestic chain saw manufacturers to establish businesses. Modern chain saws are much lighter and easier to maneuver. The men are cleaning up the damage from a windstorm in the 1950s. They are shown at the Gauthier property in Grant. The man on the left is Bernard "Bill" Plete. He grew up in Hinckley and settled on Fairchild Road in the town of Remsen. He was the son of Philip "Bill" and Anna Plete. The man on the right is unidentified. (Author's collection.)

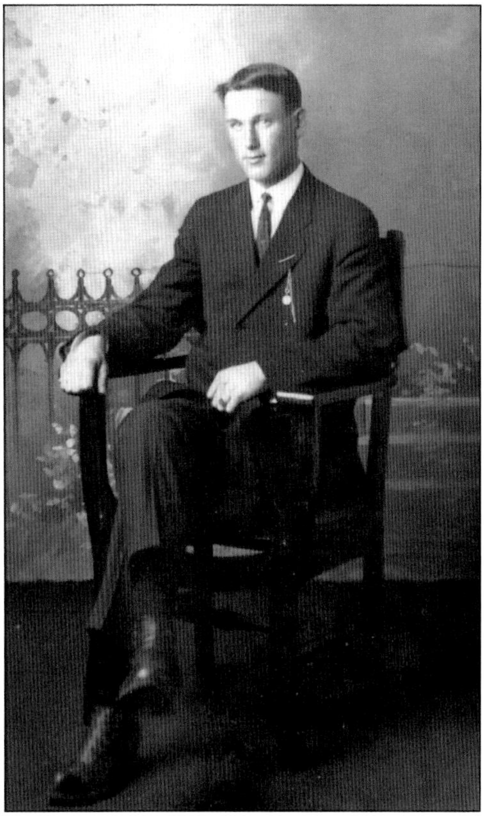

Adirondack guide Harold "Dick" Harvey guided in the southern Adirondack region. The tradition of guiding is deeply rooted in this area. Dick lived in Wilmurt, which has long since been absorbed by the town of Ohio. He married Helen Hicks, who died when she was 29. They had one child, a daughter named Anna. Dick died in his 50s in his daughter's home in Hinckley. (Author's collection.)

The Harvey family homestead was located on Dagenkolb Road in the town of Ohio in the southern Adirondacks. This is where Adirondack guide Harold "Dick" Harvey grew up. He was a popular guide in the West Canada headwaters area and the Black River wilderness area around Noblesboro. (Author's collection.)

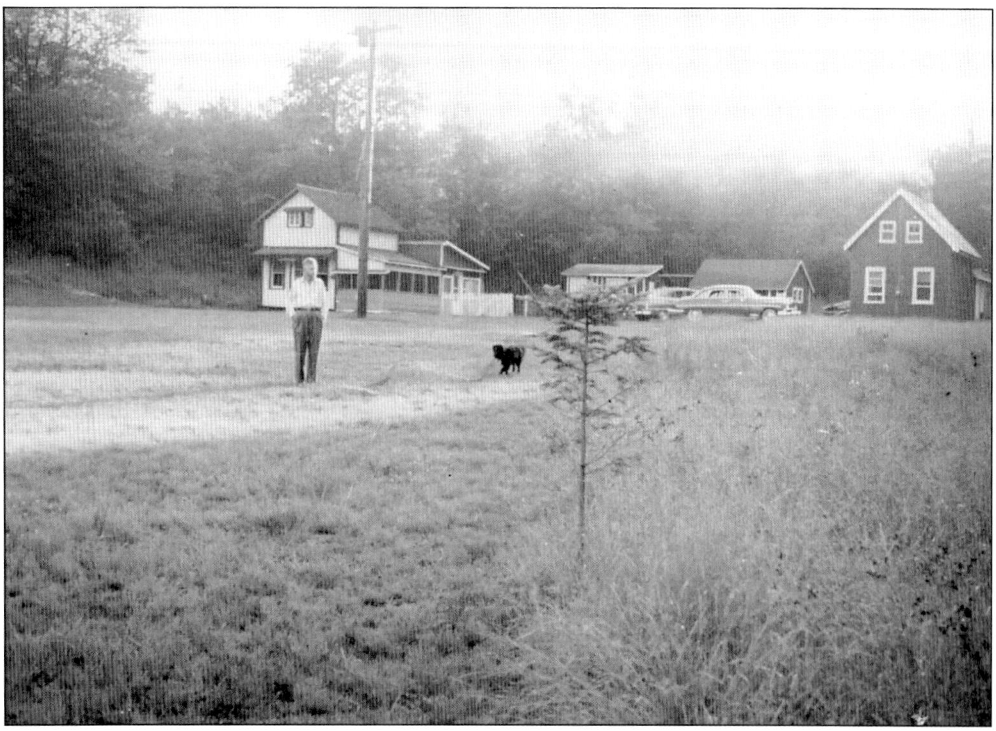

The woman shown watering her garden plants is Helen Hicks Harvey, wife of Harold "Dick" Harvey, the Adirondack guide. They married on June 30, 1913. Both she and her baby died during the birth of her second child on February 17, 1920. She left behind her husband and a young daughter. (Author's collection.)

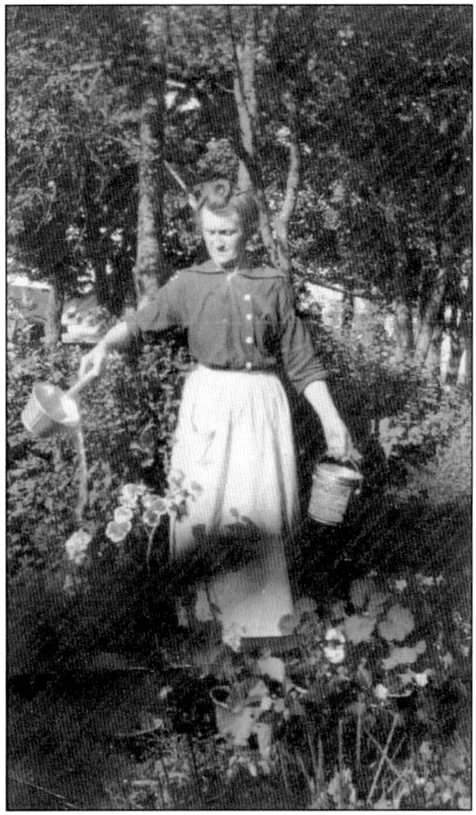

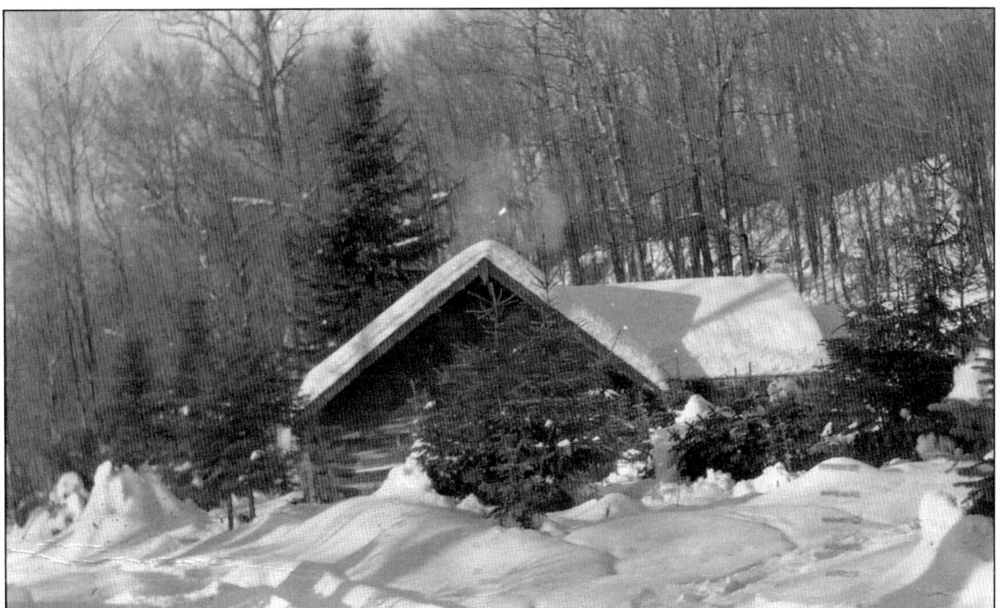

The humble home of Harold "Dick" Harvey was located in the now dissolved town of Wilmurt. Harvey was the son of William "Bill" Harvey and Ann Clancy Harvey. He had several siblings. (Author's collection.)

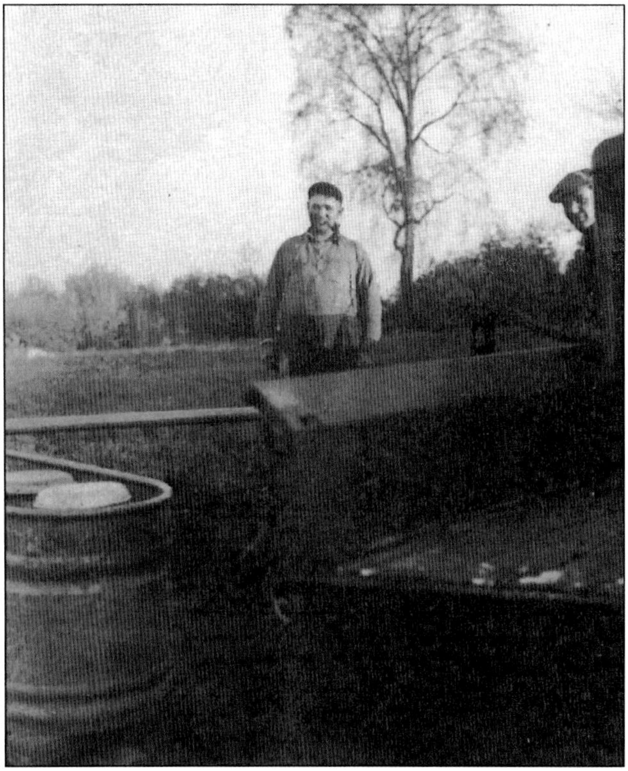

Donato "John" Plete is pictured at the family farm on Briggs Road in the town of Remsen near Ninety Six Corners. He was born in Italy in 1890. His family lived in the Little Italy district of Hinckley before being relocated prior to the construction of the Hinckley Dam. When the Plete family lived on the farm, the road was known as the Plete Road. The farm was sold in 1947. (Author's collection.)

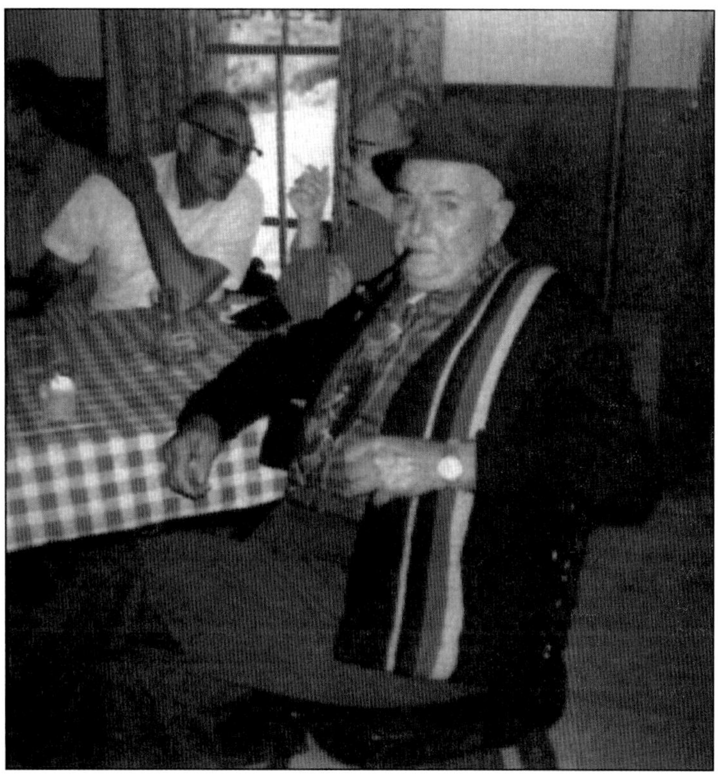

Donato "John" Plete made his living as a dairy farmer in Remsen. He married Eliza Roby in 1923. She died in 1941. They had no children. In 1942, he married Margaret Fitzsimmons. After the farm on Briggs Road was sold, he settled into a new home across the road. (Author's collection.)

Three

Old Gang Mills

The Hinckley Area

Little remains of the era when Hinckley was a robust, thriving, and industrious community. The factories have been demolished, and the taverns and hotels have closed. But this tiny community on the banks of West Canada Creek was at one time home to thousands of people and numerous businesses.

Gardner Hinckley and Theodore Ballou owned and operated sawmills on the West Canada Creek north of the area that would become Hinckley, in Noblesboro and Wilmurt. They believed that the sawmills were too far from the cities of Herkimer and Utica, however, and relocated downstream in 1849. The village that was established there came to be known as Gang Mills. The name was changed to Hinckley in 1891. The mills were later owned by the Trenton Falls Lumber Company and later still by the Hinckley Fibre Company. The latter produced sulphite fiber, used in paper manufacturing.

In the early 1900s, the State of New York decided to dam the West Canada Creek at the village of Hinckley to create a reservoir. This meant flooding the section of Hinckley known as Little Italy. Many families had residences and farms in this section and were forced to relocate. Construction of the Hinckley Dam began in 1911 and was completed in 1915. This created an economic boom for the businesses in Hinckley. About 500 men were employed in constructing the dam and another 500 were employed by the Hinckley Fibre Company, and they frequented the hotels and other businesses of the village. Hinckley at this time included two churches, four hotels, multiple stores, the Charles LeFevre Hinckley-Utica Bus Line, a post office, a bottling company, the Geroux ice business, and a train station that served four daily trains.

Hinckley's decline came in the 1920s, when the Consolidated Water Company of Utica bought all of the Hinckley Fibre Company property. The Hinckley Inn, the mills, and approximately 15 company-owned houses were demolished.

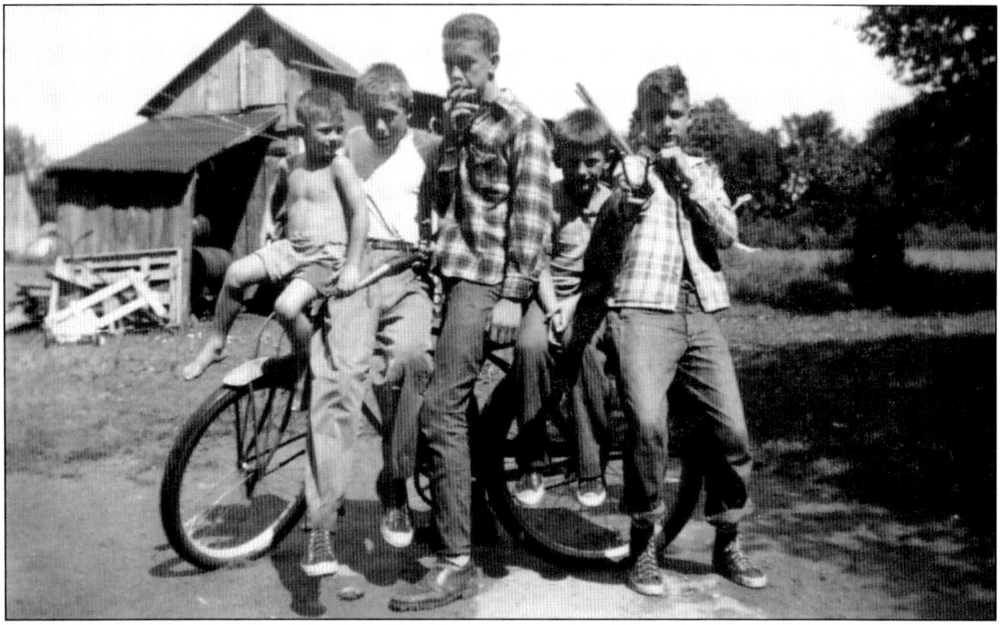

By the 1940s, most of the businesses in Hinckley has closed up or moved out. A few that remained were the Lamb Brothers' store (later Flip's Store), the Hinckley Hotel (later Nancy's), and Smith's garbage disposal company. The boys pictured here grew up playing in the crumbled ruins of the factories and mills that once lined the creek. The foundations have faded with time, but some remnants of the once-thriving village do remain. (Author's collection.)

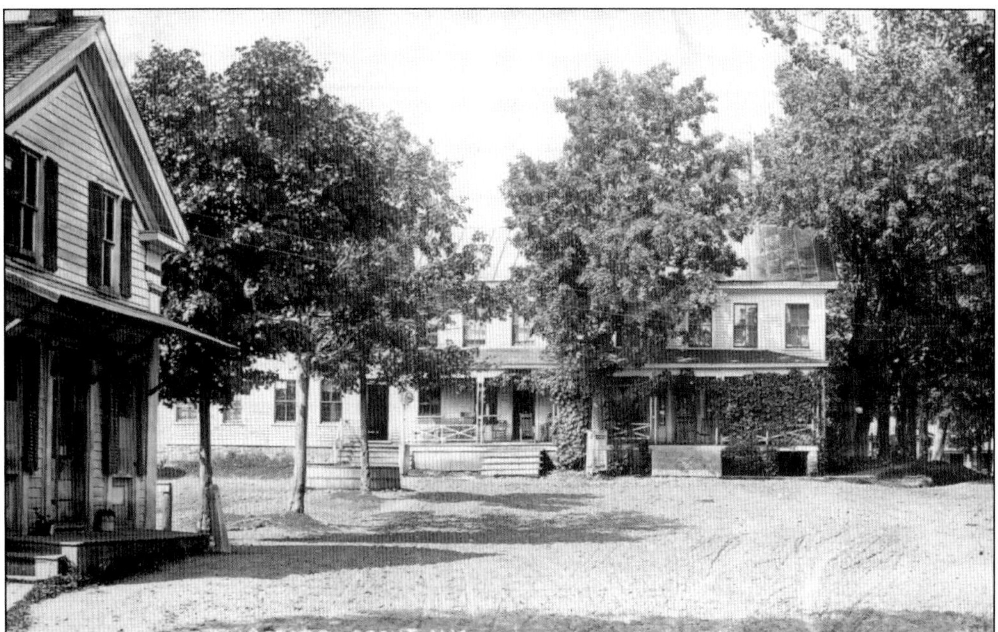

Grant is a community located five miles east of the village of Hinckley on the banks of the Hinckley Reservoir. The American Hotel and corner store in Grant are shown in this photograph. They were two of the busiest places in Grant. Before becoming Grant, the community went through many name changes over the years. (Author's collection.)

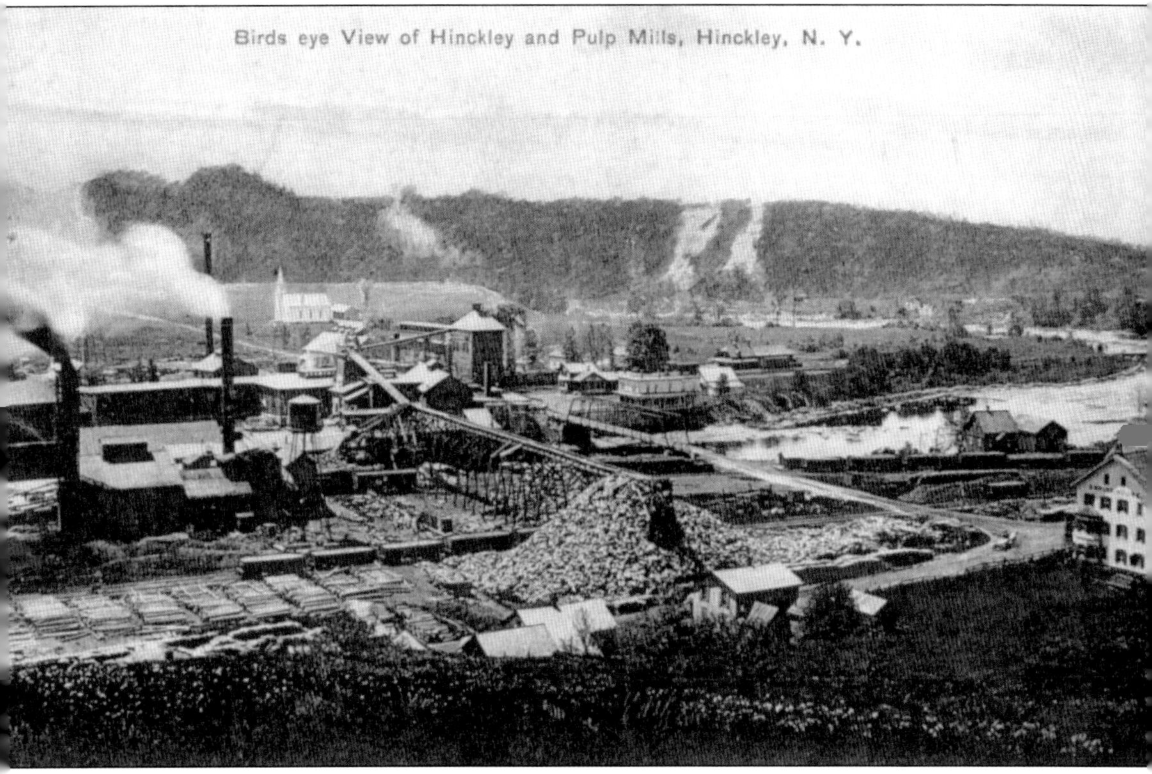

This view of Hinckley and the pulp mills shows the cluster of industry and residences in the village of Hinckley on both sides of the West Canada Creek. The large log conveyor is at the center. The Empire House is to the right of the large log pile. The railroad trestle can be seen at the far mid-right at the bend of the creek. (Courtesy of Jeanette Walter.)

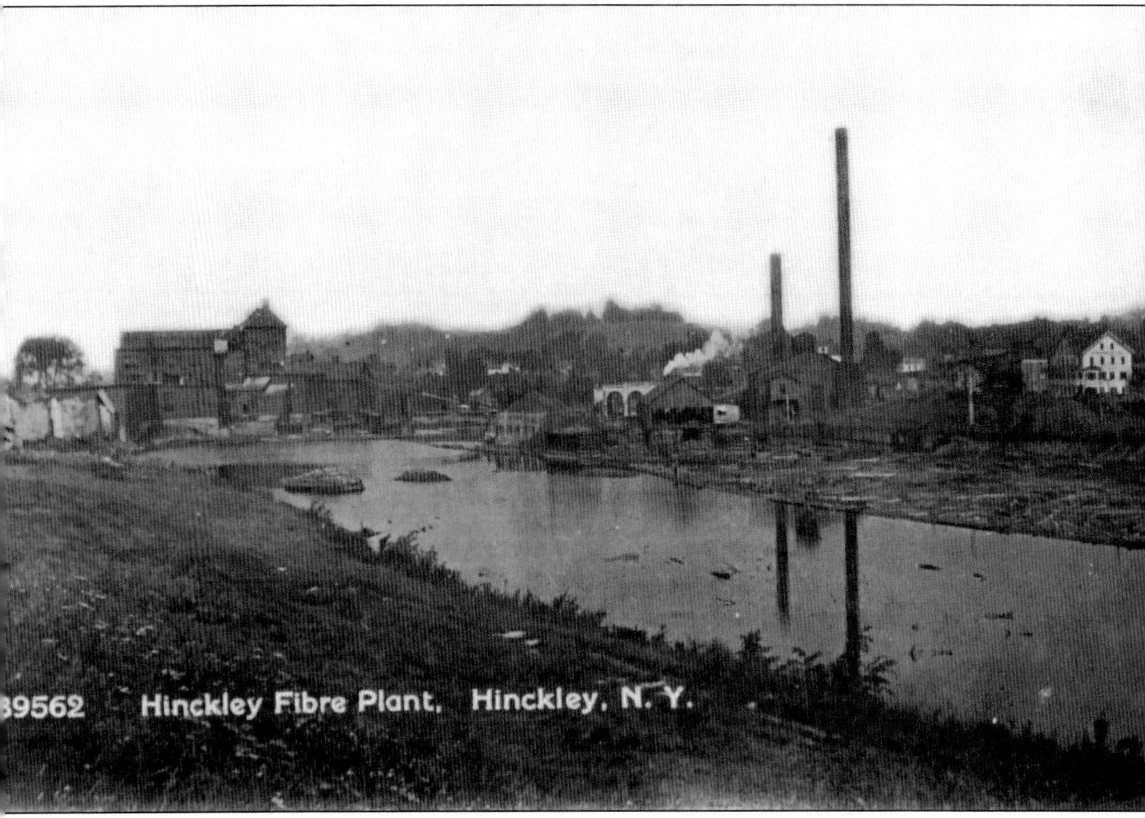

The Hinckley Fibre Plant was one of the largest businesses in Hinckley. In 1916, the company reported the highest earnings in its history. W.A. Stewart was president of the company. N.J. Catrow was named vice president. The role of secretary and treasurer was filled by W.E. Becraft. (Courtesy of Jeanette Walter.)

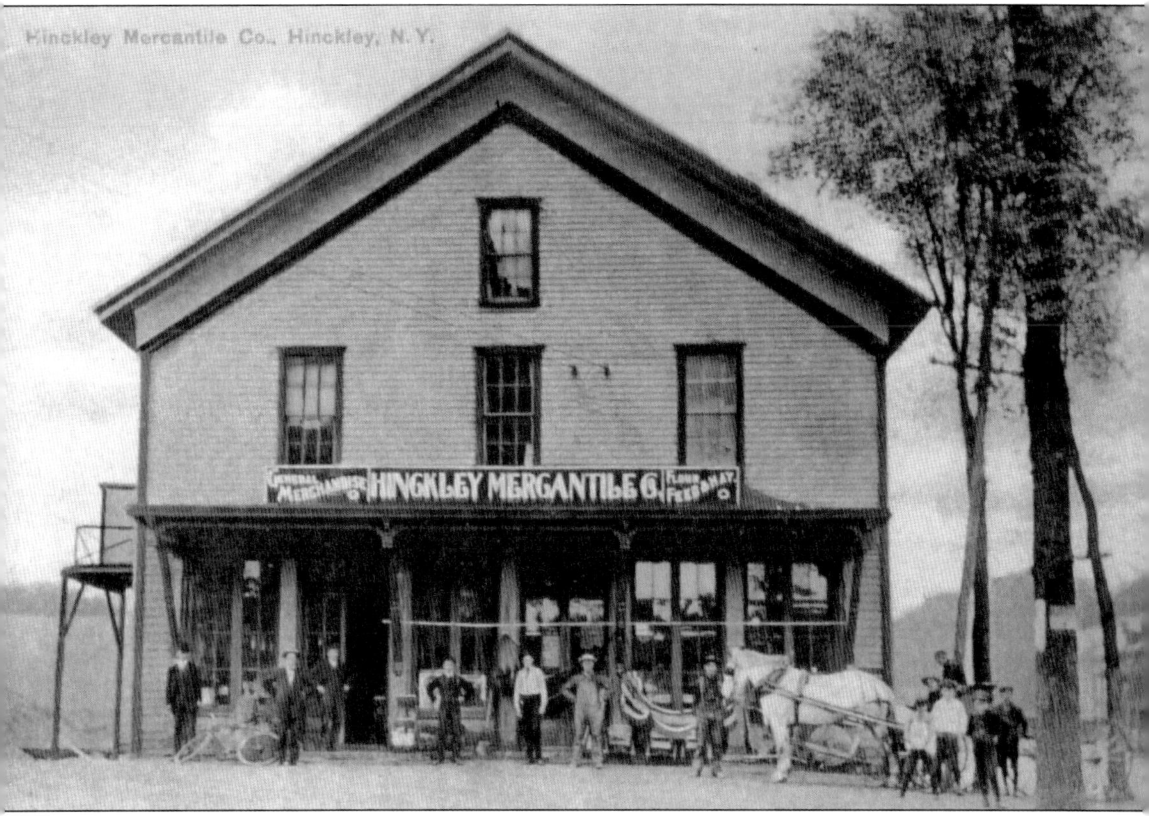

The Hinckley Mercantile was built by carpenter James Walters in 1860 for Hinckley and Ballou. It stood two stories tall. Its dimensions were 80 feet by 40 feet, with a cellar underneath. Hinckley thought the building was too large, but Ballou approved of its size. He called it the "Jim and Ballou building." The store was stocked with all kinds of goods, like most general stores of the time. The first crackers to be sold in the region were sold at the Hinckley Mercantile. The photographer and author Howard Thomas, of Prospect, had an interesting dilemma involving tennis balls and the Hinckley Mercantile. Thomas enjoyed playing tennis as a youngster. At that time, the only place one could purchase tennis balls was the Hinckley Mercantile. Unfortunately for Thomas, every time the Prospect boys came to Hinckley, the Hinckley boys met them with the intention of a territorial brawl. Purchasing tennis balls became quite a problem for Thomas. (Courtesy of Linda Bailey.)

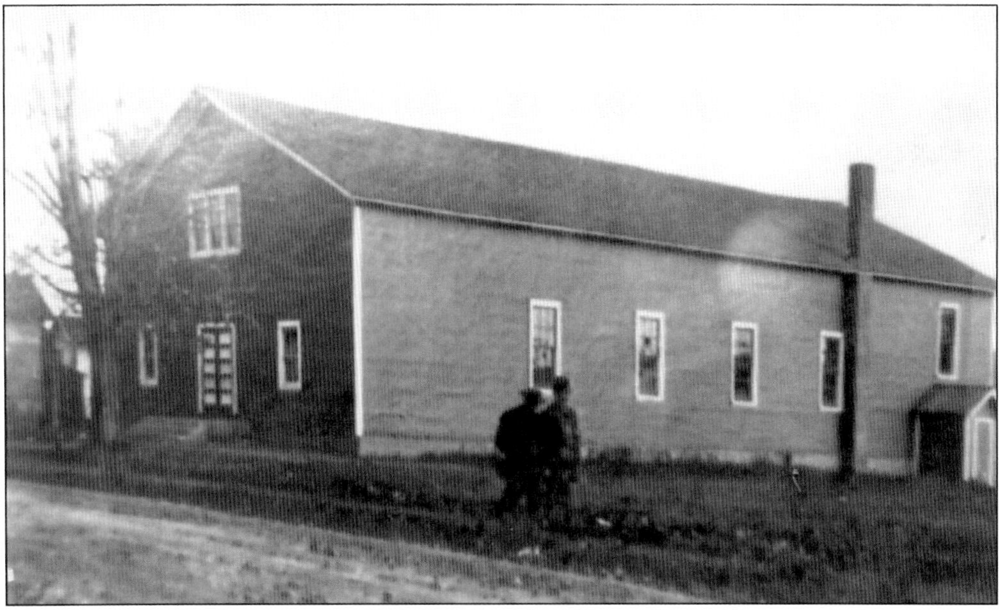

The town hall (above) was centrally located in the village of Hinckley on a hill overlooking the West Canada Creek. The Catholic congregation wanted to establish a facility in the same location. The town hall building had the same dimensions as the building that the Catholics were using at the time, so they asked the town board to switch locations. Their request was denied. Coincidentally (perhaps), the town hall burned to the ground shortly after. The lot was then given to the Catholic congregation, and St. Ann's Catholic Church was built. There is a small cemetery in the churchyard. The church (below) was an active place of worship until it closed in the early 21st century. The congregation partnered with St. Leo's in Holland Patent, and the new church became the congregation of St. Leo's and St. Ann's. The building still stands and has been for sale for many years. (Both, courtesy of Linda Bailey.)

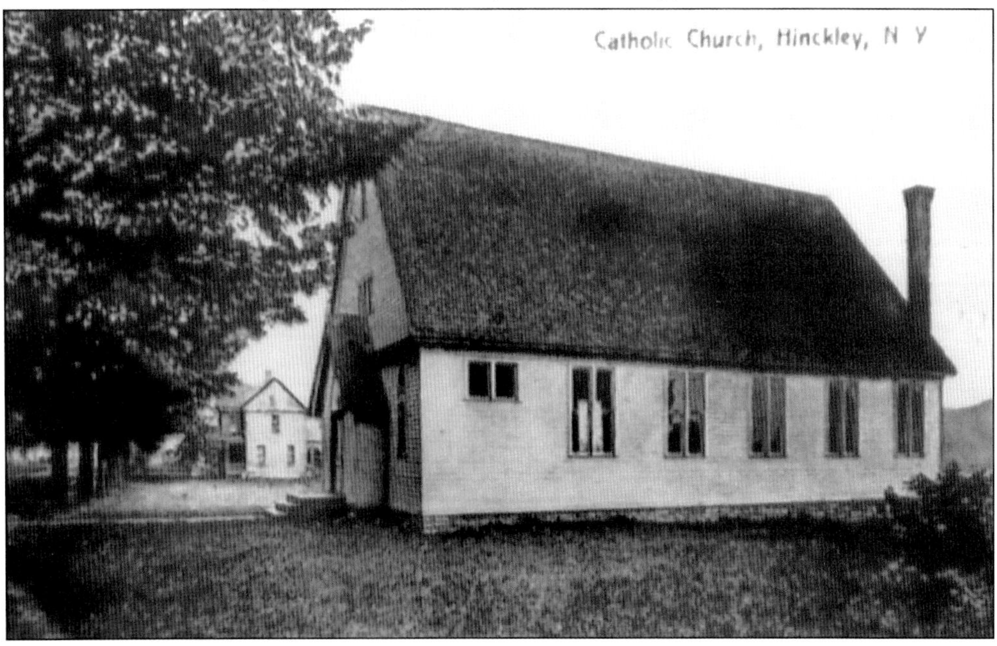

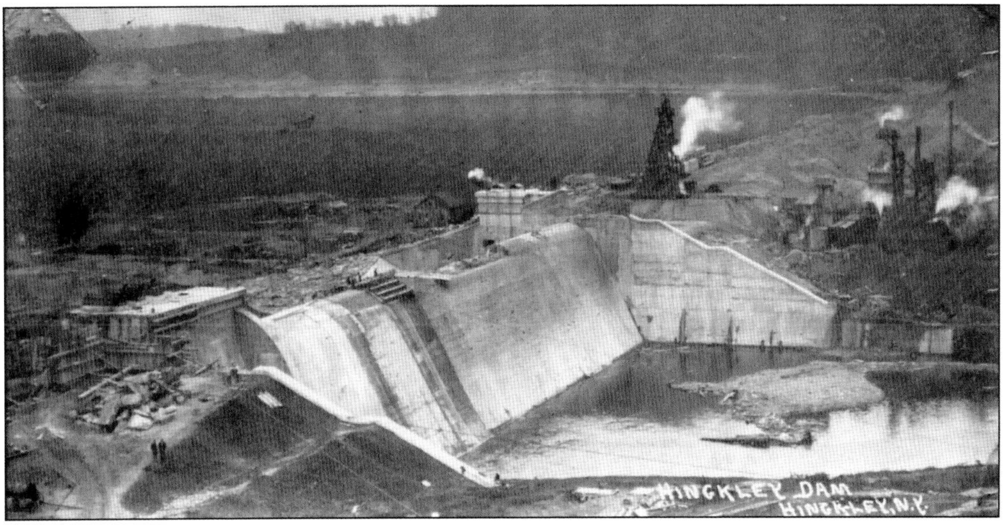

Hinckley Reservoir was constructed by the State of New York and completed in 1915 for the Erie Canal. It supplies drinking water to about 130,000 people in the Utica area and the Mohawk Valley. It is also used to regulate the water level in the Barge Canal. The village of Hinckley was a place of industry in the late 1800s and early 1900s. Business boomed while the village became an active workplace during the construction of the reservoir and dam between 1911 and 1915. The dam depends on 117,000 cubic yards of concrete and 600,000 yards of dirt fill to hold back the water. There was at least one known fatality during the construction, a worker named Alfred Thorp. These photographs show the progression of the construction. (Both photographs by LeRoy Thomas, courtesy of Jeanette Walter.)

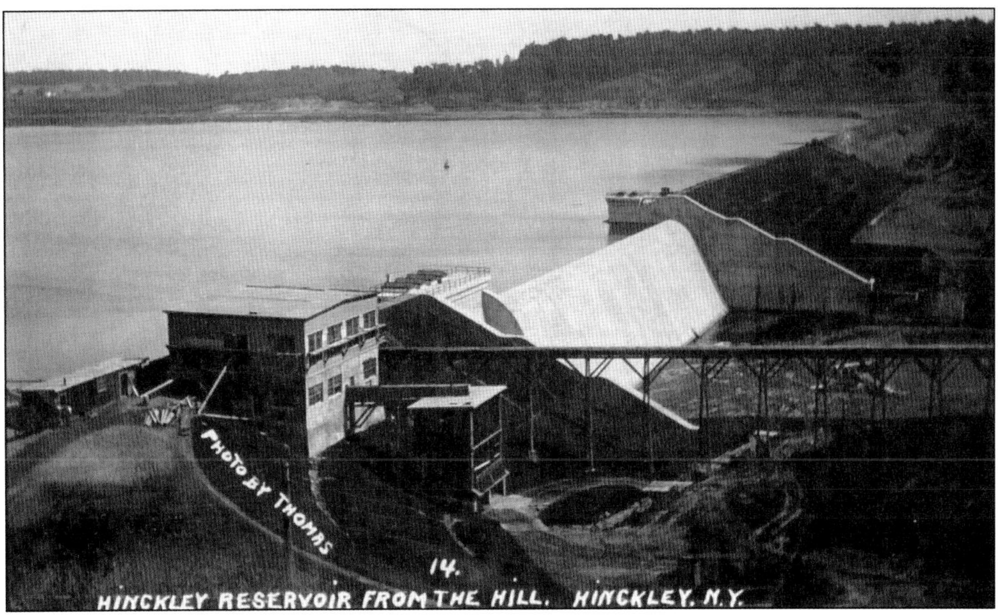

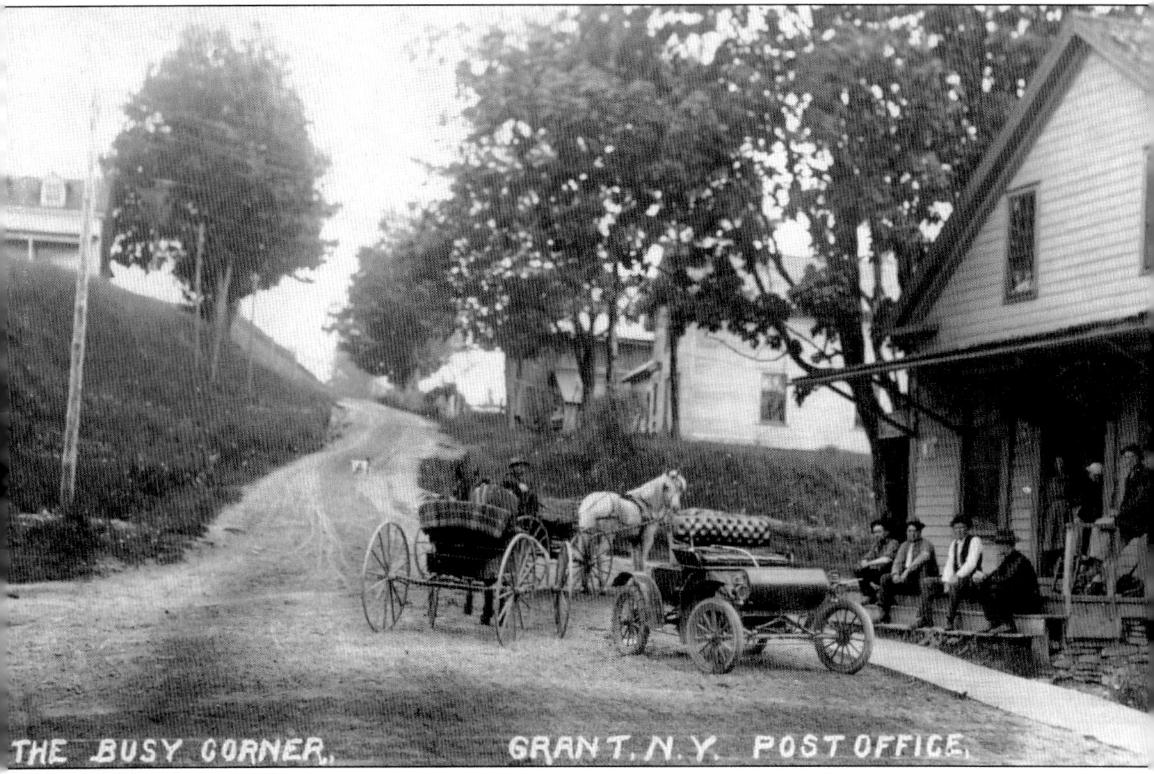

Isaac Woodin was the first settler in 1816 in a small village known as Potter's Bush on the Black Creek. The creek is a tributary to the Hinckley Reservoir. The settlement was renamed Postville in honor of John Post. After that, it became Booth. This community went through many changes before the name Grant was chosen for the hamlet. The location in this photograph was the busy corner in Grant where Stormy Hill Road, Pardeeville Road, Grant Road, and South Shore Road converged. The building where people are gathered is the post office. The building no longer stands. Grant is now a quiet, rural residential hamlet. Woodin Corners Cemetery is located about three quarters of a mile outside of the settlement on Grant Road. Other prominent settlers of the area were Jonathan Millington, Farley Fuller, George Taylor, Roscum Slocum, William Buck, Jethan Carpenter, and a family named Coon. (Author's collection.)

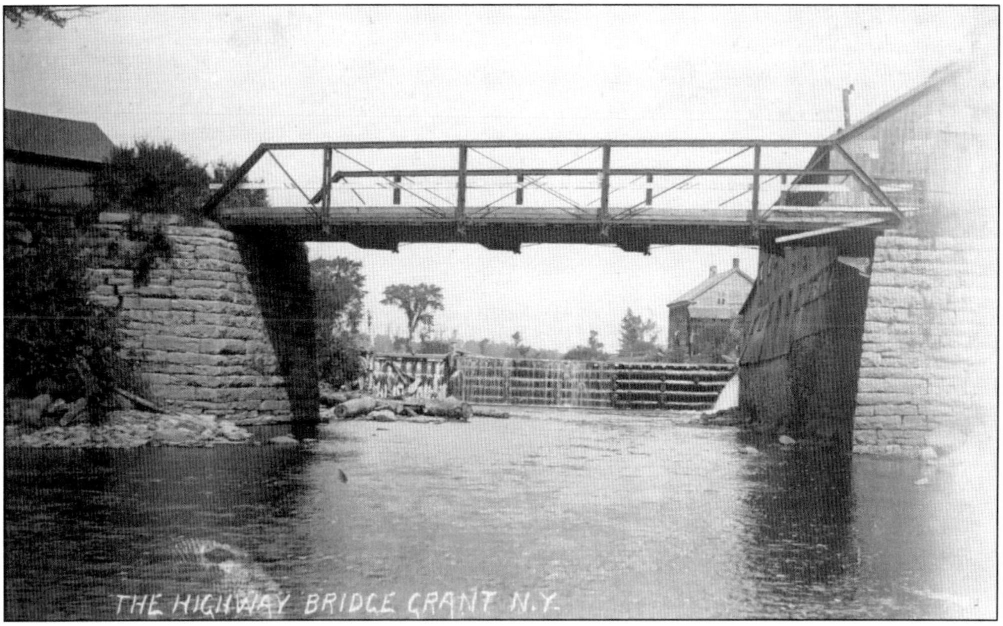

The bridge in Grant spans the Black Creek, which flows into the Hinckley Reservoir in Grant. The Black Creek is not to be confused with Little Black Creek, which is a tributary of the Black River. Both creeks are used for fishing and recreation. (Photograph by LeRoy Thomas, author's collection.)

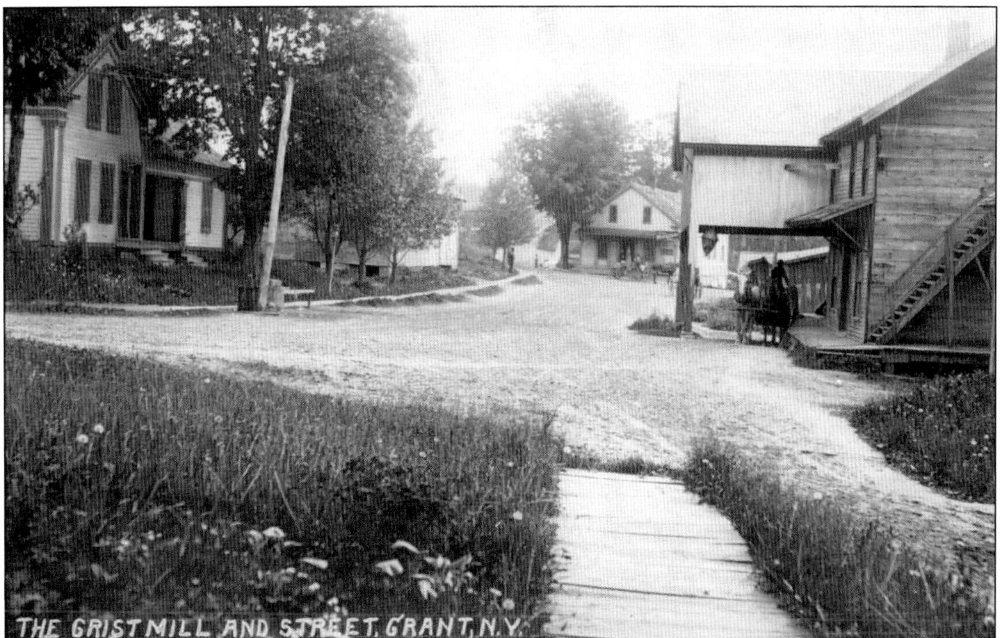

The gristmill (at right) was photographed from the bend of Pardeeville Road. A gristmill is a facility where grain is ground into flour. Most mills were built on rivers to strategically harvest the waterpower for the mill wheel. The post office is at the intersection. Notice the wooden sidewalk. (Photograph by LeRoy Thomas, author's collection.)

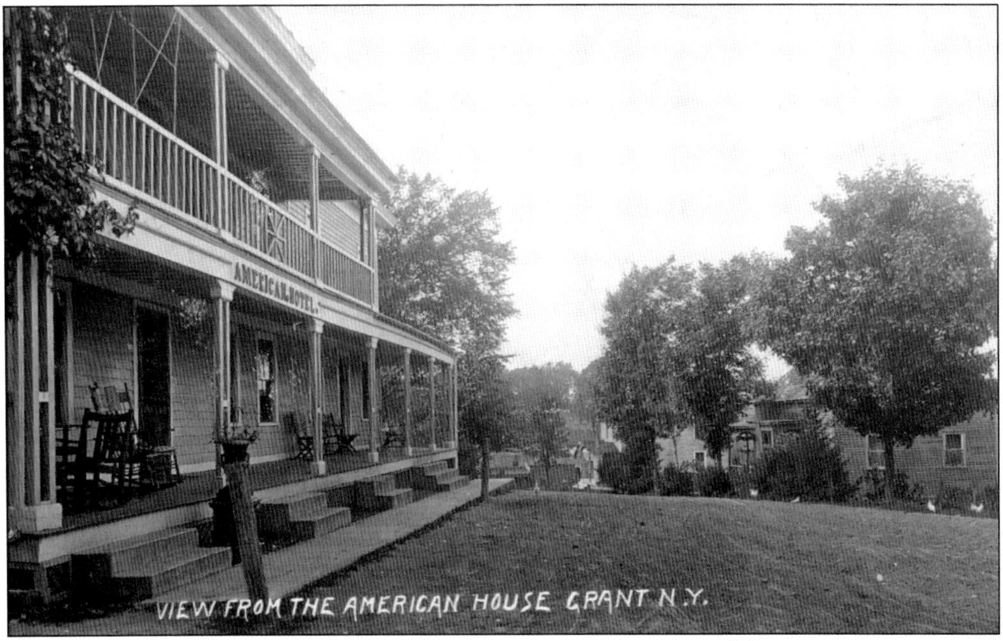

The American Hotel, also known as the American House, operated for 30 years in Grant. It was a large three-story structure with a two-story porch. The third floor housed a ballroom. The hotel burned down in 1915. A handyman was rescued from the blaze only to die a few days later. (Author's collection.)

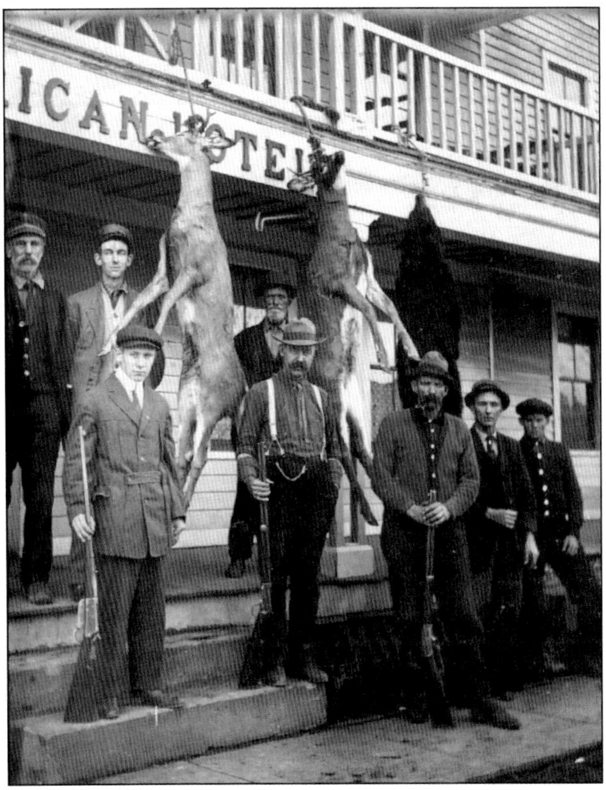

Sportsmen are gathered on the front porch of the American Hotel showing off their trophies. Two bucks and a bear are strung up from the second-floor balcony. The American Hotel was a popular gathering place for locals and travelers alike. (Author's collection.)

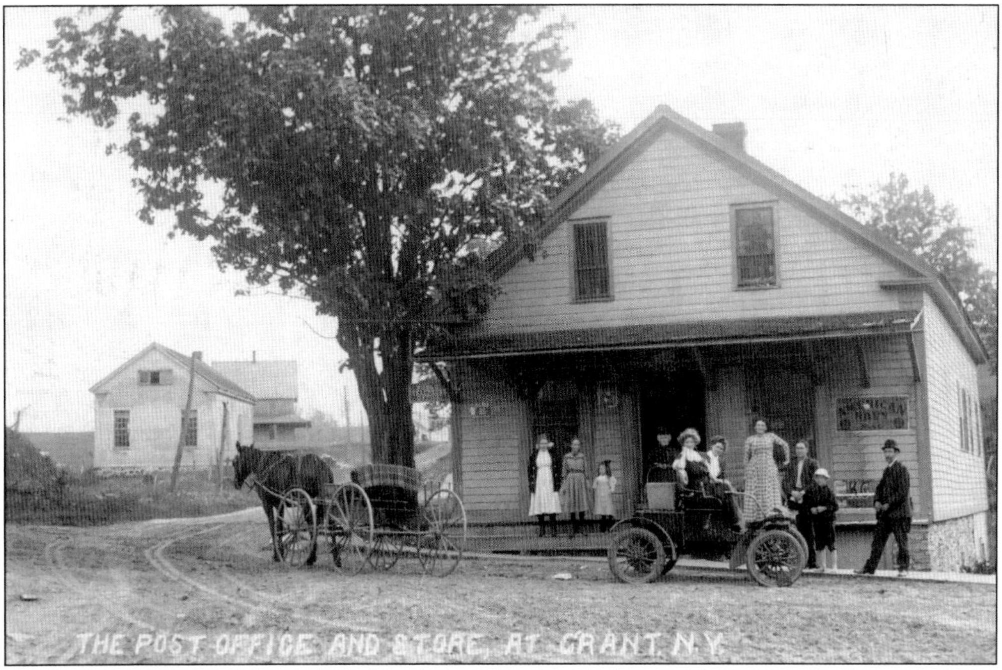

Grant used to be named Booth. After the assassination of Pres. Abraham Lincoln in 1865, the community decided to change the name. It was renamed after Civil War hero Ulysses S. Grant. This image shows a crowd gathered at the post office and store in Grant. (Photograph by LeRoy Thomas, author's collection.)

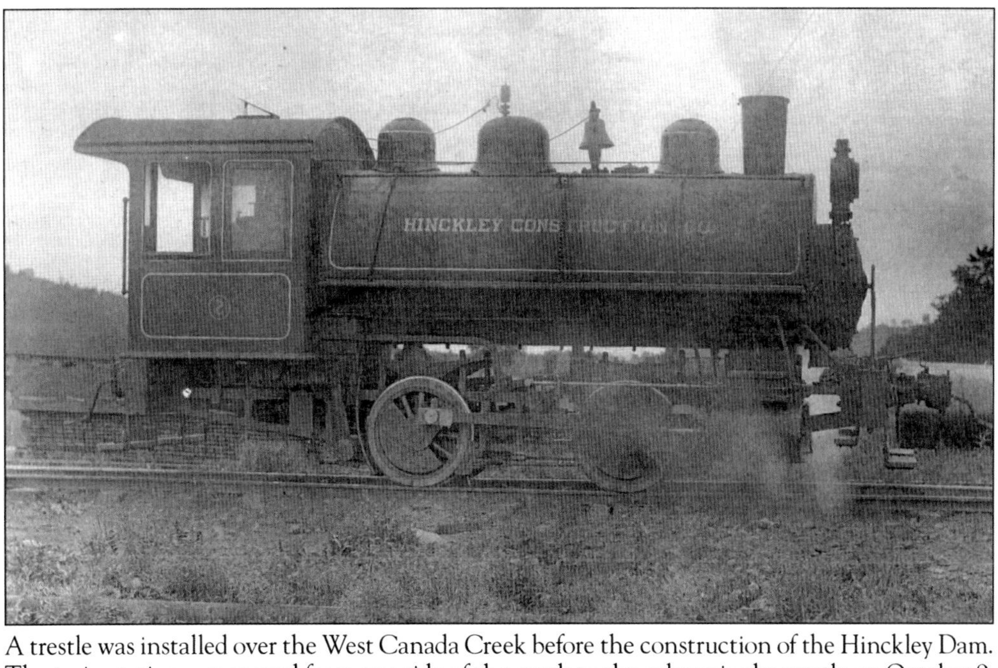

A trestle was installed over the West Canada Creek before the construction of the Hinckley Dam. The train station was moved from one side of the creek to the other via the trestle on October 9, 1896. Trains ceased coming to Hinckley in the 1930s. (Courtesy of Linda Bailey.)

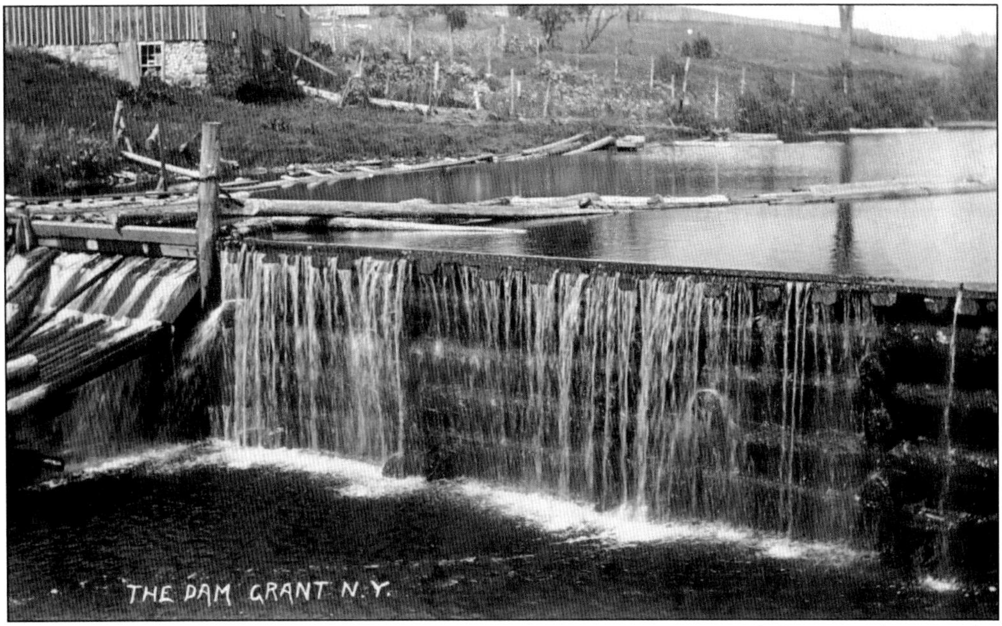

It was standard practice to dam the waterways in communities to control the water for use. The dam in Grant is shown here in an undated photograph. (Photograph by LeRoy Thomas, courtesy of Jeanette Walter.)

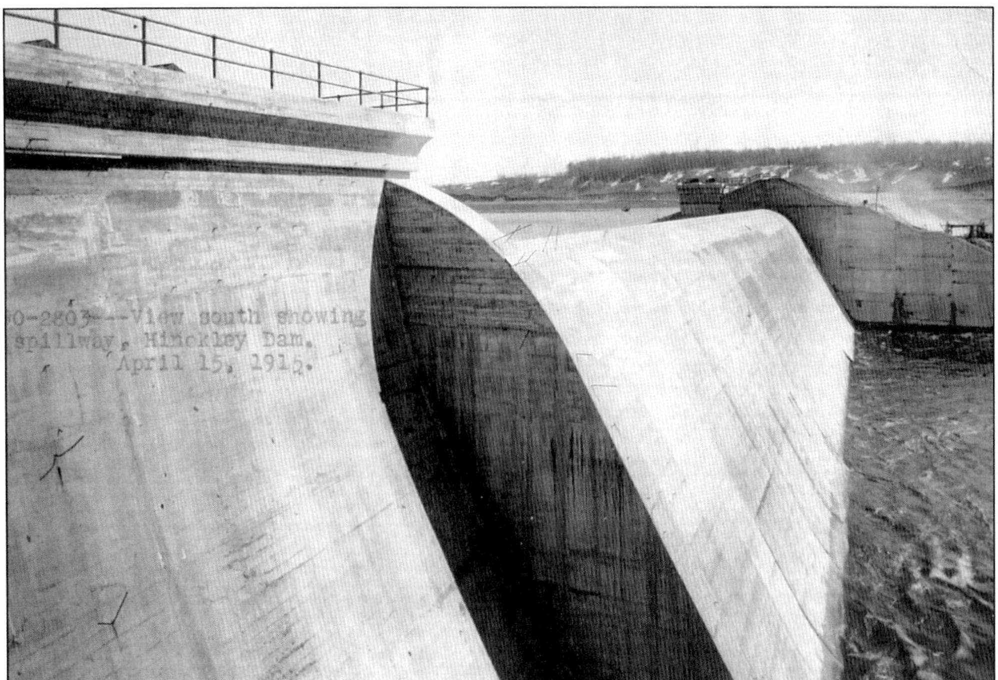

Villagers were fascinated by the Hinckley Dam when it was completed. It was a marvel for its time. Local newspapers described it as having "mammoth proportions." Fishing has long been a popular pastime in the Hinckley Reservoir. (Courtesy of Linda Bailey.)

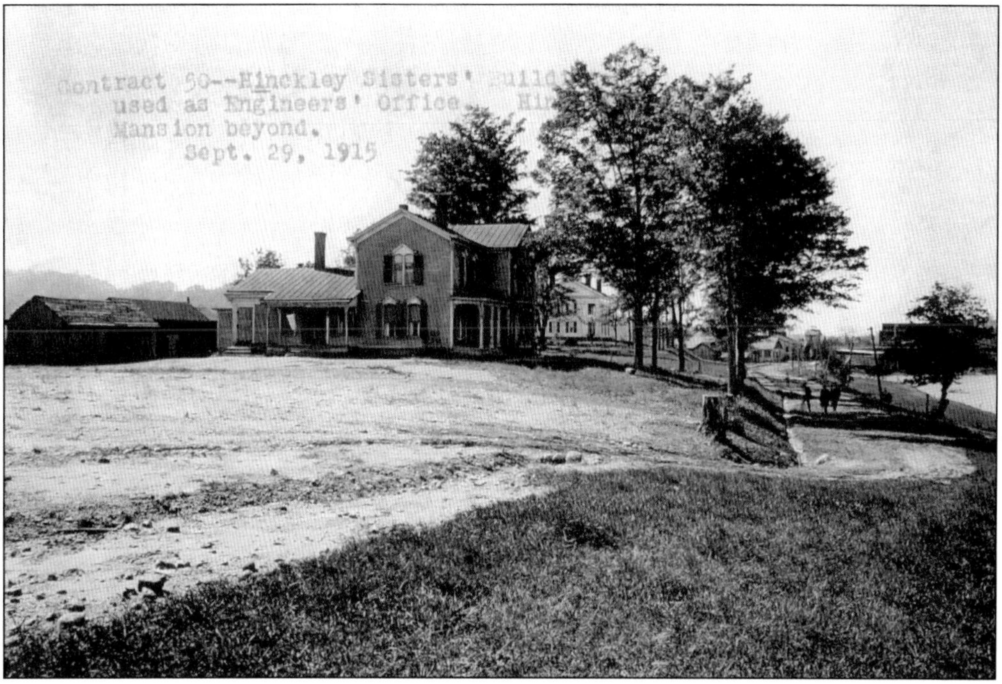

The above image of the Hinckley sisters' home was taken on September 29, 1915. At that time, it was being used as the engineer's office for the construction of the Hinckley Dam. The Hinckley family homestead is visible beyond. Seen below, the Hinckley mansion overlooked the village from the opposite side of the creek. This photograph was taken the same day as the one above. This home is one of the few structures that has withstood the test of time in Hinckley. (Both, courtesy of Jeanette Walter.)

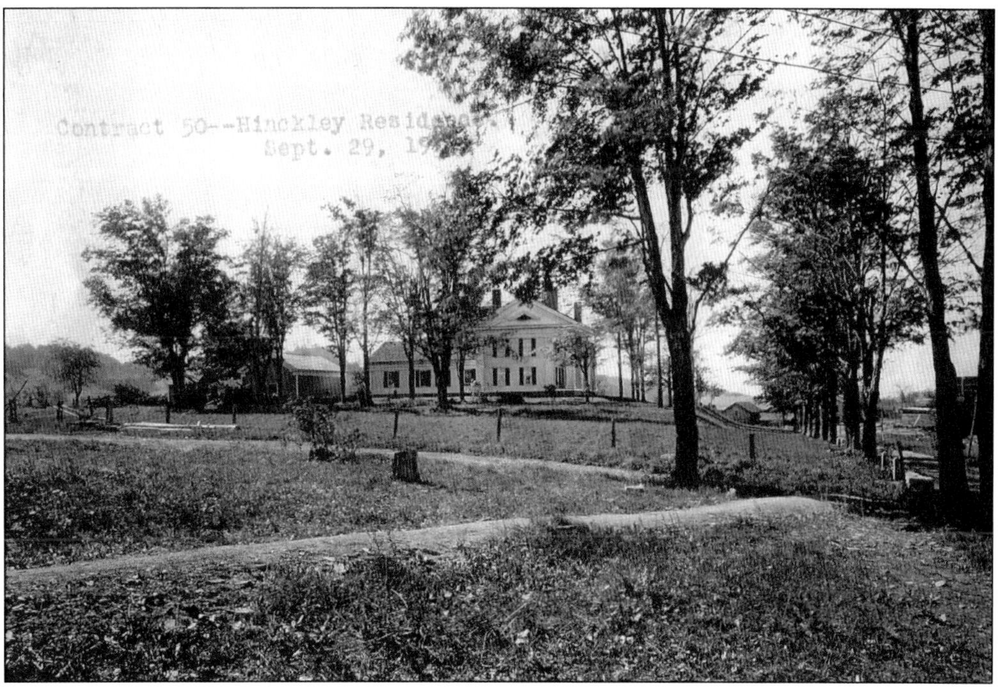

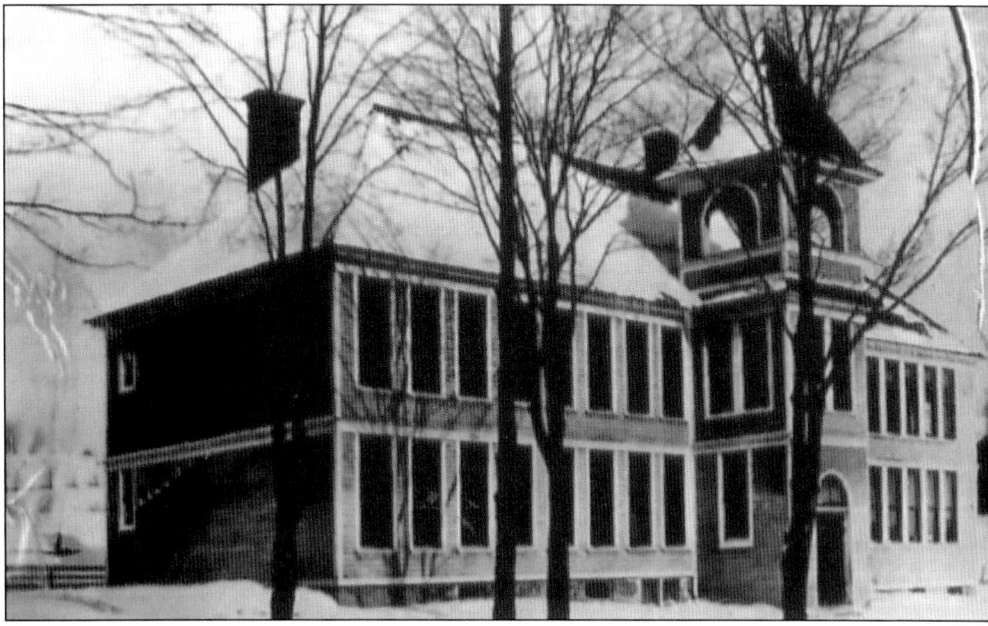

The rising population in the village of Hinckley necessitated the building of a schoolhouse. The Hinckley Union School was constructed in the center of the village on Main Street. The building sat empty for many years after the district was absorbed into the Holland Patent School District. (Courtesy of Linda Bailey.)

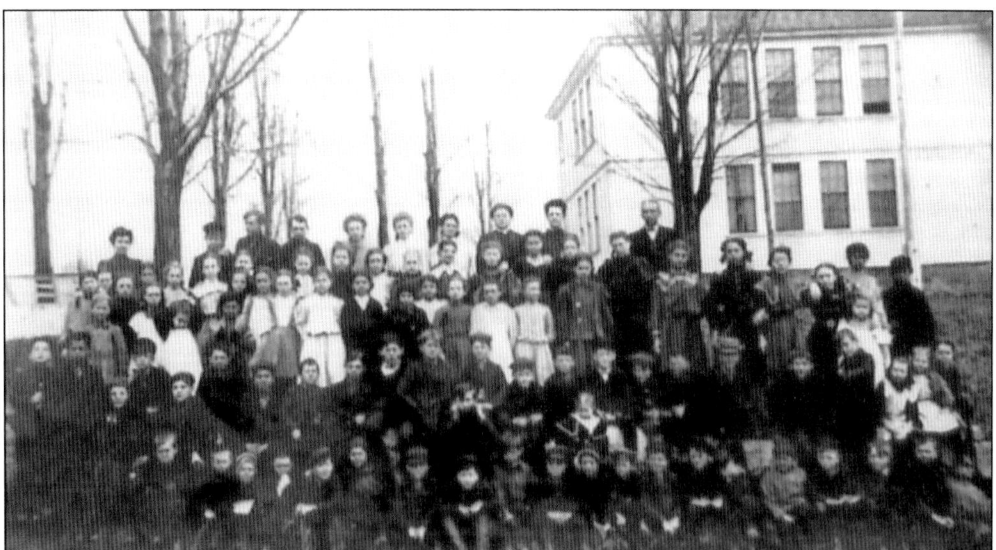

Students pose for a photograph on the lawn of the Hinckley School. The population of Hinckley decreased after businesses moved out and the plants were demolished. The village eventually became too small to support the school. (Courtesy of Linda Bailey.)

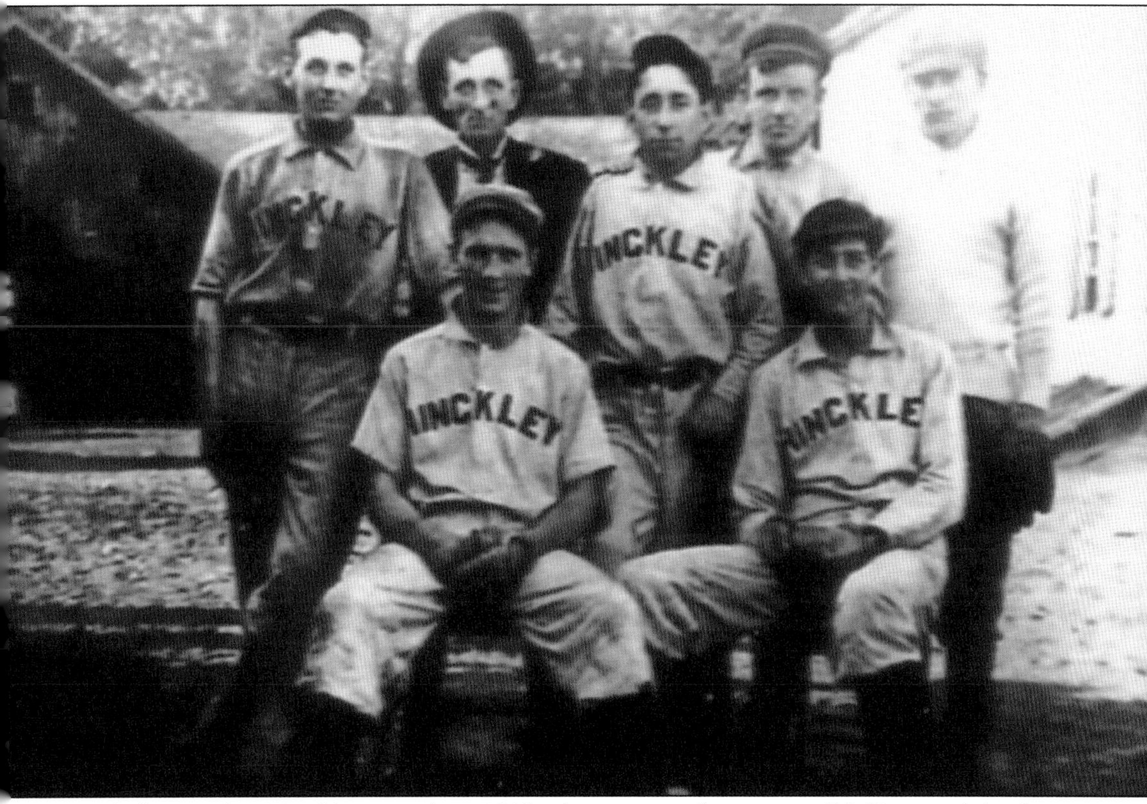

Baseball started in Hinckley as early as 1895, when it was a boomtown. E.J. Hargrave's lumber company employed 300 men in town. Many more worked there in other industries. Many good baseball players had come with Hargrave from Michigan to work. These men made up the first baseball team in Hinckley. No Hinckley natives played on the team. The team did not have a place to play at first. A farmer named Van Etten offered the use of his pasture, across the creek from the village near the Methodist church. The villagers rallied together to get the pasture in condition to play baseball on. This area became known as Van Etten Park. The baseball team earned a great winning reputation. The local folks supported this team with great enthusiasm. (Courtesy of Linda Bailey.)

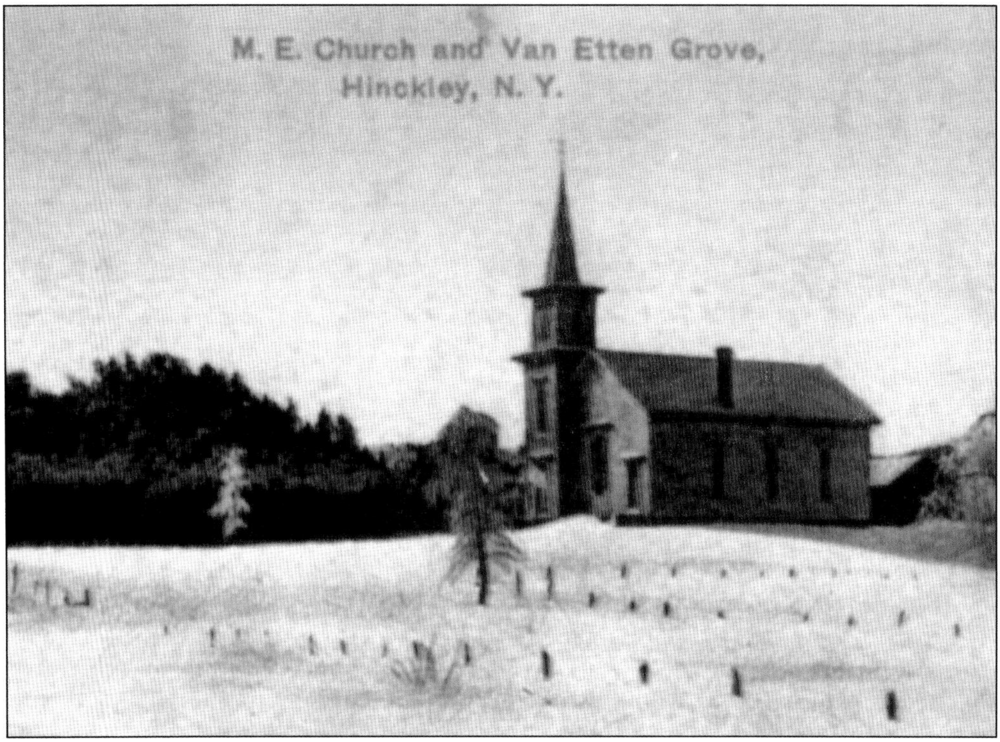

The image above shows the Methodist church and Van Etten Grove. Van Etten Grove or Park was the site of Hinckley's baseball field. The view below shows the perspective from the Hinckley homestead on the east side of the creek. Life in the early years of Hinckley centered on the lumber baron and Hinckley's family. He was a strict Methodist who preached temperance. He had a system of issuing credit slips instead of currency as payment to his workers so that they would not be able to spend all their money at local taverns. (Above, courtesy of Jeanette Walter; below, courtesy of Linda Bailey.)

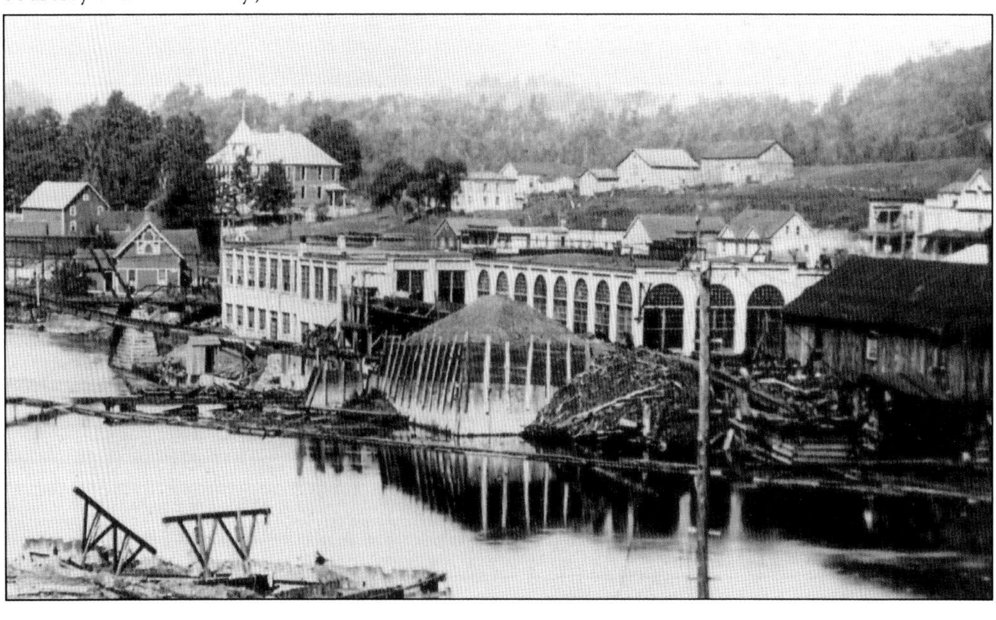

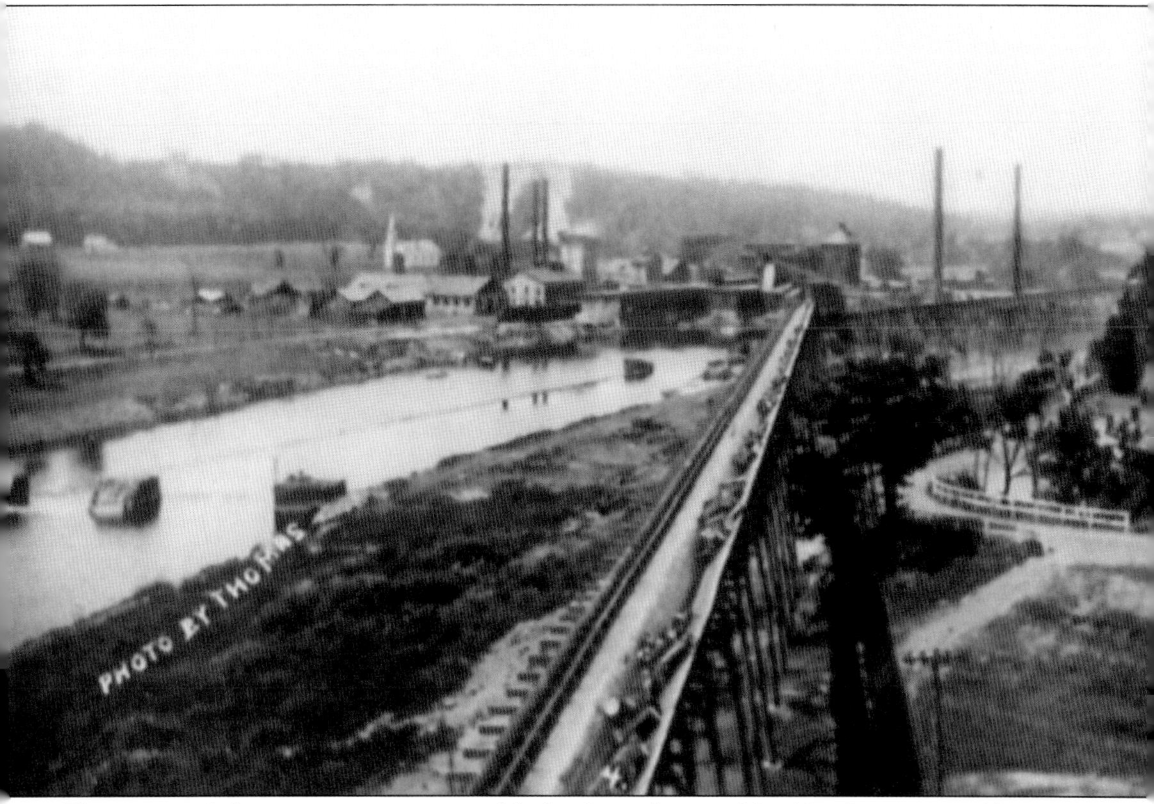

The conveyor belt was an important part of the lumber industry in Hinckley. It maneuvered heavy logs around the Hinckley Dam to the lower lumber mill to be processed into pulp or shipped out on the railroad. The lumbering village carried the name Gang Mills until 1891, when it was changed to Hinckley in memory of its founder. This was 16 years after Gardner Hinckley died. Hinckley was a man of great accomplishment. He served as the supervisor for the town of Wilmurt from 1844 to 1853 and as a member of the state assembly in 1853 and 1854. Hinckley was a Democrat until the Republican Party was organized in 1856. He then shifted parties. His family home still stands, overlooking a community that has grown considerably quieter over the years. (Photograph by LeRoy Thomas, courtesy of Linda Bailey.)

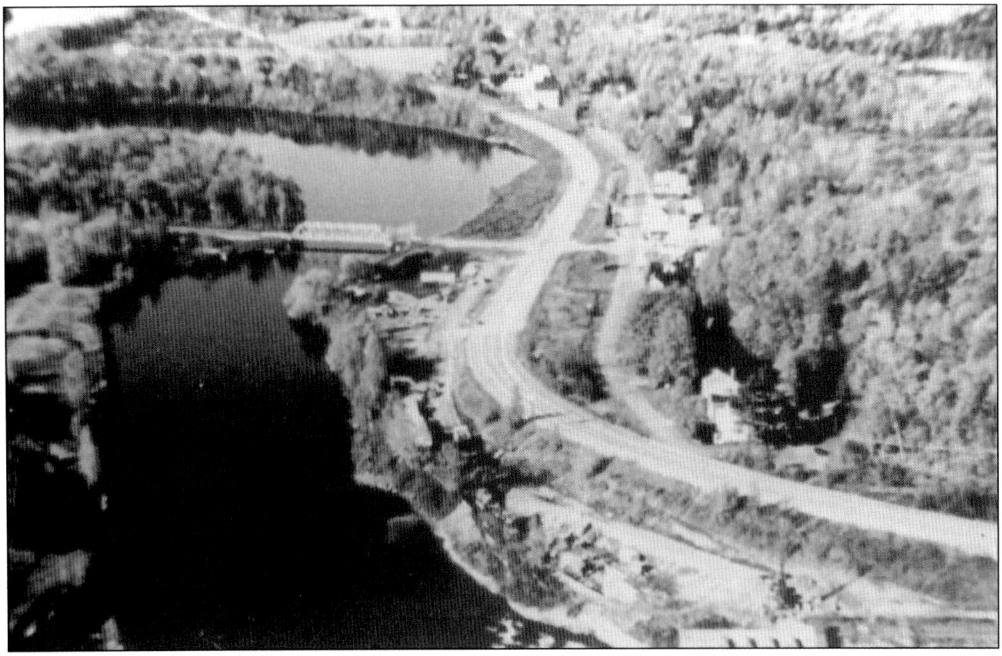

The West Canada Creek was once known as the Kuyahoora River. The name *Kuyahoora* means "leaping water." It was the name used for the waterway by the Native Americans before the settlers came to the Central New York area. The West Canada Creek flows from the southern Adirondacks into the Mohawk River at Herkimer. (Courtesy of Linda Bailey.)

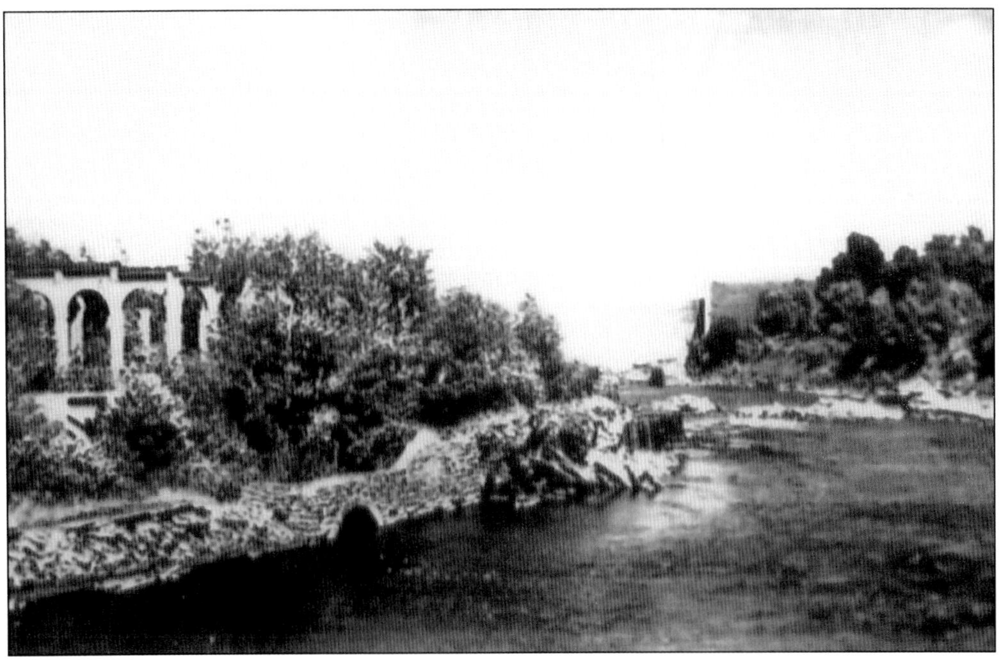

The West Canada Creek is 76 miles long. The series of waterfalls in the Prospect Gorge, principally Trenton Falls, was a major tourist attraction in the past. Some people believe that the title *creek* is inappropriate and that the watercourse should be more accurately called a river. (Courtesy of Linda Bailey.)

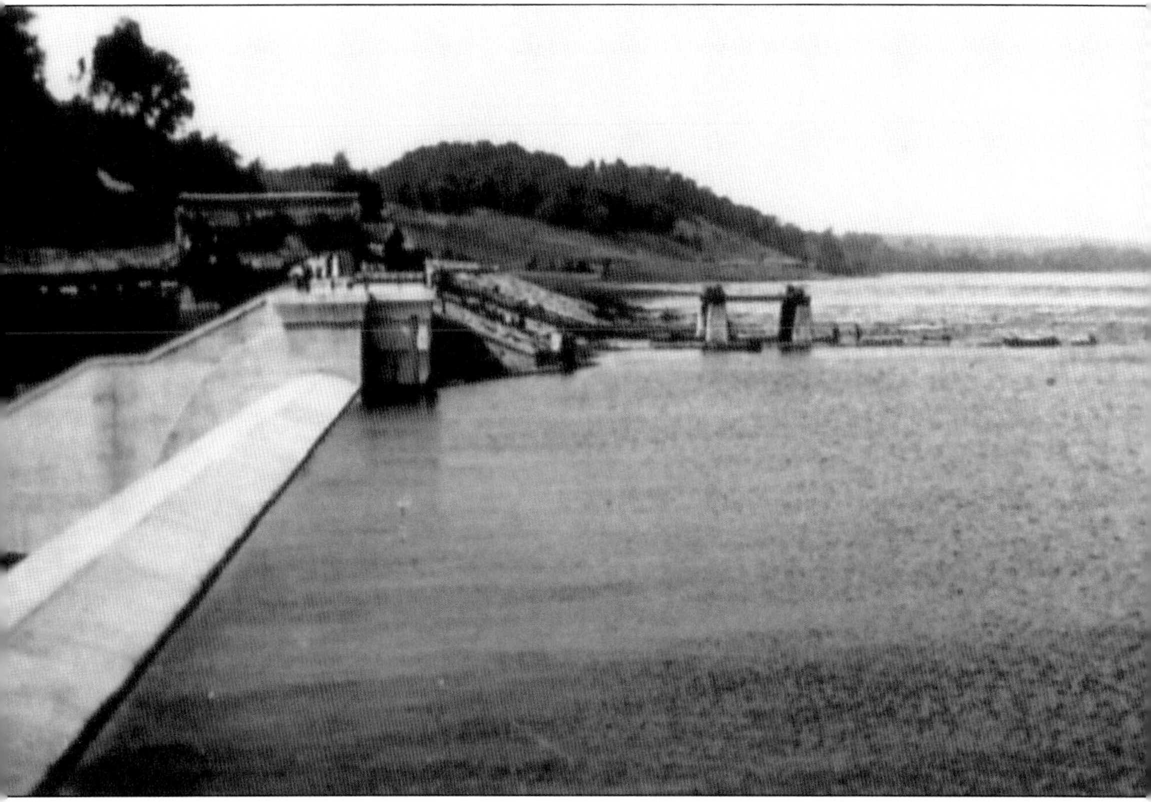

The ethnic makeup of the Hinckley community prior to the construction of the dam was mainly Italian, Polish, and French Canadian. The families tended to form neighborhoods with other families who shared origins. The Italians lived at the upper end of Hinckley in the area that was to be flooded. This community was known as Little Italy. The Polish mostly lived in a section they called Little Brooklyn on the opposite side of the West Canada Creek. The French Canadians were the roughest of the citizens who made Hinckley their home. They were rowdy loggers who worked on the West Canada. The children of the French Canadian loggers were not permitted to attend the Hinckley school with the other children. To make way for the Hinckley Dam, about 100 families, mostly Italian, had to relocate. The stone pillars here, which formed the base of the log hoist, are located where Little Italy was. (Courtesy of Linda Bailey.)

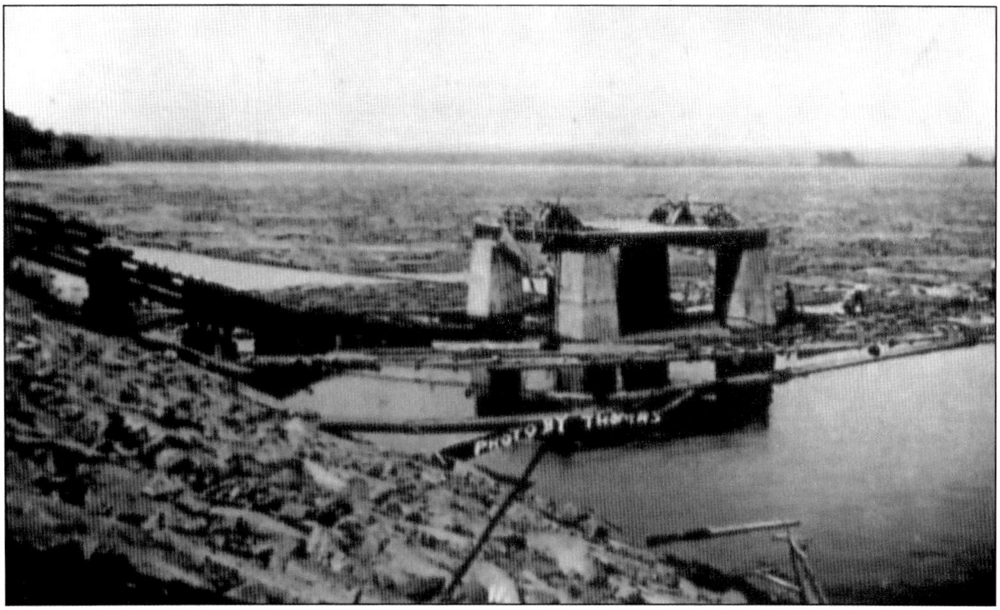

The log conveyor transported logs that were floated down the West Canada from north of the construction site. This system brought the logs over the working men and equipment via a raised conveyor belt. The destination of the logs was a lumber mill in Hinckley on the bank of the West Canada Creek. Logs were shipped out on the railroad, which used to run from Hinckley. The logs were often stacked in piles taller than some of the buildings in Hinckley. The conveyor was located approximately where Route 365 runs past the dam today. (Above, courtesy of Jeanette Walter; below, courtesy of Linda Bailey.)

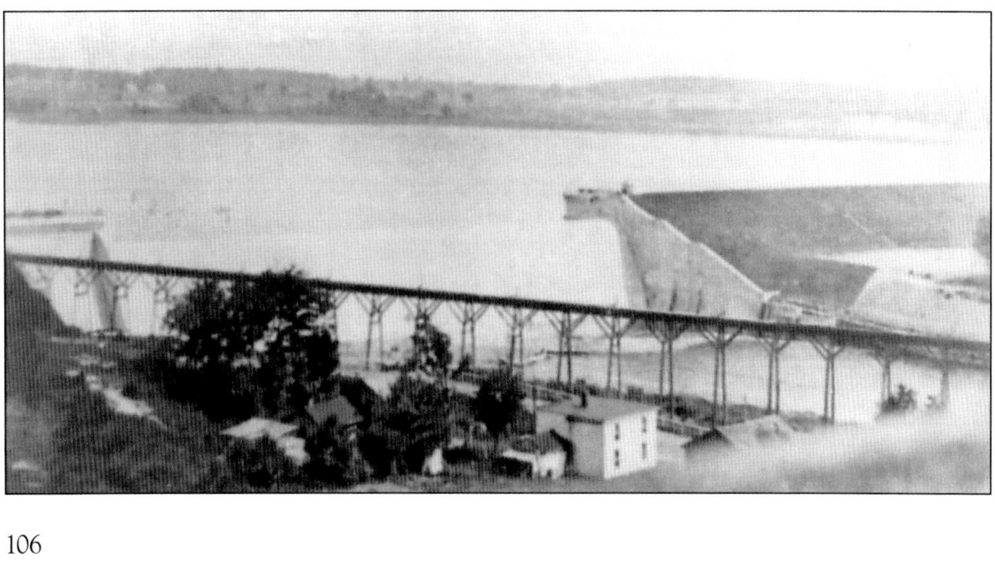

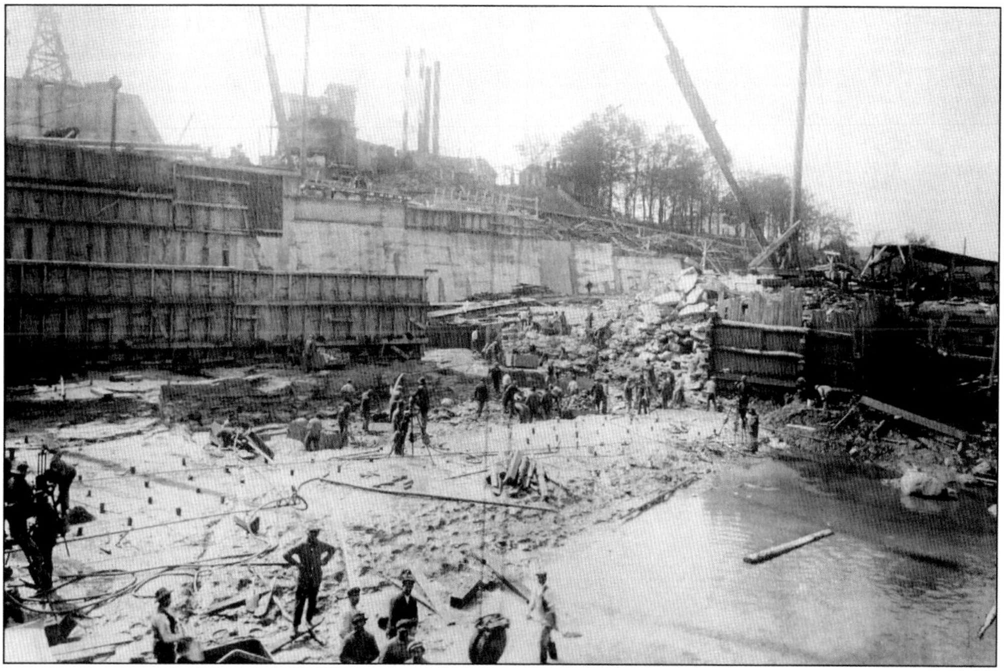

The mills dominated the landscape of Hinckley at the beginning of the 20th century. The log conveyor is in the foreground. Logs are stacked underneath. The Methodist church, located on the east side of the creek, is visible in the background. All of the mills in this photograph have since been demolished. (Courtesy of Linda Bailey.)

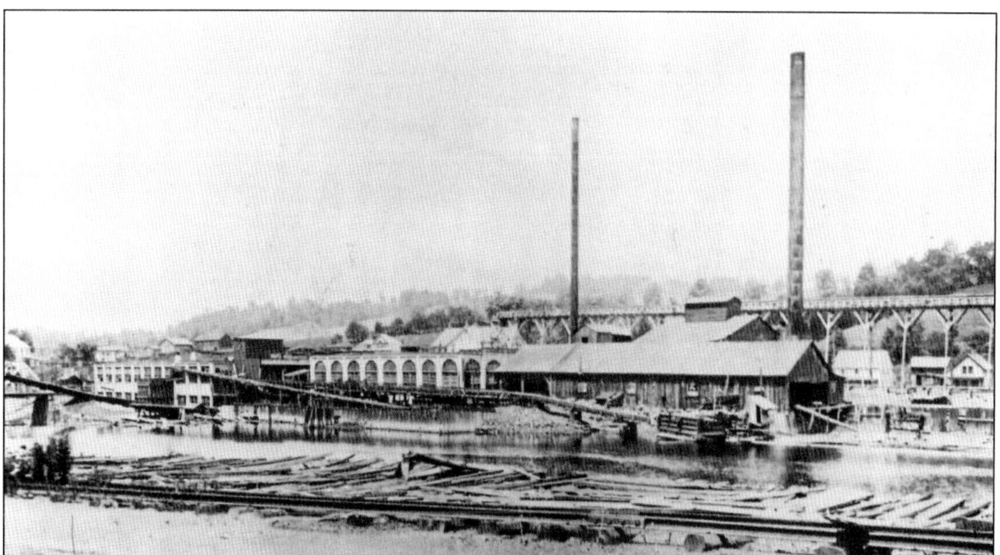

This image of the mills in Hinckley was taken from across the creek looking towards the village. Railroad tracks are in the foreground. The log conveyor can be seen behind the mills. Notice the tall chimney stacks that belonged to the Hinckley Fibre Company. (Courtesy of Linda Bailey.)

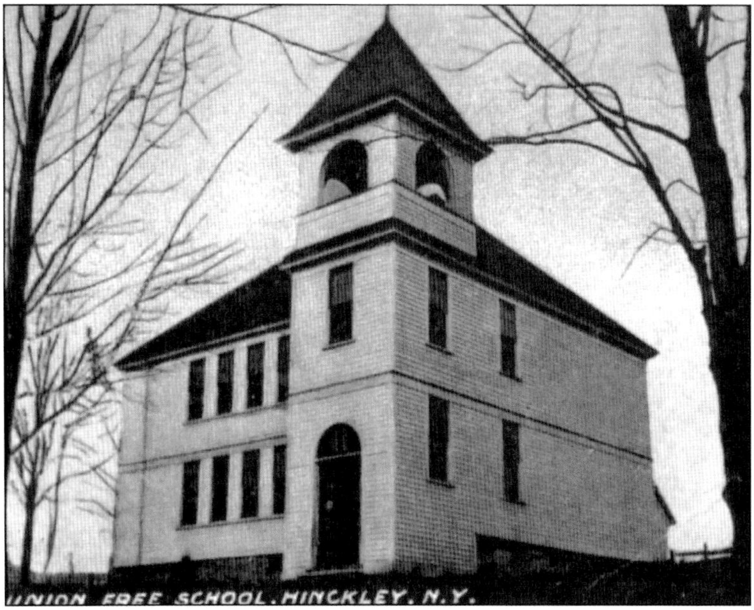

The Hinckley Union School was at one time a busy educational establishment. Members of the board of education included George McKee, John Smith, and Leonard Jones. The librarian was William Wilt. The teachers at that time were J.J. Evans, Margaret Pritchard, and Olive Havens. (Courtesy of Jeanette Walter.)

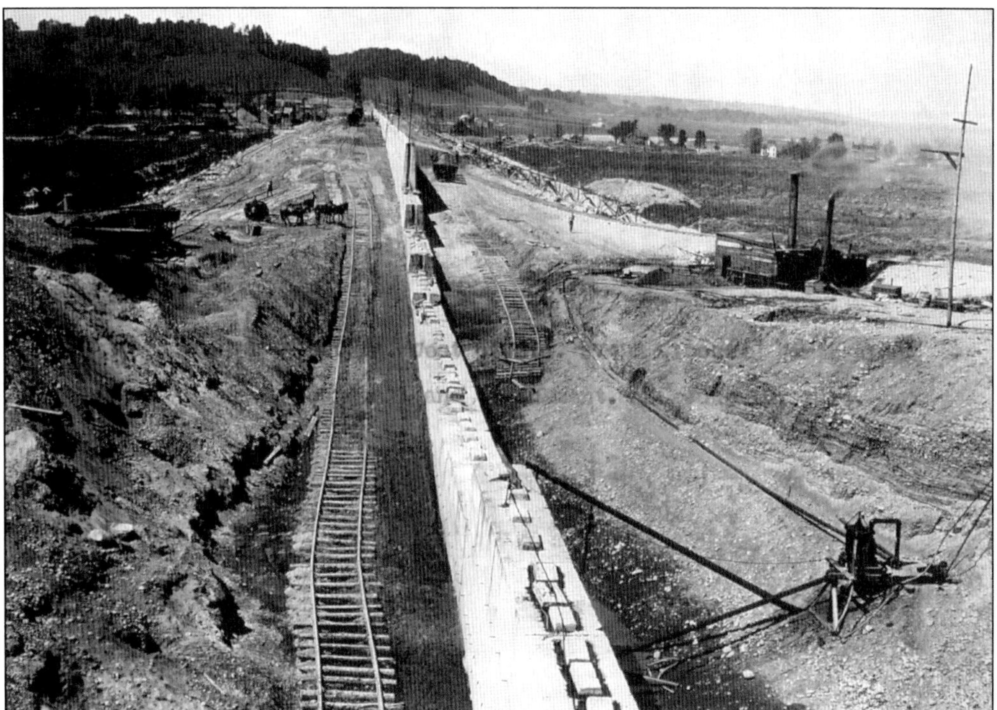

During Hinckley's industrial era, there were multiple railroad tracks throughout the village. They are all gone now. (Courtesy of Linda Bailey.)

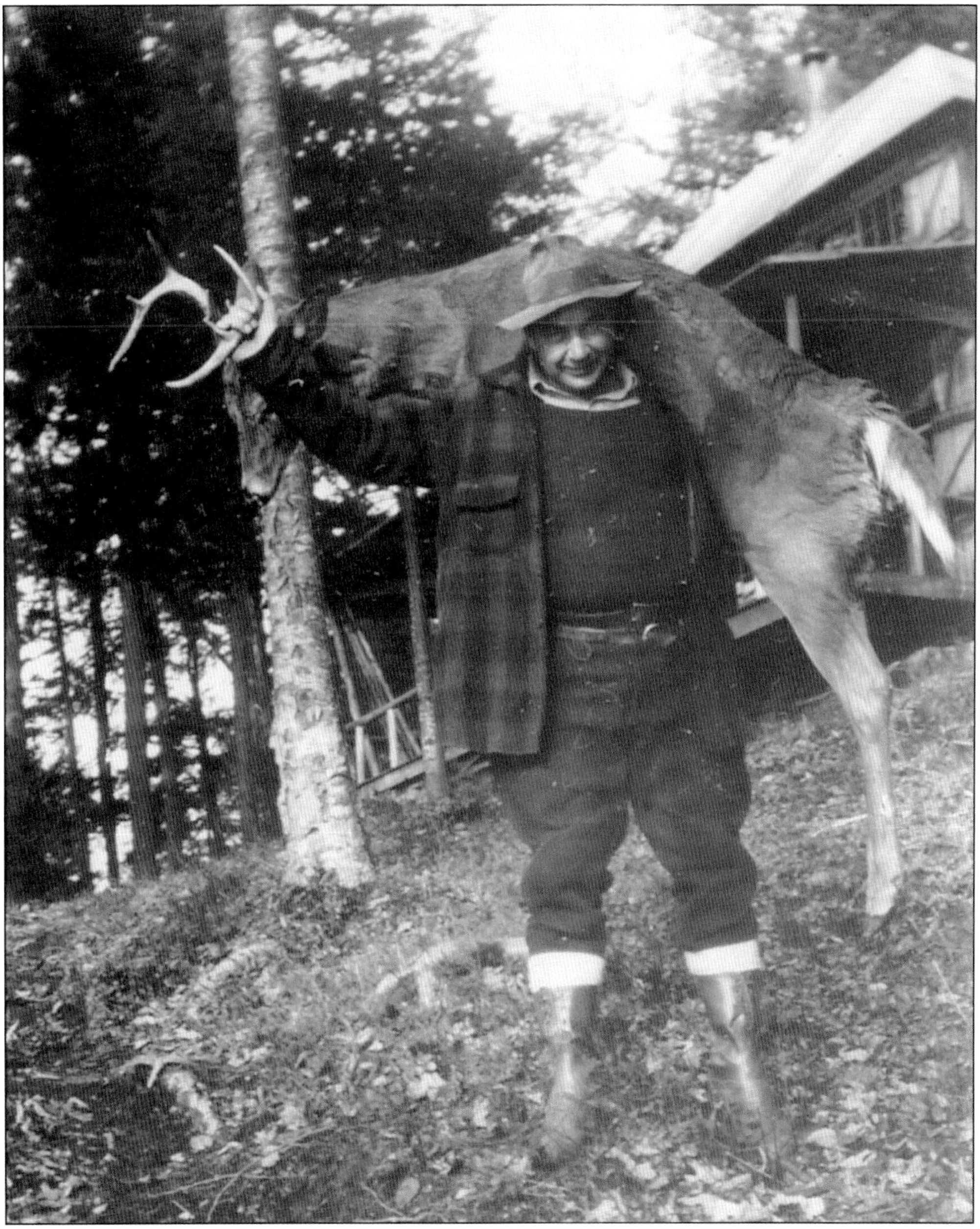

Many locals made their living as Adirondack guides. Guides knew where to hunt and fish; they knew how to build boats and shelters of native material; they knew how to cook what they caught and how to navigate and survive in the vast wilderness of the Adirondacks they called their backyards. These men and women began to hire themselves out to the visitors, or "sports," as they were called. Pictured here is local guide Philip "Bill" Plete. He guided in the southern Adirondack region for the Adirondack League Club. Plete also worked for the New York State Department of Transportation for 25 years. When the Adirondack League Club was established in 1890, it was met with resistance from many locals. The club posted land that those natives had been hunting on for generations. This caused strife and led to a string of vandalism by some hometown vigilantes. (Author's collection.)

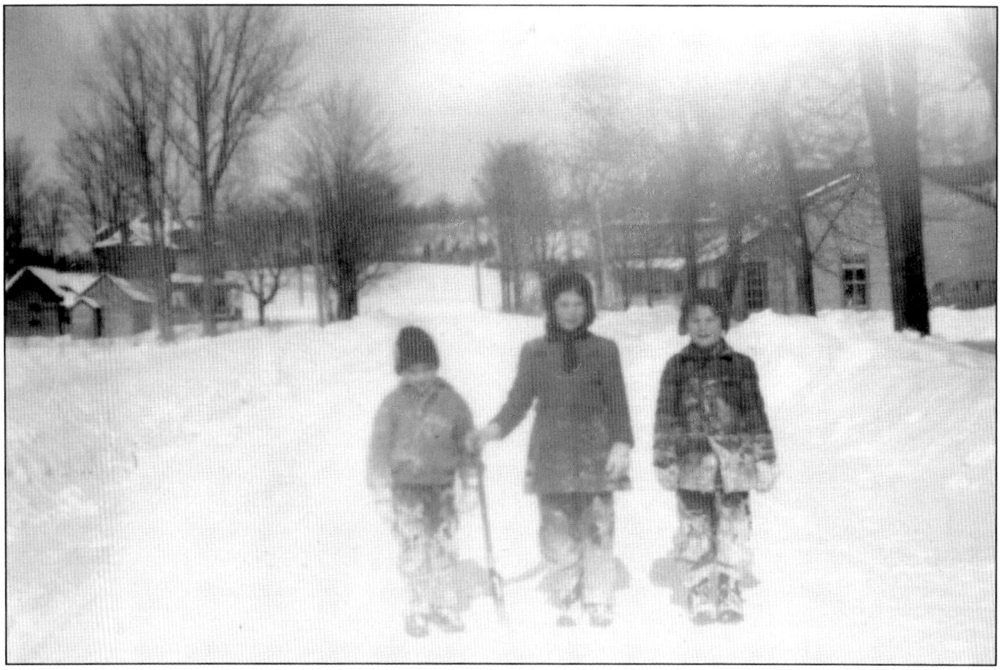

Growing up in small towns, children spent a lot of time outdoors. The kids pictured here are taking a break from playing in snow in the village of Hinckley. Rural communities like Hinckley had lots of opportunity for outdoor recreation. The people in the photograph are unidentified. (Author's collection.)

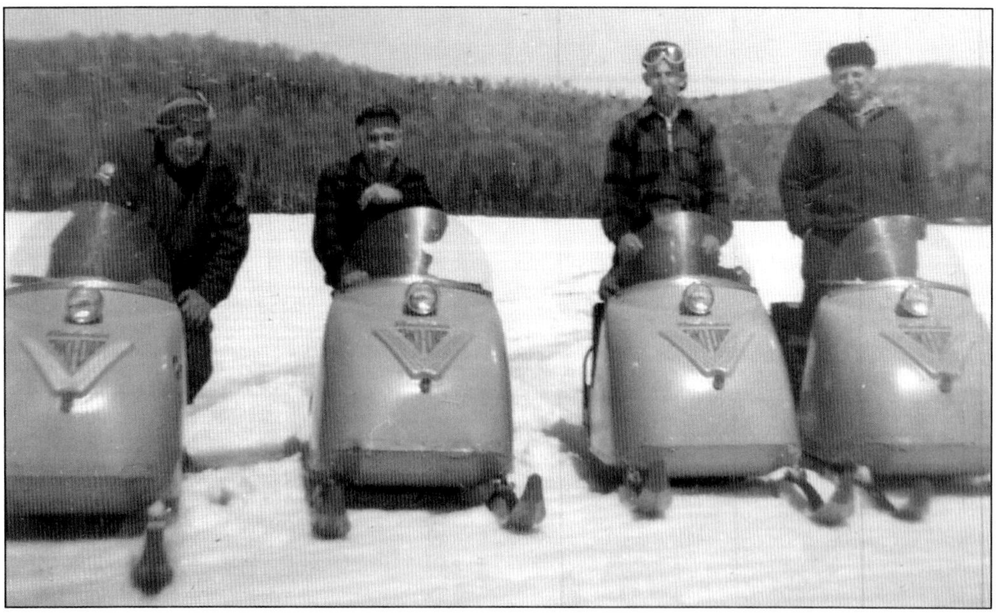

This group from Remsen and Hinckley enjoyed a day of snowmobiling in the middle of winter. Modern snowmobiles began being produced in the 1940s. Iron dogs, as they were known, were used mainly by hunters and trappers in cold-weather climates. From left to right are Phillip "Bill" Plete, Elsworth "Bud" Worden, Pete Briggs, and unidentified. (Photograph by Art Johnson, author's collection.)

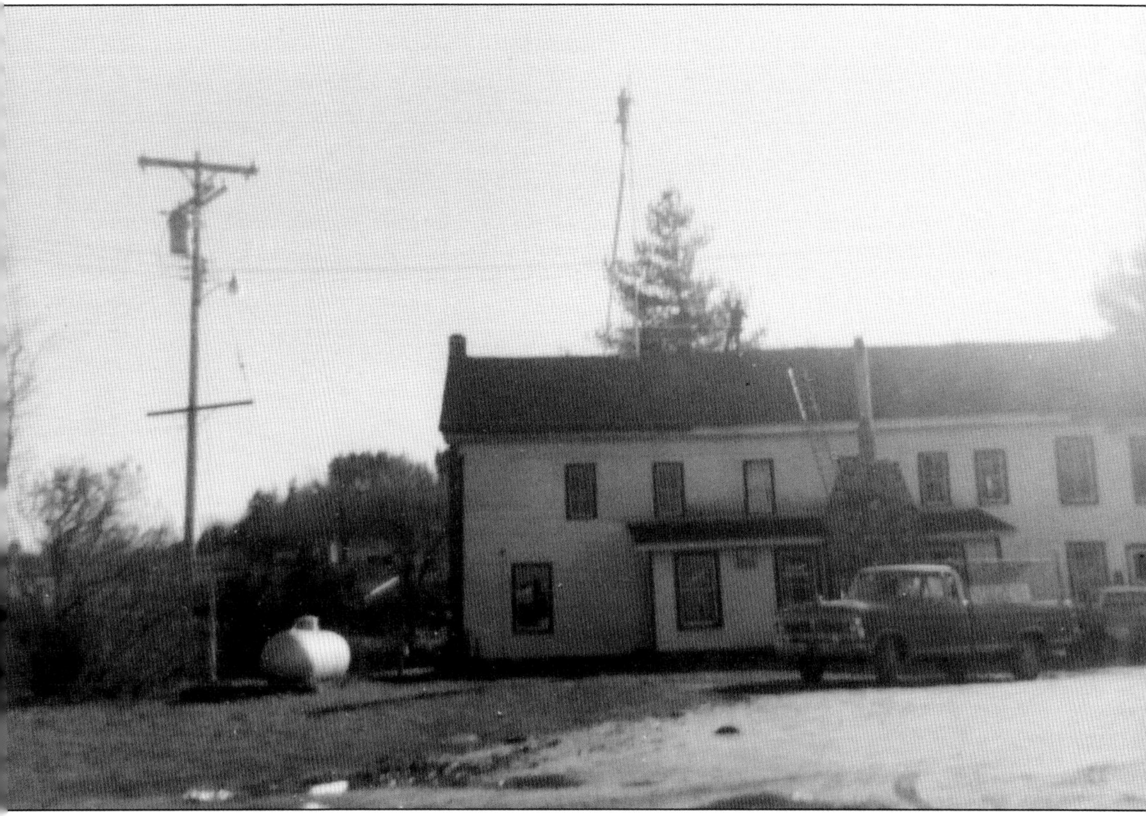

The Grant Hotel was the main inn in Grant after the American Hotel burned down. It was sold many times through the years. At one point, the proprietors were Frank and Anna Barley. A short, pudgy, traditional Italian woman, Anna could often be found in the kitchen with a rolling pin in hand. The Grant Hotel was frequented by the disorderly tavern crowd of local working men. One night, the crowd of loggers was getting too rowdy for Anna's liking. She instructed her husband to quiet them down. He, as the story goes, attempted halfheartedly to hush the rollicking mass. When the group persisted to get louder rather than quieter, Anna lost her temper. She rushed through the swinging bar doors in a fury, brandishing her rolling pin. The rough-and-tough loggers were apparently no match for Anna, as they reportedly scrambled out of the barroom via the door and windows. The inn was said to have been cleared in no time. The structure still stands, although it is closed for business. (Author's collection.)

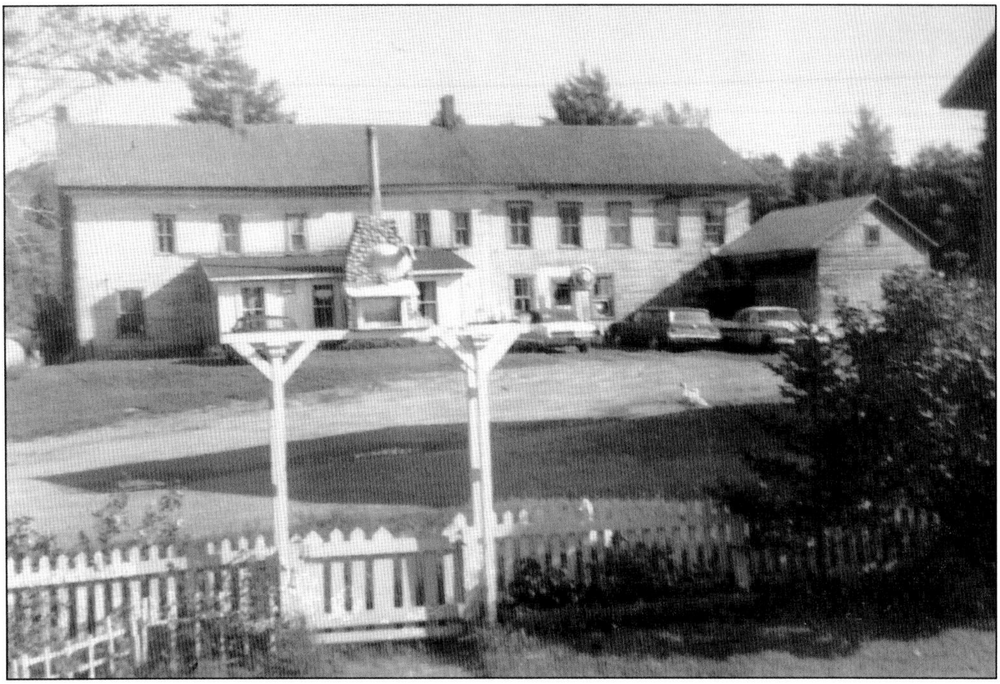

Ducks are gathered on the lawn of the Grant Hotel. One duck is perched on top of the bird feeder on the garden trellis. The hotel was a favorite stopping place for lumberjacks coming out of the forest. The inn served dinners, hosted events, and operated a robust barroom. (Author's collection.)

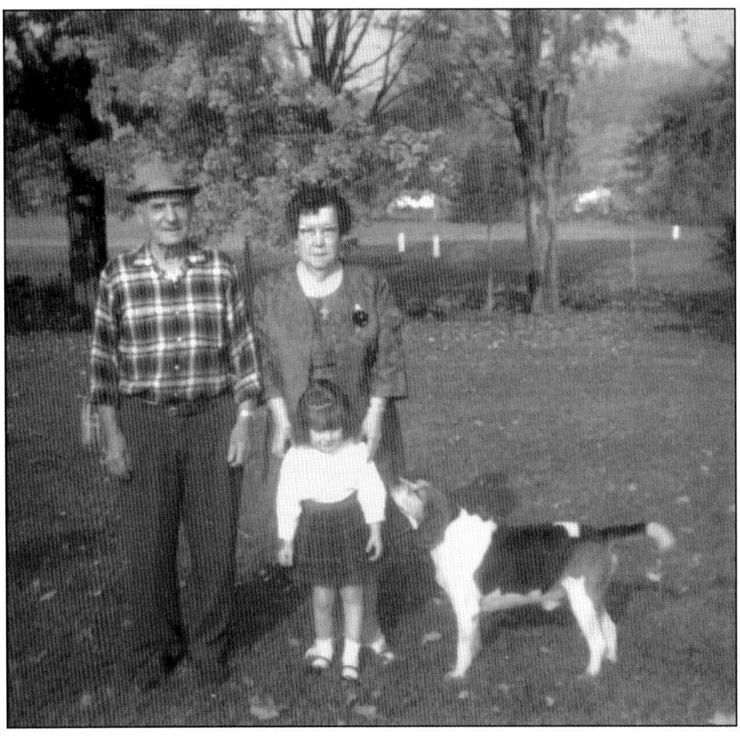

Myrtle Dykeman lived in Grant behind the Grant Hotel. She was the widow of Emory Dykeman, who was the highway superintendent of the town of Russia. She made pies for the Grant Hotel. Her friend in the photograph is Tom Clifford. They are pictured with young Wendi Plete. Both Myrtle and Emory are buried in Woodin Corners Cemetery. (Author's collection.)

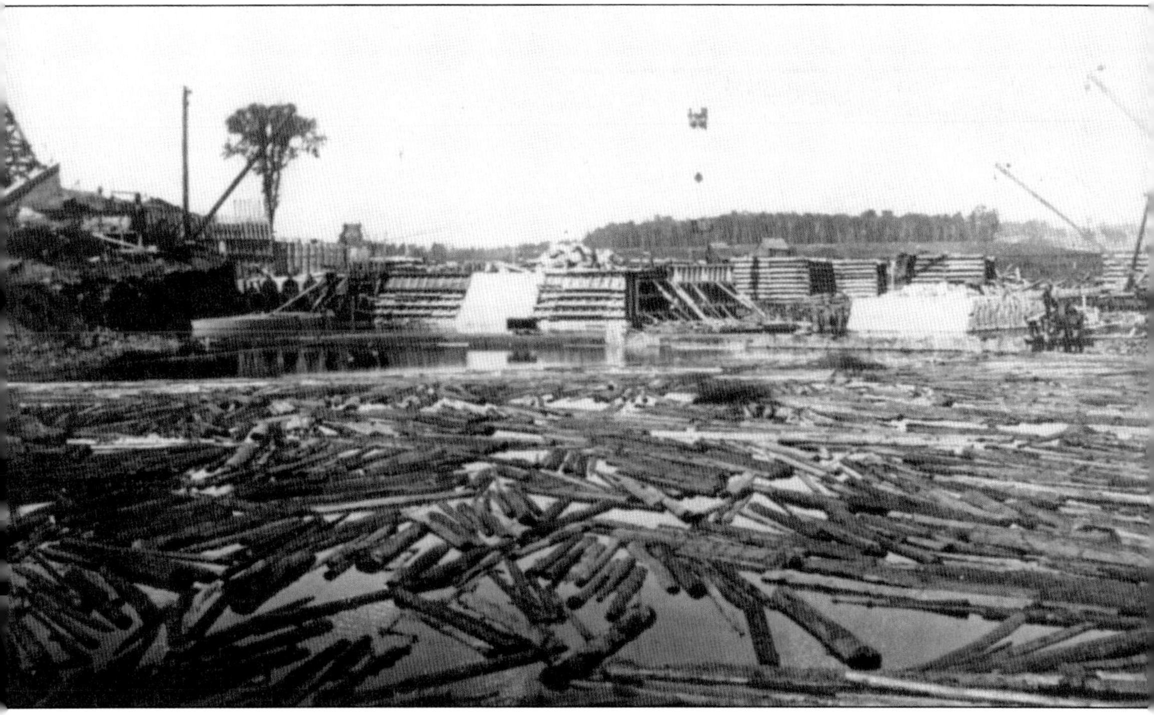

This photograph, which dates to around 1911–1913, shows the logs collecting in the West Canada Creek at the base of the dam, which is under construction. Gardner Hinckley, whom Hinckley is named after, built his sawmill three miles above the Prospect Falls. He was partnered with Theodore Ballou. They called in carpenter and millwright James Walters, a graduate of Fairfield Academy. They built a mill that had a set of saws on each side, with gang saws in the middle. The gang mill they constructed was the first of its kind in the area. That is how the area first came to be known as Gang Mills. Hinckley built his home on the east side of the West Canada Creek and became the founding father of a quickly growing village. Buildings were constructed on both sides of the creek in short time. Gang Mills became a roaring lumbering village that provided headlines for the local newspapers on numerous occasions. (Author's collection.)

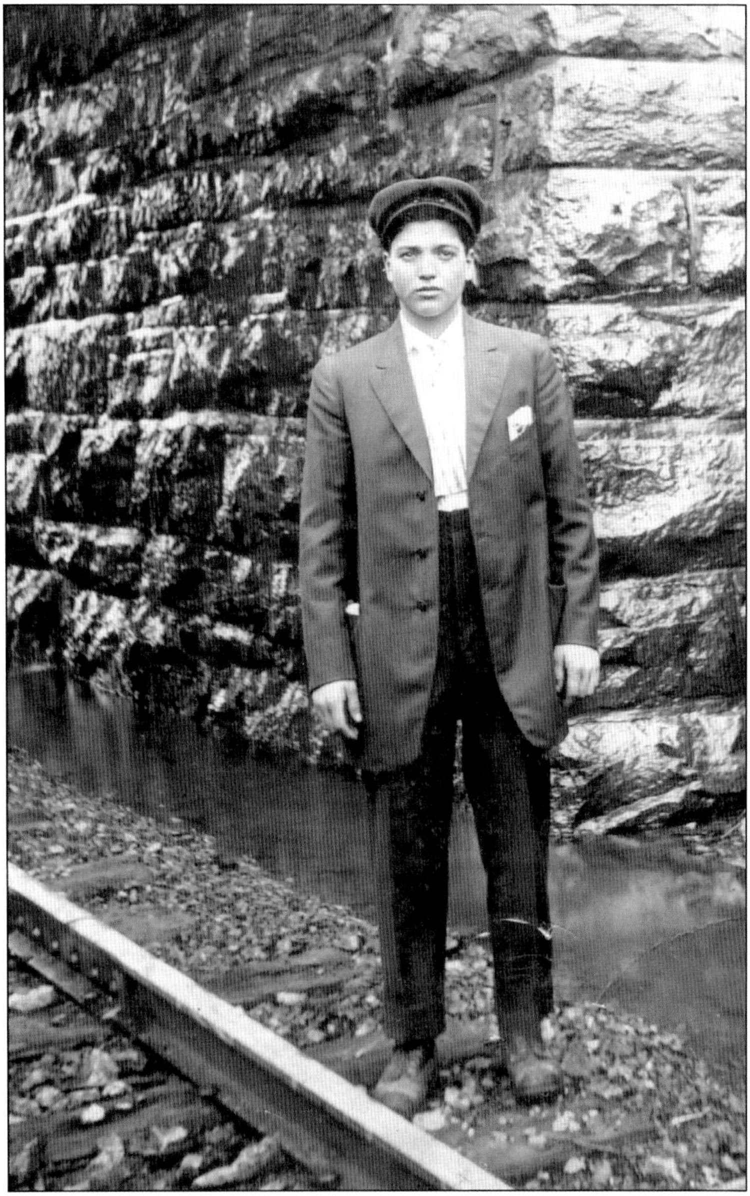

Up until the United States entered World War I in 1917, its leaders tried to remain neutral. President Wilson even issued a proclamation of neutrality. But German forces challenged American neutrality by repeatedly attacking unarmed British and American vessels. The United States responded by joining the war efforts. When the First World War threatened America, many local young people answered the call. Charles "Charlie" Plete is shown before leaving for military training. He served with the 310th Infantry, Company C. He was a sergeant at the time of his discharge. While serving in France during the war, his unit was attacked with mustard gas, which left him with long-term health problems. The entrance of American forces marked a turning point in World War I. By 1918, approximately 50,000 American soldiers had died in the Western European battlegrounds. Upon returning home, Plete worked at Revere Copper and Brass in Rome. He belonged to the Enlli Church on Fairchild Road. Plete died in 1946. He is buried in Fairchild Cemetery in Remsen. (Author's collection.)

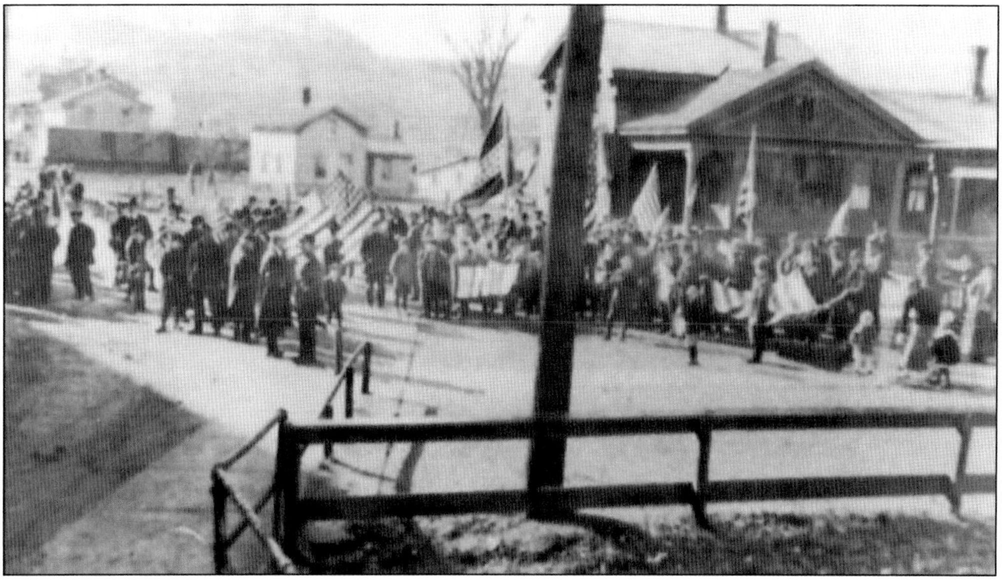

Armistice Day marked the end of hostilities on the western front of World War I. Representatives of the Allies and Germany signed an armistice treaty in the early hours of November 11, 1918, in Compiègne, France. It took effect on the 11th hour of the 11th day of the 11th month. In these images, the streets of Hinckley are filled with villagers who gathered to celebrate the end of the Great War. Many are waving American flags. Scenes like this played out all across America on this day. Armistice Day is commemorated every year in the United States as Veterans Day. The Hinckley Dam can be seen in the photograph below. It had been completed only three years before. (Both, courtesy of Linda Bailey.)

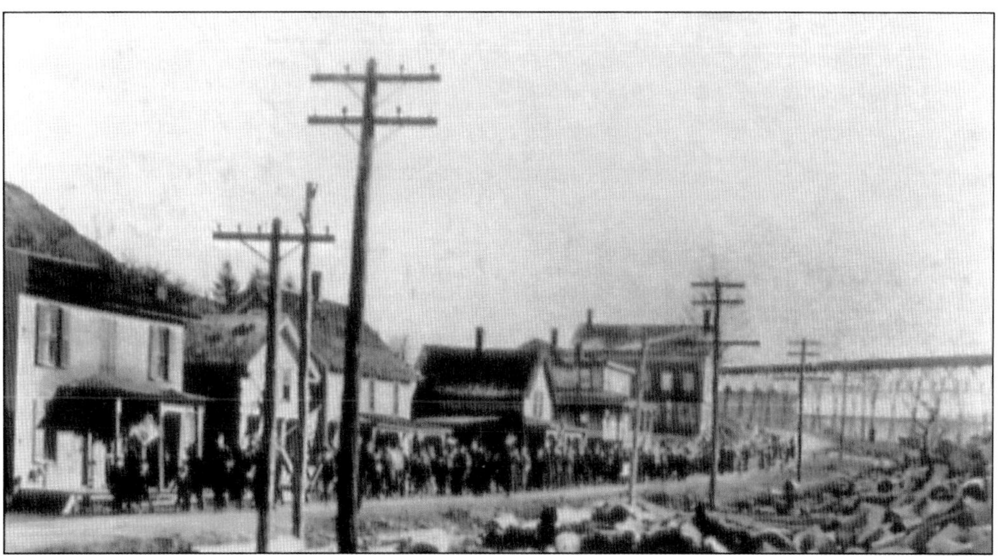

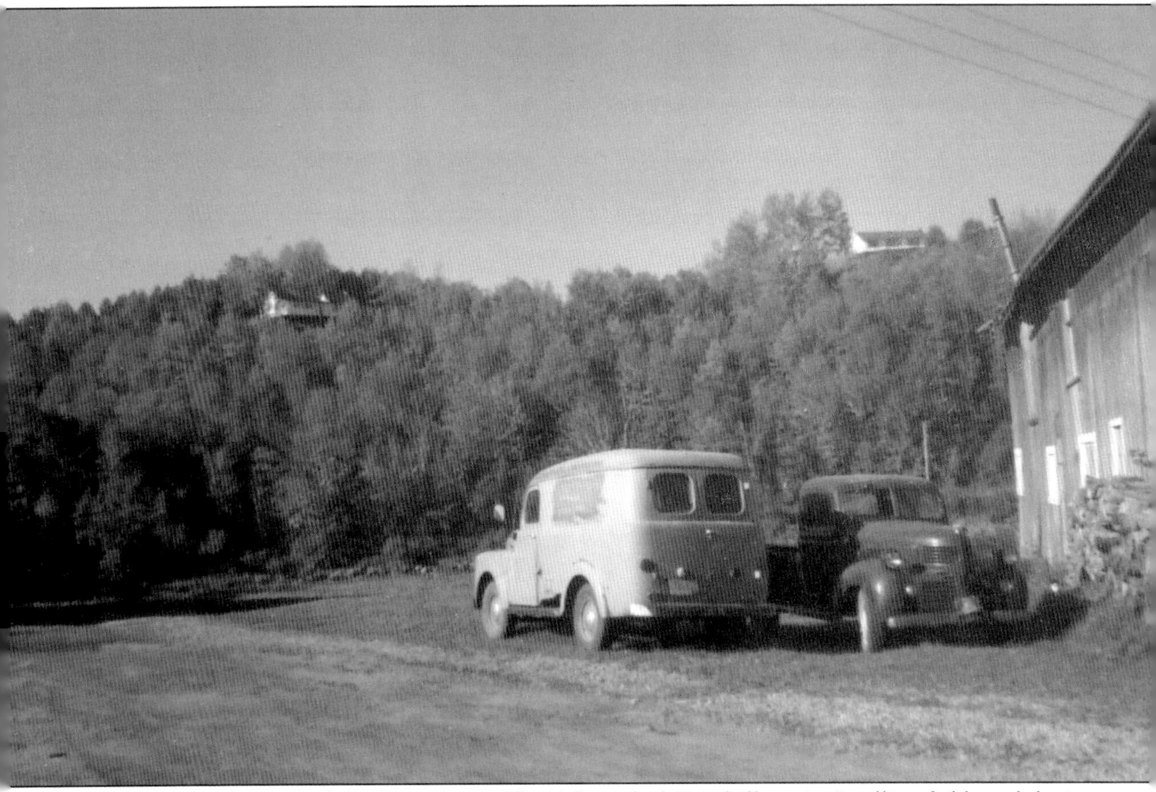

This image shows the hillside in Grant. The Adirondack Foothills region's rolling fields and sloping hills has inspired artists for hundreds of years. Each of the four seasons highlights a unique feature of the natural beauty of the landscape. The region is home to hundreds of different species of animals, including black bears, white-tailed deer, bald eagles, and brook trout. (Author's collection.)

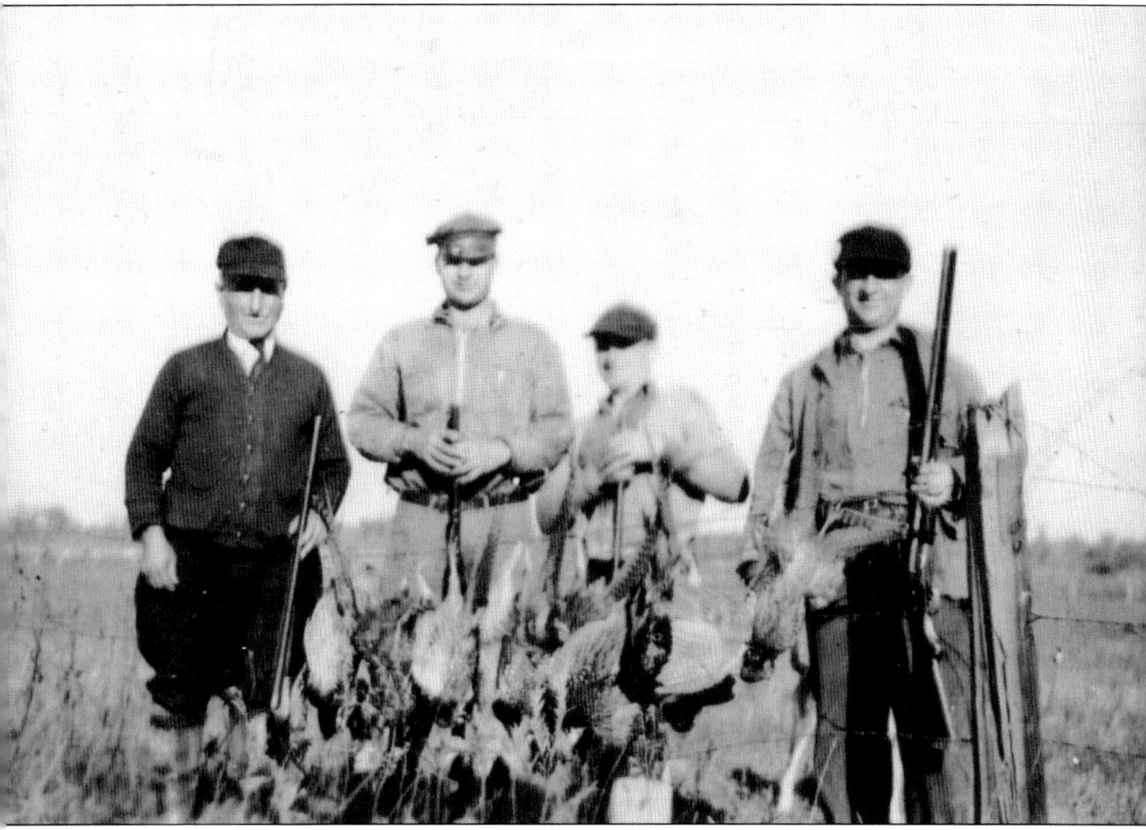

Hunting in Central New York has a long history. Sportsmen hunted wildlife most commonly for food, sometimes for recreation. Regulation of hunting within the United States dates from the 19th century. Many modern hunters see themselves as conservationists and sportsmen in the mode of Theodore Roosevelt. Some of the animals that were hunted in Central New York include white-tailed deer, turkeys, rabbits, and black bears. Many pheasant hunters can attest that these birds are very crafty and successfully outsmart even the most experienced hunters and dogs on a regular basis. These early-20th-century sportsmen are showing off the game from a day's hunt. Notice the man of the far left wearing a necktie. He is probably a sport, a visitor who contracted local guides to lead him on hunting, fishing, and hiking trips. The men are unidentified. (Author's collection.)

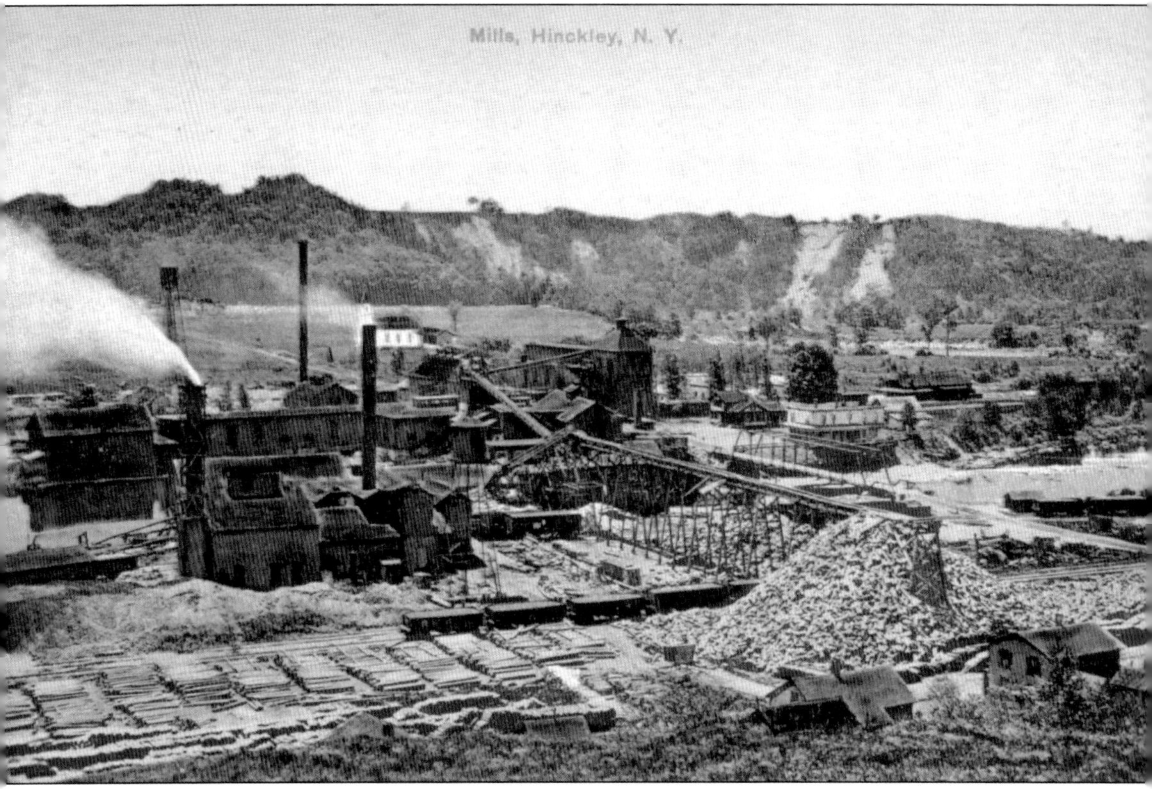

The namesake of Hinckley, Gardner Hinckley, was born on October 12, 1808. His parents were Elijah and Sally Vincent Hinckley. Gardner lived on his parents' farm in the town of Russia until the death of his father in 1822. After that, he lived and worked on the farm of his guardian, William Graves, of Gravesville. Two years later, at age 16, Gardner purchased his brother's share of the family farm. He married in 1829. His wife, Elizabeth, was the daughter of Mr. and Mrs. Esek Atwood. The Atwood family began in Vermont but, following the death of Elizabeth's mother, moved to Wilmurt, north of Hinckley. Gardner left his farm in 1837 to become a land agent and business manager for A.K. Morehouse and lived in the Piseco Lake area for about a year before establishing his sawmills with Theodore Ballou in Wilmurt and Noblesboro. Gardner finally moved to Gang Mills (which became Hinckley) in 1849. This photograph shows some of the mills in Hinckley. (Author's collection.)

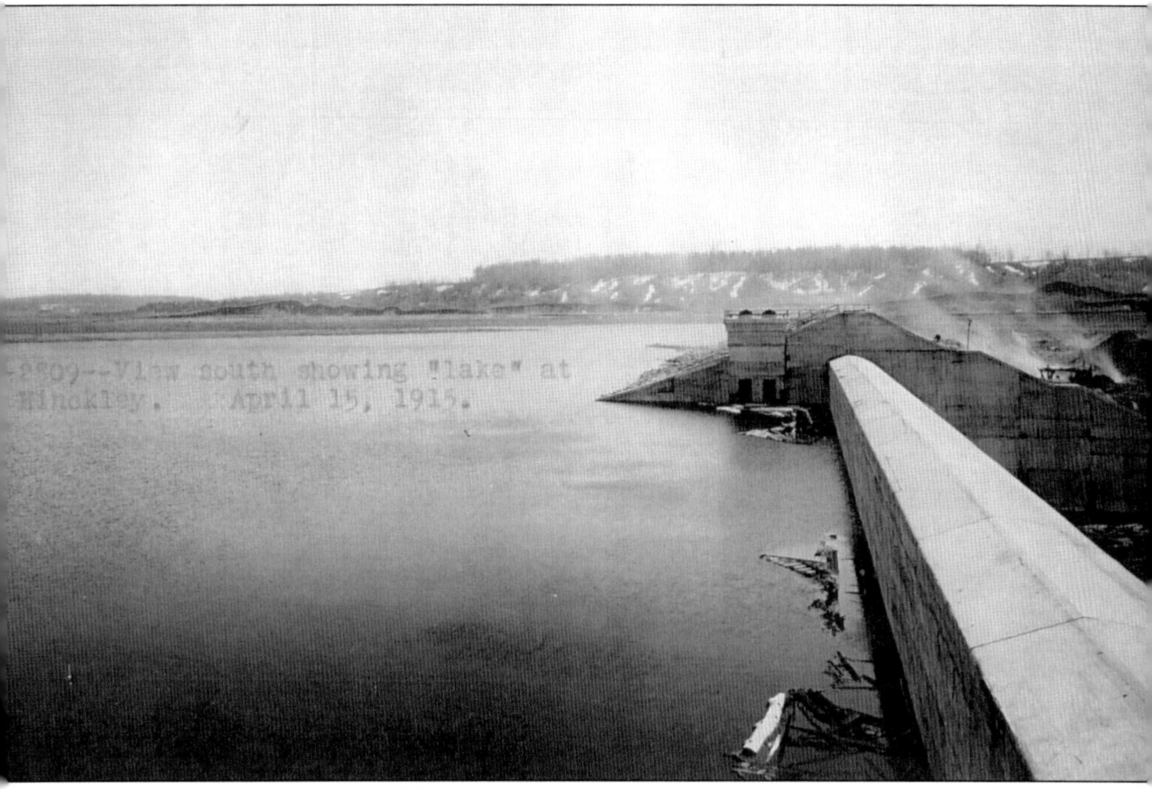

The local photographer LeRoy Thomas and others documented the Hinckley Dam while it was under construction from 1911 until 1915. The original engineer was replaced when it was determined that the work was progressing too slowly. The first water came over the dam on August 23, 1915. (Courtesy of Jeanette Walter.)

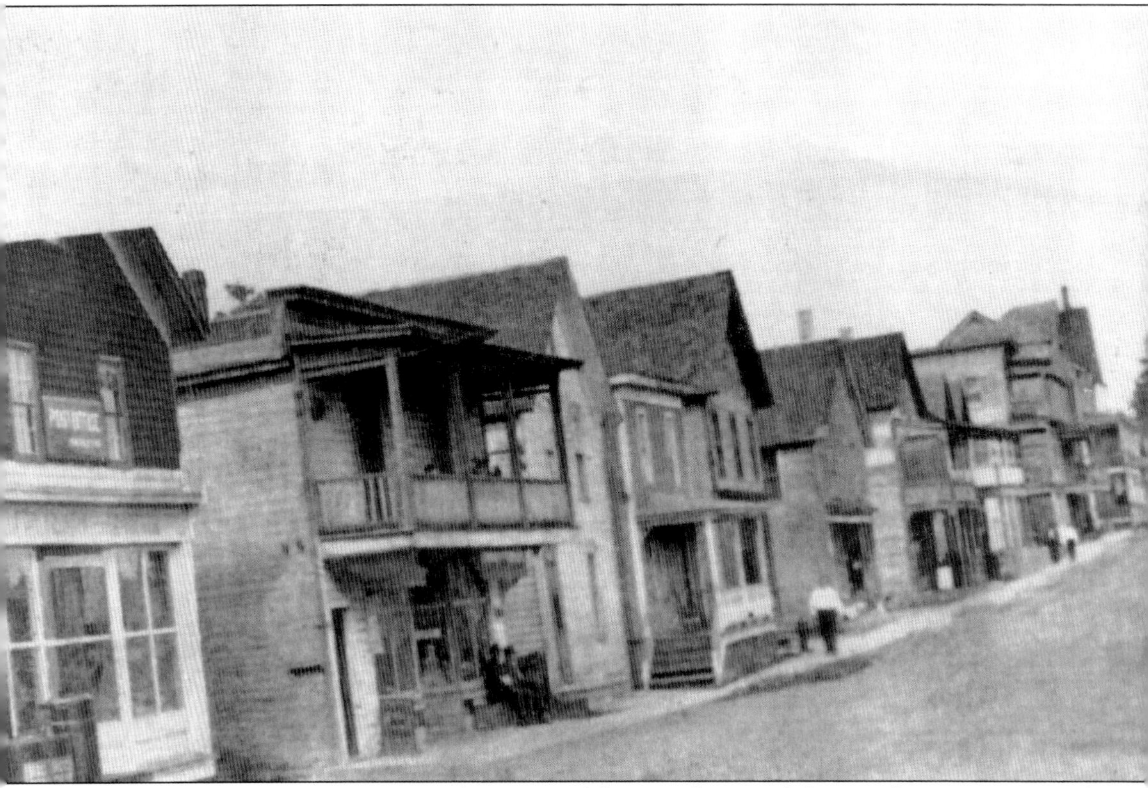

Hinckley was marketed as a tourist location to fishermen, hunters, hikers, and vacationers. Local guides were available to escort trophy-seekers to the prime fishing and hunting locations. The village was accessible by railroad, bus line, and a smooth highway for automobiles in the early 20th century. A spur of the Mohawk & Malone Railroad ran right through the village and crossed the West Canada Creek via a trestle. The remains of the train trestle can still be seen in the lower reservoir. The raised area that was the railroad still remains, mostly hidden by trees along the waterway. The first Hinckley railroad bridge was a wooden structure built in 1892. It was washed away in 1901 during a flood. Floods were frequent occurrences. A steel railroad trestle was built further downstream. Use was discontinued in the 1930s. (Courtesy of Linda Bailey.)

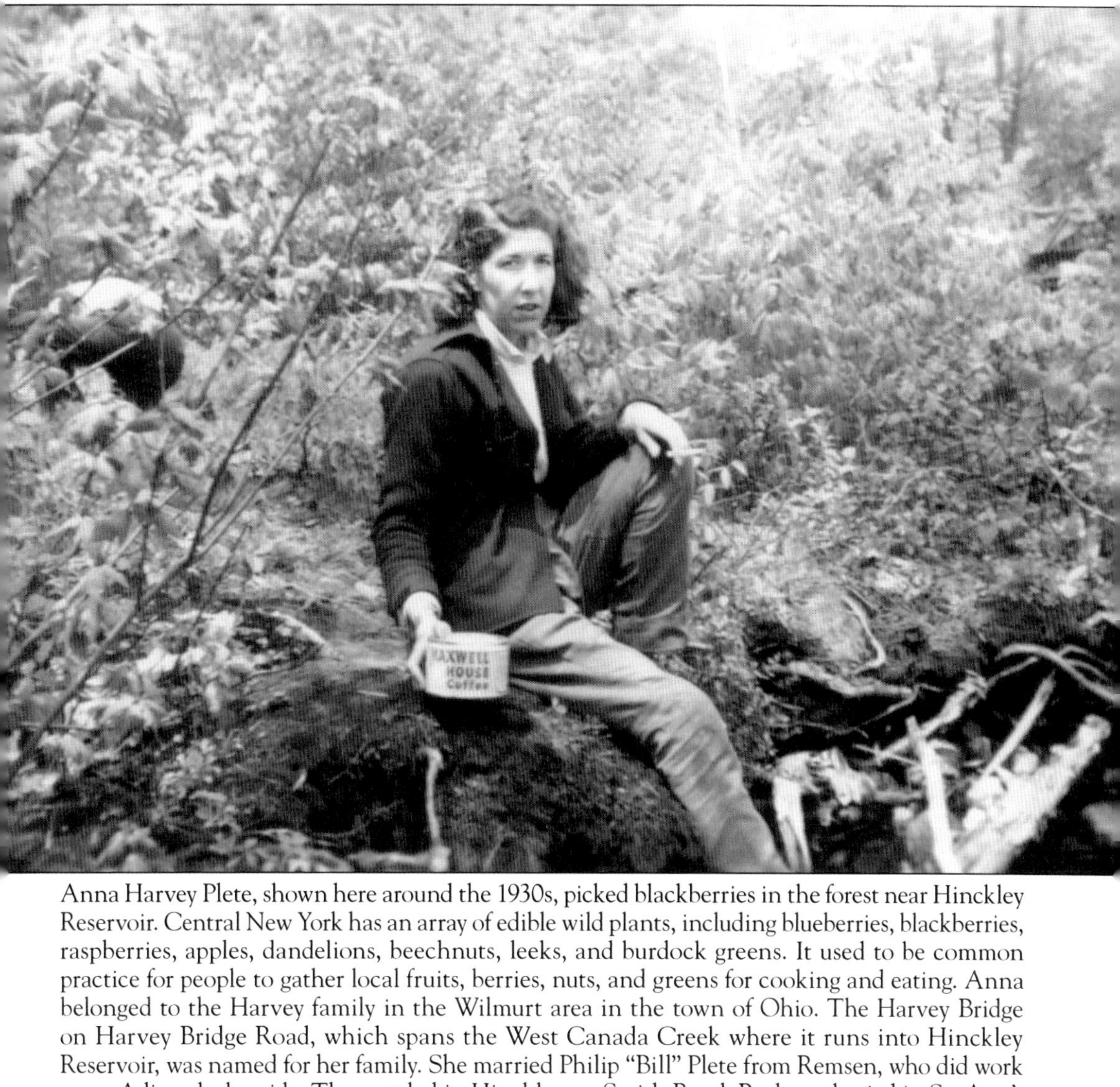

Anna Harvey Plete, shown here around the 1930s, picked blackberries in the forest near Hinckley Reservoir. Central New York has an array of edible wild plants, including blueberries, blackberries, raspberries, apples, dandelions, beechnuts, leeks, and burdock greens. It used to be common practice for people to gather local fruits, berries, nuts, and greens for cooking and eating. Anna belonged to the Harvey family in the Wilmurt area in the town of Ohio. The Harvey Bridge on Harvey Bridge Road, which spans the West Canada Creek where it runs into Hinckley Reservoir, was named for her family. She married Philip "Bill" Plete from Remsen, who did work as an Adirondack guide. They settled in Hinckley on Smith Road. Both are buried in St. Ann's Cemetery. (Author's collection.)

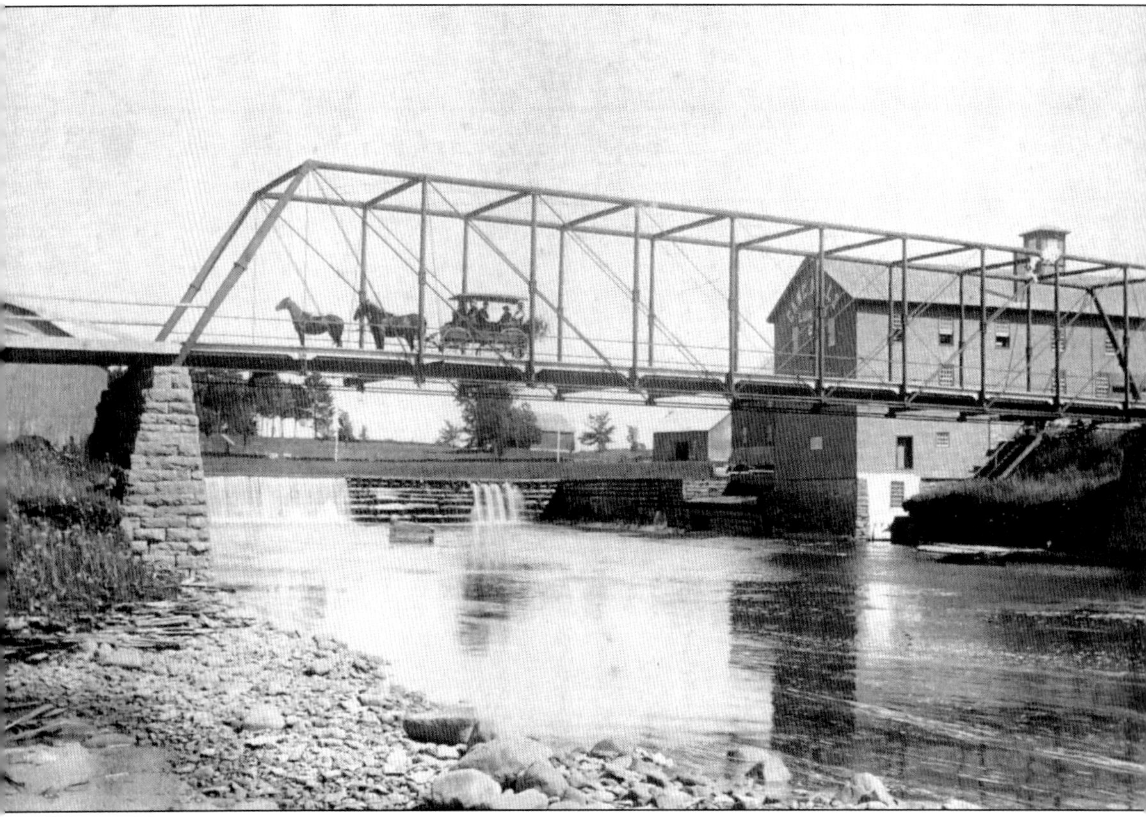

This late-1800s photograph shows the original bridge that spanned the West Canada Creek and the small wooden dam. This is prior to the construction of the Hinckley Dam, which was finished in 1915. The first bridge in Hinckley, which was known as Gang Mills at the time, was a private bridge that led from the sawmills on the north side of the West Canada Creek to the planing shop on the south side of the creek. (Courtesy of Jeanette Walter.)

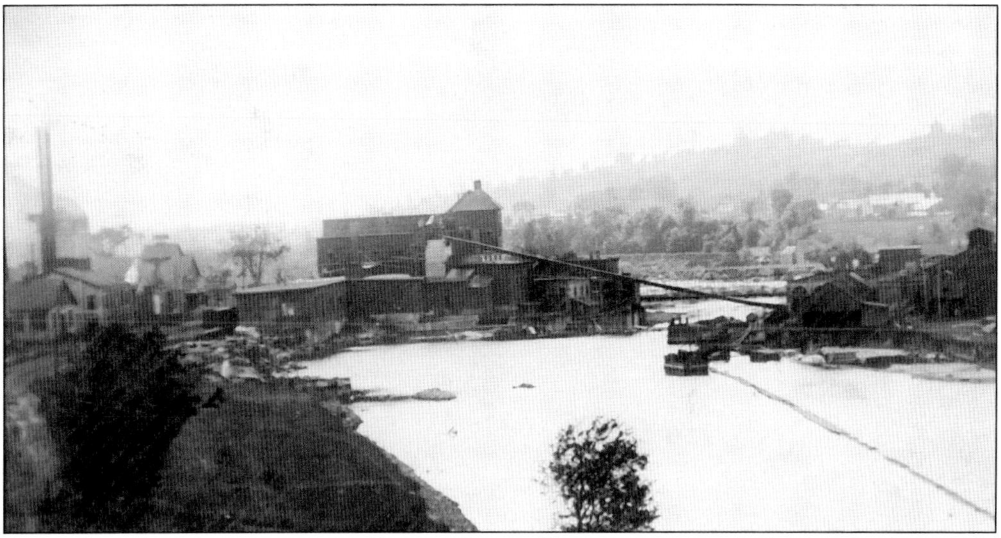

The first iron bridge erected in Hinckley was designed by an engineer named Whipple of Boonville in 1871. This bridge was severely damaged by floods many times. Floods were common on the West Canada Creek. The flood of 1901 proved to be the worst for Hinckley. In 1910, a massive flood waterlogged Herkimer. The bridge was replaced in 1913. (Author's collection.)

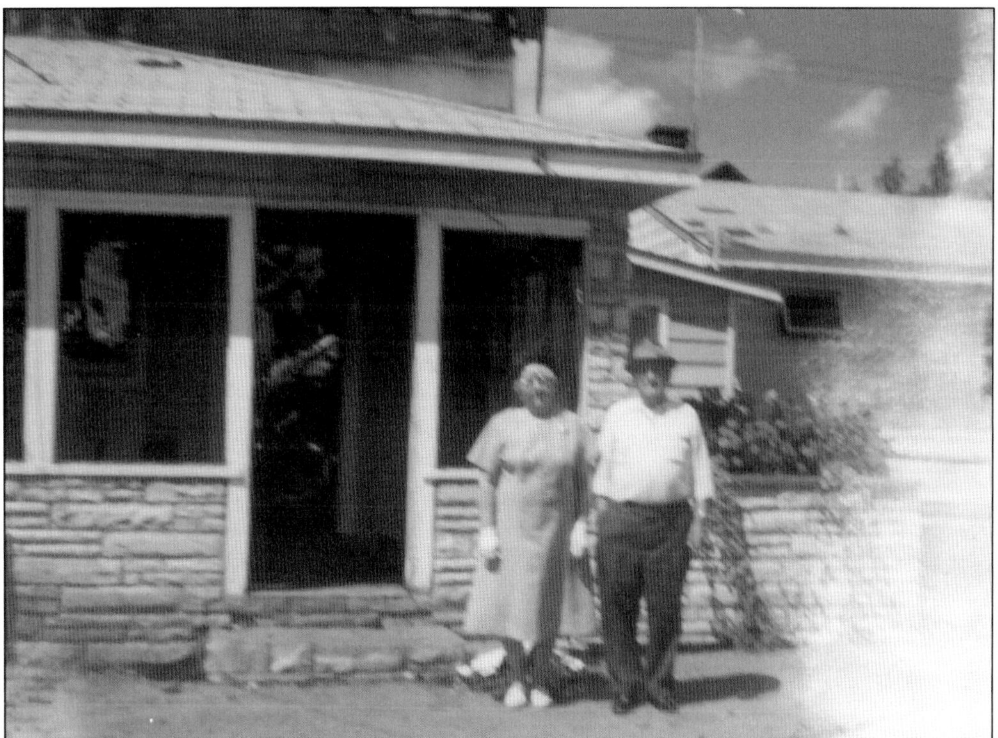

The Ohio Hotel, located on New York State Route 8, was operated by Myrtle Hicks Dykeman's sister and brother-in-law. It was popular with local loggers and woodsmen. The business is still there and has changed ownership many times. It is now open as the Ohio Tavern. (Author's collection.)

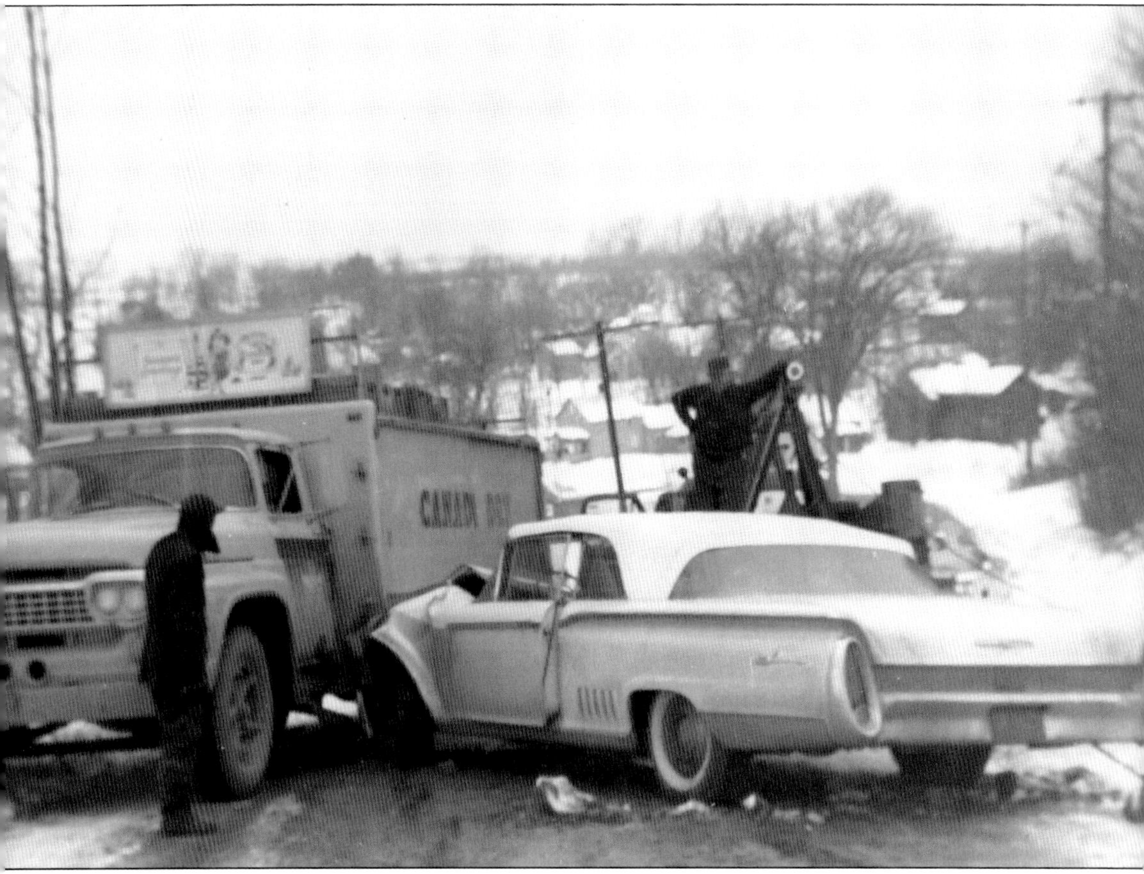

Winter driving has always proved challenging, even to the most experienced upstate New Yorkers. This wreck was in the Hinckley area and involved a Canada Dry delivery truck and a passenger vehicle. The tow truck is there to assist. The drivers are unidentified. (Author's collection.)

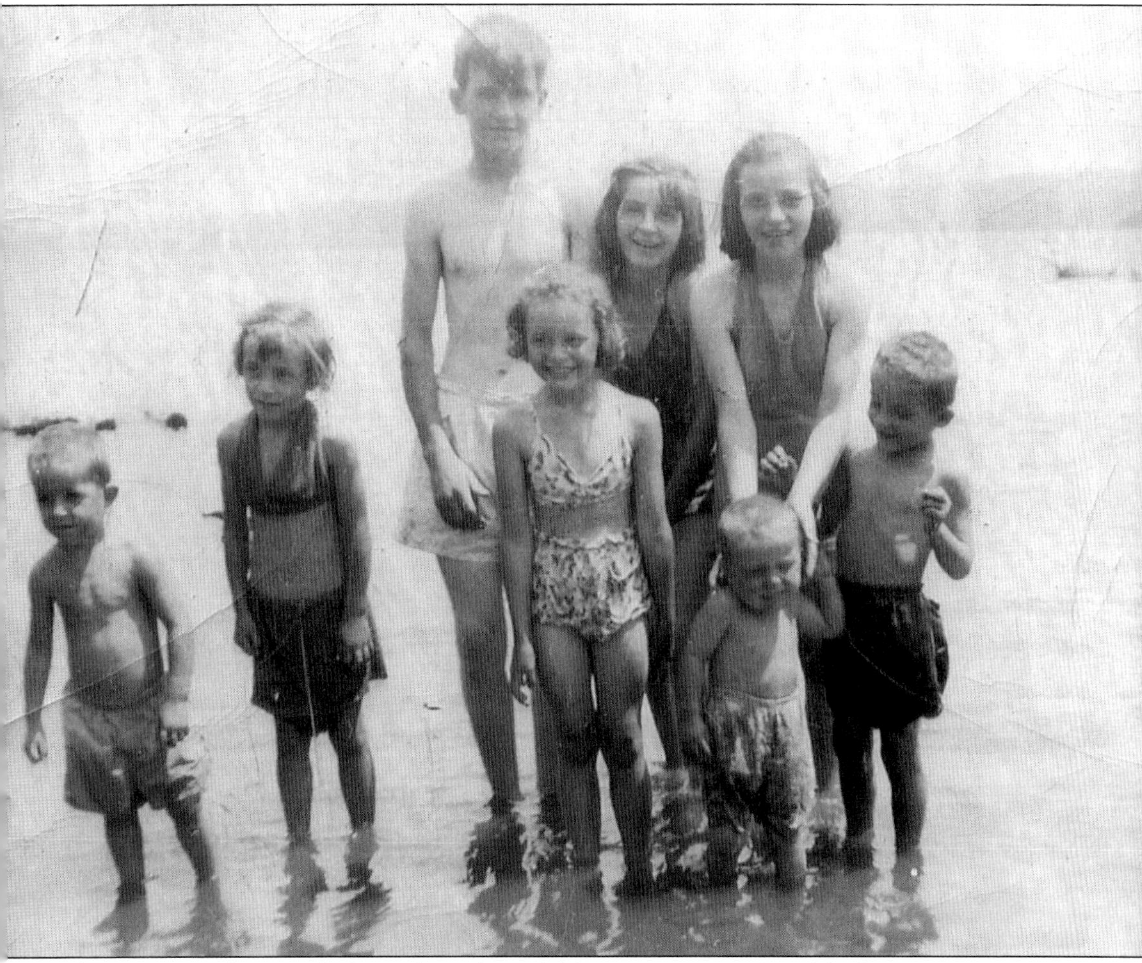

This 1940s-era photograph shows the Wilcox children swimming in Hinckley Reservoir. Gaining access to the water used to be relatively easy. There were numerous places people could go swimming. Much of the land surrounding Hinckley Reservoir is now privately owned, and public access is limited. New York State does have a park with a maintained swimming area on the Grant side of the reservoir. The upper portion of the Hinckley Reservoir is located in three towns—the town of Remsen, the town of Ohio, and the town of Russia. Numerous hamlets within those two towns are located on the shorelines of the reservoir or nearby, including Northwood and Grant. The lower portion of the Hinckley Reservoir is located in the town of Trenton, with the hamlet of Hinckley on the shoreline. Pictured are, from left to right, William "Bill" Wilcox, Margaret Wilcox, Joseph "Joe" Wilcox, Elaine Leathem, Helen Wilcox, Elizabeth "Bit" Wilcox, and Patrick "Pat" Wilcox. (Courtesy of Helen Griswold.)

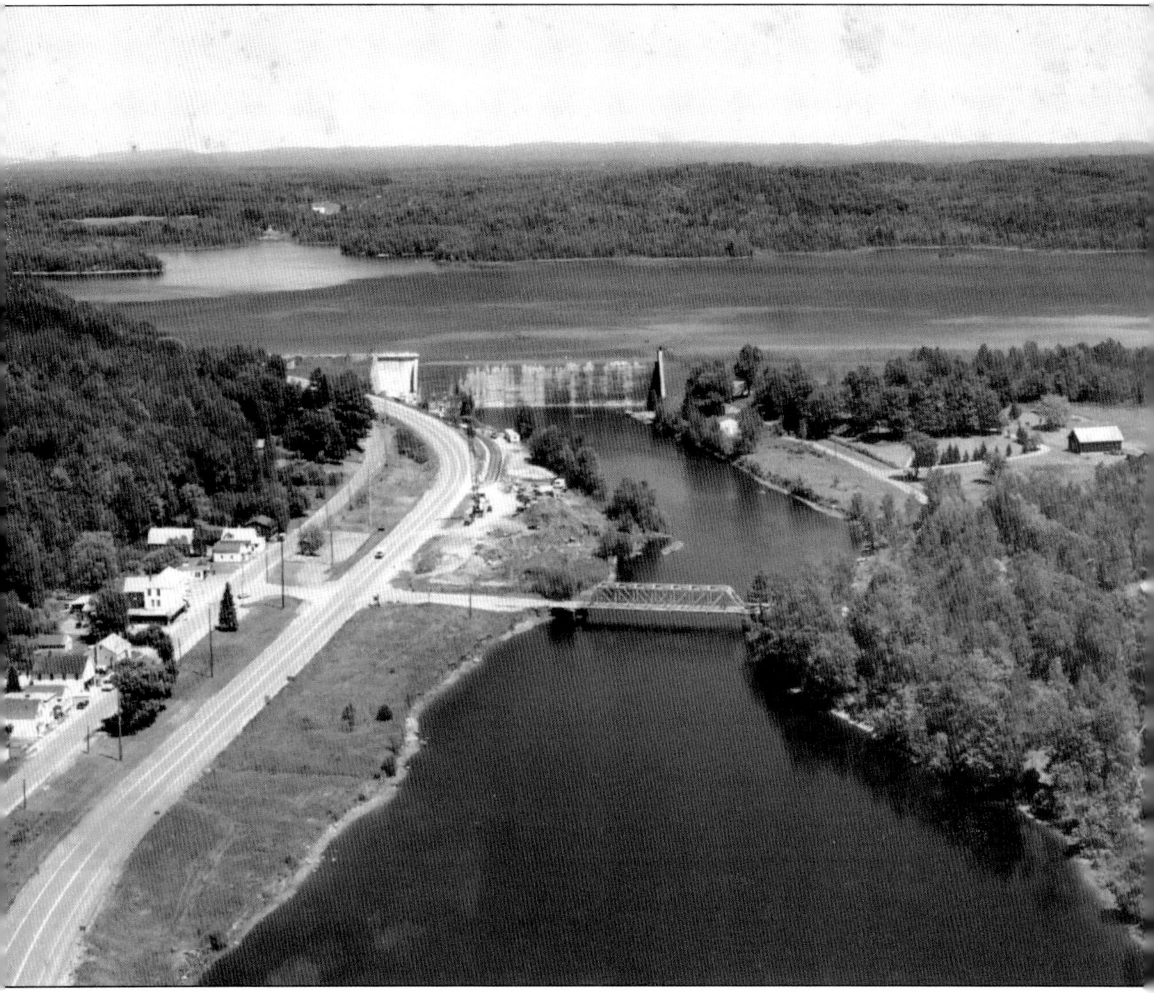

This aerial view is looking towards the dam and reservoir in Hinckley. Both the upper and the lower bodies of water are visible. The mills are gone. Many of the businesses and residences have been demolished. The massive log conveyor has long since been dismantled, and trees have grown and filled in the area where the railroad tracks and train station were. The Methodist church is gone, Van Etten Park is now overgrown, and little remains of the industrious era in Hinckley's past. New York State Route 365 passes the village and follows the shoreline of the lake. The combined length of the lower and upper lakes is approximately 13 miles. There are few businesses left operating in the area. Northway Stop and Shop, located on the shore on the Hinckley Reservoir in Remsen, is the only convenience store on the route between Barneveld and Speculator. (Author's collection.)

Bibliography

Davis, Margaret P. *Honey Out of the Rafters*. Self-published, 1976.
History of Oneida County, The. Utica, NY: Oneida County Historical Society, 1977.
Jones, Mary Helen Eppright, and Lorena Start Jersern. *Steuben: The Baron and the Town*. Remsen, NY: Remsen-Steuben Historical Society, 1994.
Roberts, Millard. *A Narrative History of Remsen and Steuben*. Self-published, 1914.
Thomas, Howard. *Tales from the Adirondack Foothills*. Prospect, NY: North Country Books, 1956.
Utica Observer Dispatch, 1913–1916. Retrieved from Fultonhistory.com.